On the Hard

in Paradise

Over the glad waters of the dark blue sea,
Our thoughts boundless and our souls free,
Far as the breeze can bear, the billows foam,
Survey our empire, and behold our home!
                                            Lord Byron

On the Hard! in Paradise

When vacation paradise
becomes home,
and the thread holding a family together
is tied to a dock

Connie Fleenor

Mangrove Books

Published by Mangrove Books

Copyright © 2012 by Connie Fleenor

All Rights Reserved

Published by Mangrove Books, Antelope, CA

www.mangrovebooks.com

Cover Design by Jeff Huber

Illustration by erica Art & Design

ISBN-978-0-9846750-0-5

Library of Congress Control Number: 2011918442

Library of Congress subject headings:

 1. Virgin Islands—Description and travel. 2. St. Thomas—Description and travel. 3. Virgin Islands—Social life and customs. 4. St. Thomas—Social life and customs. 5. Sailing. I. Title

Fleenor, Connie.

On the hard in paradise/Connie Fleenor.

Printed in the United States of America

ACKNOWLEDGEMENT

I want to thank again here the friends who offered praise, solicited and unsolicited, for this project. Their encouragement helped keep me writing through multiple drafts and edits. I also want to thank Erica Celeste Thomas for the beautiful interior illustration. And, I need to single-out Jeff Huber for a special thank you for his help bringing this project to the form you see before you. Without his generosity and talent you'd be holding a pile of loose papers with a clip-art cover page. Finally, I'd like to thank all contributors to the self-publishers yahoo group; the new members who asked questions so I didn't have to ask all of mine, to the professionals who generously share their insight and patiently answer the same questions again and again.

DISCLAIMER

This memoir is my story, I don't expect everyone to agree with my perspective or my memory. I hope I haven't offended anyone, if I have, I must have been talking about someone else.

Many have dedicated books to their mothers,
but none more gratefully than I,
for my mom.

On the Hard

in Paradise

Each new wave rearranges the patterns in the sand
so we may pretend our footsteps are the first.

Rancho Del Fuego

*O*wning land does strange things to a person. We lived in our country home for just two weeks when a new unseemly side to my usually openhanded nature showed itself. I was standing near the large black oak tree that filled the center of our circular driveway when I heard the distant sound of engines polluting my country quiet. I looked up in time to see three ATVs cutting the corner of my property and disappearing over a hill. I wasn't well acquainted with that hill because it was an inhospitable area of poison oak, and the rutted dirt path was too steep for my lazy, pampered horses. Nevertheless, I seethed like an irate cattle rancher besieged by sheep herders. A git-my-gun attitude swept over me and for a moment I understood the feverish territorial barking of dogs. The next day I did the human version of peeing on bushes: I posted NO TRESPASSING signs.

My husband, Brian, never before lived on land either, and he wanted to give a name to our ninety-two acre parcel. "How about the Lazy S?" he asked.

"You're kidding, right?"

"Lazy S, Lazy Ass, get it?"

"Appropriate, but no."

"The guys at the OFBC think we should call it the compound." Brian had coffee six mornings a week with a gossipy group of codgers who referred to themselves as the Old Flyers Breakfast Club. Occasionally he said Farts or other 'F' words depending on the company or the mood.

"It sounds like we'll be posting gun turrets and brainwashing followers. I don't think so." I stood my ground. "When people name their property it's always either hokey or pretentious."

We dropped the subject until two years later when my son's Volkswagen bug sparked a fire that burned seventy acres and Rancho Del Fuego named itself.

Summer wildfires are an annual threat in the foothills of the Sierra Nevada. Forests turn kindling dry by June and thousands of acres burn each year. Our fire started near the seasonal pond across the road from our corral. It blazed up a grassy hill past a small stand of tall pine trees and the knoll I chose as my building site if we ever built our dream home.

A neighbor from a mile away saw the smoke and called. Seth, our thirteen-year-old, answered the phone. "Yeah, the fire department is on the way," he said.

"Are your dad and mom home?"

"No, but my brother's here."

"Are you boys okay? How close is the fire to the house?"

"The fire's about fifty feet away," Seth said.

Twenty-two-year-old Josh sprang across the kitchen and grabbed the phone from Seth. "It's okay," he said, "The fire's five hundred feet away, on the other side of the driveway and heading away from the house." When he hung up the phone, Josh turned to his younger brother. "How far is your bedroom from where we're standing?"

"About ten feet," Seth said.

"Right. Now how far is the back door?"

"About twenty feet."

"So that makes the shop what?"

"A hundred feet?"

"More like a hundred and fifty, but you get the idea, right?"

"I get it. Whatever. It's still too close," Seth answered.

After the air tanker and helicopters had flown away, the fire trucks rumbled off, and the twenty-member work release crew was counted and escorted back to where ever they came from, the firefighter in charge met with us. He wore the same yellow shirt and green cargo pants as the crew. His closely cropped, graying hair scarcely showed beneath his yellow helmet. A wide mustache formed a black arch over his mouth. As stoic as we were emotional, he listened patiently as we babbled.

"We're really sorry about this," Brian and I said.

"Thank you so much," I said.

"You guys are great. We appreciate everything," Brian said, "Who do we call if we see smoke?"

"Do you think those pine trees will live?" I asked.

"We've got really great water pressure in our wells." Brian loved to talk about our water pressure. He could work the gallons-per-minute statistics into any conversation within ninety seconds.

The firefighter waited for an opening then said, "It looks like we got it all, but I'll have a crew out tomorrow to check for hot-spots. Don't know about the pines." He gave us a number to call, and as he climbed into the cab of his truck, he looked up toward the burned area and said, "I've lived here all my life and that's the tallest poison oak I've ever seen."

We stared mutely after him as he drove away chased by a cloud of dust. Then we slowly turned our gaze toward what we would now call Charcoal Hill.

The pine trees did survive and the forest of poison oak came back an angry shade of red the following spring. Seth suffered three encounters with poison oak and the blisters, swelling, calamine treatments, cool-water baths and corticosteroid creams before finally learning to avoid it.

Besides poison oak and a dozen or so ponderosa pines, Rancho Del Fuego had twenty or thirty acres of meadows where oat grass and star thistle elbowed one another for room. Two seasonal ponds covered an acre each, and the view in any direction was of hillsides ornamented with nearly every kind of oak tree that grew in California. Year round the oak trees invited us to study them. In winter when the blue, California, valley, and other deciduous species had dropped their leaves a variety of evergreen live oaks colored our hills.

Brian wasn't the only one who liked to name things. To make conversations simpler I tried naming places. I called a grassy slope where Brian and I had seen a bobcat, Bobcat Hill. It was easier than saying, the hill over there east of the lower pond where we saw the bobcat. A large, rough boulder in a shaded draw west of the house became Horseshoe Rock; and a secluded corner where my dad said he would choose to build a house became Dad's Meadow.

But Brian's brain retained different information than mine. He could tell you how much power we saved in a month by switching to energy-saving light bulbs, whereas I couldn't tell you if we were saving kilograms or nanoseconds. But he never remembered the names I gave places, so conversation with him was generally made more difficult.

"I saw a coyote today in the middle of the Racetrack," I'd say.

"Where?"

"The Racetrack. By the upper pond."

"What racetrack?"

This was hopeless. "The path around the upper pond where it was so muddy last time we rode. I've been calling it the Racetrack. I thought you knew."

"Maybe I did. I don't know. What about it?"

"Never mind."

In January, Seth and I bought a fistful of fir tree saplings from the Forestry Service for a dollar apiece. Our property elevation was lower than recommended for fir trees, but for $20, we took a shot at home-grown Christmas trees. As we dug holes with a garden spade and patted muddy soil around thread-like roots we named them too. For a while, he and I knew parts of Rancho Del Fuego as over by Michael Jordan, or near Ross, Joey and Chandler. Brian never seemed to remember what we were doing. When the warm weather came and the saplings began to die, he simply rolled his eyes when we reported Bonnie and Clyde dead on Horse Poop Hill.

For three years, we enjoyed country life on Rancho Del Fuego. I spent my time writing, riding and learning woodworking. I had a corral built and bought two Quarter horses before we even moved into the house. Nearly everyone I knew rode with me at one time or another. For some, it was their first time on horseback, for my father-in-law it was the first time in nearly sixty years, since he was a teenager on his family ranch in eastern Washington.

Our patio was the sight of nearly as much activity as our living room. We ate breakfast there on weekends and barbequed with friends. When the weather turned hot, Brian installed a misting system on the pergola, and we swayed in a hammock under its refreshing mist on summer afternoons. In cool weather I slipped out to the heated spa on a daily basis.

I loved the quiet of the country; hearing through open windows the sound of acorns dropping through the leaves, and my horses shaking off dirt after a roll on the ground.

Rancho Del Fuego's isolation encouraged wildlife visitors. Our front yard was on a route wild turkeys followed daily one summer. Each morning, nine females and two toms appeared from the woods west of the pasture and passed by, like neighbors out for a stroll. I enjoyed visiting deer, even when they ate our apples.

I didn't, however, enjoy the three-quarter-mile rutted dirt road that was too long for our budget to pave. We shared the road with neighbors who resented all traffic past the rubbish heap they burrowed into each day after work. I didn't love the neighbor's gate that crossed the road and had to be manually opened and closed to drive through rain or shine, dust or mud.

Then the stock market plummeted, leaving us, and many other stunned Americans, reviewing our unexpectedly diminished options. The plans we'd had for improvements to the rutted road and the house at Rancho Del Fuego were no longer practical, and there was only so much we could do ourselves.

My son, Josh, stayed at the ranch while on breaks from college, together he and I made some improvements. Using rocks collected on the property, we built a wall that framed a backyard from a portion of the large open meadow behind the house. Our inability to make the wall run straight and even had the unexpected benefit of a homey, vintage look that fit beautifully against the backdrop of oaks.

I had concrete poured for a new, larger patio. Brian and Josh built the pergola, and Josh built a counter next to the spa. He helped me create an herb garden on the narrow slope between the new patio and the old; we remodeled a tool shed into a tack room and built stalls for my Quarter horses. My bond with my middle son was strengthened by the concrete we mixed and the nails he drove into boards I held in place.

Some projects were a group effort. In one weekend, the kids and I transformed the barren space between the driveway and the house into a landscaped oasis of evergreen shrubs, stepping stones and blooming flowers nestled against a boulder that Josh and Cameron, Brian's oldest son, delivered in the front-end loader of our John Deere. On the last day of the year, we hacked a new riding trail through the brush between Dad's Meadow and the Racetrack. I called it the New Year's Eve Trail.

Brian occasionally participated, but not often. His passion was flying and his time was spent at the airport. Our marriage got louder and rockier with his absences from home. His failure to help on projects was the primary subjects of dispute. Eventually, we made the difficult decision to sell Rancho Del Fuego.

When an offer came in on the property, I was visiting my daughter Rose, a business major at San Diego State University. Brian called to tell me the news and share an idea he hatched to start another business together.

With a buyer for the ranch, we examined our lives and saw opportunity. Four of our five children had fled to college and, at the moment, neither of us had a job. After selling our first business, Brian worked for a start-up company; and I was enjoying an early retirement. But the start-up failed and with the stock market decline I slipped from the giddy position of forty-something retiree to jostling for space in the unemployment line alongside others wearing the same disenchanted look. After a short, intense period of studying Brian's idea, we decided to make lemonade of our unemployment lemons and start another Internet business. This time, we'd take it to the beach. We would live on a boat and sell wireless Internet access at marinas in the Caribbean. I'd always dreamed of living in a foreign country, of seeing another culture from the inside. I wanted to know what similarities and differences might exist between me and women from another part of the globe… and maybe even learn to speak French.

As it turned out, the United States Virgin Islands was the logical place to offer wireless Internet access, so we wouldn't be moving to a foreign country—but it was far enough to satisfy the romantic adventurer in me.

We announced our decision to mixed reactions from family and friends. Some offered enthusiastic congratulations, then turned to spouses with a can we go, too look. These bold friends were married to less adventure-loving souls and some to resolute wives who clung to mortgages on their beautiful homes like a Labrador onto a sock. Some warned against a decision so obviously based on a foolhardy desire to enjoy the hell out of ourselves.

Our friend Dennis was helping Brian weigh and stow boxes and luggage in our airplane. "If you're still in the islands in the spring maybe I'll fly down after the Florida Sun-n-Fun Air Show."

"Come!" Brian said, "We'll be there two or three years at least."

Dennis paused a moment, then said, "You're both my friends, but do you think . . . well, that's a long time . . . the two of you . . . on a boat."

"I know," I said. "But, we're going to give it a try."

"The OFBC started a pool. I've got three months," Dennis said, then winked at me. Brian was studying the aircraft weight and balance chart.

"Pool. There's a pool betting how long Brian and I can stay on a boat together? Can I get in on that?" I winked back.

Our friends had good reason to be skeptical about the durability of our relationship in the confines of a boat. We had created the marital equivalent of an Ironman triathlon, and our energy was giving out. After meeting and falling blindly in love, we plunged headlong into what was the second marriage for both of us. Seven months later, we moved to a new house in a new town and gathered our blended family under one roof. Finally, to make things interesting, we started a business together. Statistically, we were more likely to open the door to Ed McMahon than make this marriage work.

However, we had learned in our years together that starting a bold venture was what we did best. It was our strongest compatibility. This might just be the shot in the arm our marriage needed.

Seth, hearing our plans to take him four thousand miles away to live on a boat, was beset by ambivalence. The boy was already confused as to whether life was an awesome journey filled with wrestling trophies and BMX bikes, or just one day after another that sucked of acne, burned-out teachers and twice-daily hour-long rides on a school bus. His brothers and sister, however, were unreservedly envious. They, too, wanted travel and adventure, and each one immediately began plans for extended visits.

Sausalito Sailing Camp

Brian looked forward to realizing a long-held dream of once again living on a sailboat, but there was a problem: I knew nothing about boats or sailing. As a twenty-year-old student at San Diego State University, Brian spent a year living on *Cleodoxa*, a boat he co-owned with a guy named Randy. Ever since Randy took both halves of the 32' sloop and disappeared, Brian had wanted to own another sailboat.

I was willing, but completely unqualified to act as crew. So before leaving California, we signed up for sailing lessons. It would be a refresher course for him and an introduction for me. Five days immersed in all things sailing; six to eight hours on the water each day; evenings studying the international rules; even sleeping on a boat. The Modern Sailing Academy in Sausalito, California called it their Basic Coastal Cruising course. I called it sailing camp.

Sausalito is nestled on the western shore of Richardson Bay north of San Francisco. It rests in the afternoon shadow of a five-mile-wide mountainous, blue-green, tree-covered peninsula that is home to the Golden Gate National Recreation Area on the northern side of the Golden Gate Bridge. Besides a small marina this Bohemian community hosts an extraordinary number of art galleries and restaurants, and few of those T-shirt and souvenir stores that litter Fishermans Wharf.

Our camp counselor, Carl, a blue-eyed Norwegian with short, blond hair, and no other resemblance to Dolph

Lundgren, introduced us to our vessel, a 32' Pearson Sloop, and fellow students, Bill and Frank.

After exchanging greetings, Bill looked at me and said, "I tried to get my wife to come."

Frank added, "Me too, but she doesn't even like boats."

Brian beamed. Sailing camp was off to a good start.

I've never excelled at any sport or activity, but I'll try anything, and if nudged, I'll take on a challenge. I got my pilot's license because Brian flew airplanes and he encouraged me. I learned how to handle handguns when Brian signed up for a four-day gun course in Pahrump, NV, and I wanted to go along.

I have interests of my own, but even those I don't pursue ardently. The horses on Rancho Del Fuego were mine, and I can ride, but I'm no expert. If I'm on a galloping horse don't ask me where we're going. Ask the horse, because my hands are clutching the saddle horn.

We strapped on bulky orange life-vests and spent most of the first day learning rules and nautical terms. We practiced getting in and out of the slip without scratching off the paint, or worse.

Learning to speak Nautical is like learning any foreign tongue. It is a colorful language of baggywrinkles, bobstays, coxswains, ratlines and lubberlines; of charley nobles, lazy jacks and travelers; of cuddys, gaffs, halyards, twings, vangs and yawing. Some terms evoke the image of large, creaking wooden sailing ships crossing the wide Atlantic to new lands, with captains' utterances of fo'c'sles and mizzens, burdened vessels and belaying orders.

One of the first lessons was those things that look like ropes, and indeed would be ropes if used to lead a horse or tie a truckload of furniture, become sheets when attached to a sail for changing direction. Unless it is attached to the kind of sail called a jib, in which case it's called a barber hauler or a twing. However, if it is used to raise or lower the sail then it's called a downhaul. If you detach the sheet or the barber hauler or downhaul from the sail and leave it lying on the deck, it becomes a line, unless you use it to let down the anchor, then you'll call it the rode. It doesn't turn back into a rope until you take it off the boat.

There were also important verbs to learn. For example: a sail doesn't flap, it luffs. And if someone tells you to fall off, they aren't suggesting you go for a swim, they want you to turn the boat away from the wind, also called jibing. An order to come about or head up means turn into the wind, this is the same as tacking. Fend-off means keep the boat from running into whatever it is the captain has gotten alarmingly close to.

The trick to getting the boat into the slip was to completely ignore all instincts. Each of us demonstrated the same instinct to turn in and cut the engine too soon. In the best case, we sent our crew scrambling to fend-off from the dock. Worse timing meant pivoting a dead in the water boat on the outside corner of the dock arm, and crewmembers grabbing a dock line and making the precarious jump to the dock to pull the boat into the slip. This was not a good maneuver to screw up. Two days later I found an even less popular way to screw up. More about this later.

At the end of each day, we showered in the marina facilities, drove a short distance to town for dinner, then returned to our boat to study for Friday's exam. Soon we were sleepy and it was time to scooch feet first into our bed… I mean bunk, or is it berth… I hoped that wasn't on the test. Brian and I slept in a low, narrow V-shaped space with a four-inch cushion that compressed flat if too much pressure was focused in one spot. So, after much wriggling to get underwear back where it belonged we laid motionless until falling asleep to the sound of water softly lapping the hull.

Tuesday and Wednesday were spent on the meat and potatoes of sailing. We tacked and jibed from Sausalito out to the dark blue of San Francisco Bay and around Angel Island to Tiberon. In the narrow three-quarter-mile passage between picturesque Angel Island and the Tiberon Peninsula, Carl lectured on give-way rules, and I wrestled with the definition of leeward and windward. This was certain to be on the test because it defines which of two converging boats has the right-of-way.

I was glad Brian enjoyed sharing his love of sailing with me, but I really didn't display the instincts for this stuff. It didn't matter how many times Carl and Brian explained the difference between coming about and falling off, or even if they drew diagrams. When someone said, "Get ready to come about." I had to carefully review. Facing forward on the boat, I recited to myself, "Okay, come about means we're going to change direction going into the wind. Now, the sail is poofing out that way, so the wind is coming from this way, so we're going to… "

"Coming about! Connie, release!"

Once we got into a routine, it was easy to perform the duties of crew. I did the opposite of what I did on the last turn. If I pulled on a sheet last time, the next time all I had to do was be ready to unwind it from the winch.

It wasn't so easy when it was my turn to act as captain. Late Wednesday afternoon I had the helm. I was tired, I'd been piloting for a while and we were heading toward the rough water of San Francisco Bay where the wind blew in from the Pacific under the Golden Gate. Carl was standing on the steps into the salon with his head and shoulders sticking up through the opening. He faced where I stood at the wheel. I looked at him and said, "I'd like to be relieved, I'm getting tired."

"Give it ten more minutes," he answered and I reluctantly agreed.

Brian called out, "You're luffing."

Maybe after sailing hours a day for weeks on end, steering a sailboat would be easy and natural, but it wasn't yet. It was stressful and tiring. I don't mind being corrected as long as it's done tactfully or gently. But I'm far too sensitive, and Brian is far too insensitive. I glared at him to mind his own business, then looked up at the sail and fell off just a little.

Learning to fly an airplane I never failed to stomp out of the cockpit in an angry snit if he'd been in the plane with me.

My altitude might drop and he'd snap, "You're off altitude."
As I slowly began the correction, he'd snap again, "You're off altitude."

"I heard you! Would you just let me fly the plane?"

"You have to stay on your altitude. Are you remembering your scan?"

"Yes, I'm remembering my scan."

"Well you were losing altitude."

"I was barely off. Do you want to fly the plane?"

"No, I want you to fly it right."

By the time I'd made my approach to land and he'd critiqued me right down to the roll-out, I'd be fuming mad and swearing never to get in a plane with him again.
When I finally got my pilot's license, I had to admit that though my instructor, an amazingly composed young woman named Sue, had taught me how to fly, Brian taught me to fly well.

Years later, Brian got his instructor's certificate and took me up for a refresher lesson. He was a different person altogether, quick to praise and allowing me my slow corrections. I, on the other hand, still need to be treated with kid gloves when it comes to criticism.

I stayed at the helm another ten minutes as Carl instructed, then he said, "Okay, turn her around then Bill can bring her in."

"Okay. Ready about," I called to my crew.

"Ready on port," Frank answered,

"Ready," Brian called.

"Coming about!" I called. Then I turned the wrong way.

The boom flew across the boat inches above the opening into the salon. Frank reacted quickly. He grabbed the sheet he had just released and swiftly rethreaded the port winch and hauled hand-over-hand to get the boom under control. Brian grabbed his sheet and spinning it like a lariat unwound it from the winch.

Carl popped back up out of the salon where he'd ducked just in time to avoid a split skull. "What the hell are you doing?"

"Sorry," I said sheepishly. I considered adding I said I was tired, but decided to trust him to fit that piece into the incident.

The next morning we woke to the sound of Bill knocking on the boat to go to breakfast. We jerked on our jeans and clean shirts and dashed up to meet him. On the way out of the salon I turned to Brian, "I didn't even look in a mirror. How do I look?"

"You look fine."

We said good morning to Bill and on the way to the car discussed our options for breakfast. At the café, I ducked into the restroom, looked in the mirror and got angry with Brian. I wore sunscreen every day, but I hadn't used lip balm. My lips were swollen to the size of pontoons. They were like the double-D cup of collagen injections.

Every woman who ever caught a husband answering the how-do-I-look question without looking, and every man who wondered why she bothered asking, knows what was said back at the table.

That next day, we practiced man-overboard drills. After everyone took their turn at the figure eight maneuver to recover a floating dummy, Carl asked whether we wanted to spend the afternoon doing more drills, sailing out to the Pacific under the Golden Gate, or call it a day. If they'd counted all the votes there would have been one for more practice, but with three for sailing under the Golden Gate, they didn't bother to keep counting.

I zipped my windbreaker against the chill before we even reached the wind-stirred water of San Francisco Bay. As we approached the Golden Gate, the sky closed around us. Low clouds closeted us and the water grew darker as the fog grew heavier. By the time we were looking up at the bridge through the shroud of fog, I was cold to the bone and queasy from the rough waves. I looked at the men for signs of shivering or shades of green. They were all red cheeks and smiles. I closed my swollen lips around chattering teeth and fixed my gaze on the horizon. I was determined to tough it out until we cleared the bridge and turned around.

We advanced nauseatingly slowly. We were on a close reach, the wind was nearly on the bow, so most of our progress was sideways to our goal. Finally, we cleared the bridge. I relaxed a little thinking the worst was over. But the guys weren't turning around. Now I faced a dilemma. I was not about to change their opinion of me as a great sport, so I had to choose between going below and torturing my motion-sensitive stomach, or staying above deck and freezing. I told Brian I was going below. It was definitely warmer inside and I was definitely sicker. What was wrong with those men? Why weren't they miserable? Why was I? I didn't care which question was answered, but surely I deserved an answer to one of them.

I soon learned my fellow students had set the goal of sailing to a buoy at the mouth of the bay. If we'd been under power, it would have all been over in a few minutes. But every time we tacked, my misery increased. I'd have mutinied if I'd had strength. I considered going back up, but it was raining now, so I tried to watch the horizon through a tiny porthole as the contents of my stomach pounded my insides like waves on the shoreline. Any number of insect species and possibly small mammals were born, lived their lives and died during the span of time I suffered in that cabin.

Finally, good sport be damned. I stuck my head out of the salon and tugged on Brian's sleeve. I paraphrased make-this-boat-turn-around-or-I'm-going-to-die-and-leave-a-note-blaming-you into, "Can we please go back?"

Brian turned to the others and said, "Why don't we head back?"

"Okay," they said, and turned the boat around.

"How's Connie?" Frank asked.

Brian paraphrased she's-green-as-seaweed -and-would-be-angry-if-she-had-the-strength, into, "She gets motion sick."

That night I announced to Brian I wasn't going sailing after the written test in the morning. I had no plans to ever sail a boat by myself, so I didn't care if I got my logbook signed off. Moreover, I would move to Kansas and start a worm farm before spending another afternoon like that day.

Brian pleaded with me to change my mind, but the queasiness was fresh in my memory, and my stomach would not relent.

Friday morning was the sunniest yet. We took the test in the spacious, sun-streaked salon of a white catamaran docked at the end of the wharf. I told Carl I wasn't coming along for the sailing. He, too, pleaded with me to change my mind, promising an easy sail and lunch in Tiberon. I hesitated and he threw in a promise to make it a short day, so, again, I reluctantly consented.

This time I was rewarded for giving in. Friday was the finest day yet and Carl stayed true to his word. We spent a pleasant morning sailing and practicing tying knots-bowline for attaching fenders to the life lines, square knots for connecting two lines, and a half-hitch for quick release-while Carl told stories meant to encourage safe sailing. At noon we pulled up to the wharf at Tiberon, and waited patiently at picnic tables on the crowded patio of a fish and chips house for lunch. Then, getting up from the table we decided on a quick run around Angel Island before calling it a day. The best was yet to come.

Leaving Tiberon, we headed east along the north coast of Angel Island. Turning south, we rounded the eastern-most point of the island to see the sun shining on the Golden Gate Bridge. We also saw the live action version of a *SAIL* magazine cover: an America's Cup practice race in progress. Half a dozen sleek thirty-meter yachts with brilliant sails raced across the bay toward the passage between Tiberon and Angel Island. Carl ordered a heading directly across their bows. We shot glances at one another, then eagerly complied. This was cool.

We watched the world famous yachts as main sails and jibs went down and colorful spinnakers were raised. One sky-blue spinnaker filled with wind and immediately split down the middle. Moments later another, a white one, on another boat also split. We sailed so close, I counted the crew on Larry Ellison's Oracle BMW and the other yachts speeding toward us.

We passed in front of the racers then loosed our sheets, letting our sails go into the wind, we stopped to watch until the yachts were out of sight past Belvedere. We called it a day and spent the afternoon talking about what we had witnessed.

Everyone passed the written test and got their American Sailing Association logbooks signed off for Basic Keelboat Sailing and Basic Coastal Cruising. We said goodbye to Frank and Bill. They were envious of our plans to move to the Caribbean to live and work on a boat. We coaxed a promise from Frank to stay with us on a Caribbean vacation he and his wife planned for the following year. More than ever, Brian and I looked forward to sailing and entertaining on our very own sailboat.

Travels with a Fire Bucket

Our airplane was a white twin-engine Piper Aztec nicknamed Aztruck for its passenger and cargo capacity. We loaded it bottom to top with boxes and duffle bags, stuffing pillows into the gaps, and finally ourselves into the seats.

In the years since I married a pilot, I logged thousands of hours in small planes, and even got my pilot's license. But I never got over a life-long susceptibility to motion sickness. I've tried every remedy known to medicine and old wives. As a child, my mother spooned bitter yellow syrup down my throat prior to any road trip. Forty years later, I'm certain I would recognize that smell. I also remember the time she forgot to give me the medicine, and the sight of my father grabbing at bushes and skidding on his heels down a brush-covered embankment to a creek to wash out my car-sick bucket (a red pail with F I R E on the side in yellow).

By the time I was a gangly thirteen-year-old, I'd outgrown the need for my fire bucket, but never became fully comfortable with most kinds of motion. In my constant effort to enjoy the journey as well as the destination, I've used patches, pressure bands, Dramamine, Bonine, ginger tablets, and on our trip from California to the Virgin Islands, electric shock treatment in the form of a battery-operated wristband. Nothing really worked.

The first leg of our trip to St. Thomas passed smoothly. Brian leveled the airplane at 8000 feet over California's golden San Joaquin Valley. I read passages from Steinbeck's *Sea of*

Cortez aloud to him while Seth slept in back with our black and white border collie, Puck, on his feet.

When the San Joaquin Valley fell behind and we skimmed the peaks of the San Gabriel Mountains in Southern California, I got a quick look at the Mount Wilson Observatory before we began our descent into the Los Angeles Basin. We followed the ocean side of the mountains and Highway 210 toward Cable Airport in Upland. Our first stop, to say good-bye to my in-laws.

Small planes rarely have air-conditioning and on a hot day the beginning and end of a flight are miserable. Once the door shuts, there's nothing to do but open the vents and wait for the climb to a cooler altitude. Summer landings are like descents into hell. The sun beats through the large front windows and temperatures rise until you lurch to a stop, thrust the door open and emerge dripping perspiration and searching for a patch of shade.

This was how we arrived in Upland, California near Brian's hometown. I climbed from the plane sweaty and thirsty and headed straight to the airport café's covered patio. I drank a tall iced tea while Brian rearranged luggage in the back seat to get the dog off Seth's feet. Brian's parents arrived and took photos then drove us back to their place for tuna sandwiches and two hours of reassuring them they would see their grandson again before they died.

I truly envy people who don't live with motion sickness. I want to delight in the travel experience, but I tolerate it at best. On this trip, I had a lingering head cold adding its effect along with the heat, the starting, stopping and swaying about in airplanes and cars. I was piteously miserable.

Under the best circumstances, which this certainly was not, anything longer than a three hour flight is too damned long for me. Our flight east to El Paso lasted two hundred and thirty wretched, please just shoot me now minutes. Closing the door for take-off the cockpit assumed the characteristic of a prison camp hotbox and I felt a growing queasiness. I pressed the ON button of my motion relief wristband. Within minutes,

I had adjusted the power to the highest setting and shoved my twitching fingers between my sweaty legs to steady them.

There was a blessed moment of comfort when we reached altitude and a cool breeze blew through the vent onto my feet. The horizon behind us blazed a fiery red and orange sunset cloaked in deepening shades of purple. Then the sun slipped below the horizon. The sky grew dark and the air turned cold. The vent stuck in the open position and a chilling blast blew on my feet, numbing me to the knees. The iced tea that quenched my thirst hours before began pressing against my insides. I draped a sweatshirt across my shivering bare legs for warmth, closed my eyes and leaned my head against the window. I longed to be forever on the ground and wondered if I could find another way to the Virgin Islands.

I enjoyed the smooth flight to Austin the next morning until the hot, bumpy descent and a return of my nausea. Approaching an airport is the time I need to be alert. I lifted my head from where I'd let it fall against the window and tried to focus my eyes to look for air traffic and pretend to look for the runway (I seldom actually looked because Brian always saw it before I did). Once we were safely on final approach, I let my head fall back against the window.

Eating lunch revived me enough for Brian to somehow get me back in the airplane for a hop to Beaumont, Texas. It was a calm, comfortable flight and we had the Beaumont runway in sight when we had to abort our landing. A thunderstorm was making its approach ahead of us at the other end of the runway. According to FAA regulations, we had the right of way, but thunderstorms, like rhinoceroses and two year olds don't care whose turn it is. We diverted to Galveston.

The first thing that struck me climbing out of the cockpit at the Galveston City Airport was the sky. It plunged right down to our tennis shoes. No hills, mountains or even tall buildings intruded on the vast grey dome.

I grew up in the Pacific Northwest where hills go study to become mountains. Then I moved to California where fertile valleys of cotton, rice, grapes and a hundred other crops are bordered by the far-reaching Sierra Nevada. Geographic flatness was a strange sensation. I felt exposed.

Galveston Island is a thirty-mile-long, two-mile-wide barrier reef. Seawall Boulevard runs its length like a concrete police tape separating hotels on one side from the beach on the other.

We checked into a La Quinta Inn, leaving Puck to howl in the hotel while we walked to dinner. The sky had transformed into a shadowy black dome illuminated unevenly by city lights. The thunderstorm followed us from Beaumont, arriving in Galveston while we ate in an unexceptional diner on the boulevard.

Warning drops of rain fell while we browsed food-stained menus, and arrived in torrents before our dinner appeared. We gazed out the window at a bottle rolling down Seawall Boulevard as if driven by determination rather than the wind. Lightning flashed a hundred times, white threads shooting from cloud to cloud and sky to sea, like snowflakes, no two alike. The rain slowed and we considered dessert. This was my first small Southern diner. My mouth watered for homemade apple pie or warm peach cobbler. The waitress made no apologies for the selection of ice cream or tapioca.

The rain stopped before Seth's scoop of spumoni arrived in its aluminum dish, but it doesn't take a teenage boy long to eat ice cream and soon we were walking back to the hotel, sprayed now and then by gusts of wet wind.

My travel-weary body stayed stubbornly on Pacific Coast Time. I lay in bed until one a.m. listening as the air conditioner repeatedly shook itself awake, roared into action, then fell back to sleep, leaving only the sound of Seth's snoring.

Even as a toddler, Seth's snoring could be heard down the hall through closed doors. My petite grandmother had been a snorer and though loud she had rhythm. Seth's was a zoo-like medley of wheezing, snorting and honking that sets me alternately to fits of giggling and pulling the pillow over my ears.

In the morning, I was still asleep when Brian finished showering and turned on his favorite television entertainment: the weather channel. He nudged the pile of sheets where I lay. Dragging myself from bed, I splashed water on my face and brewed a cup of tea in the miniature coffee maker by the sink. When Seth got up, we all trudged to the lobby for continental breakfast before heading back to the airport. Though my cold seemed to be gone, I drank a tall glass of orange juice. I didn't want a relapse and another day of nausea.

While we were in the air, I kept my eyes closed, leaned on a pillow and turned my motion relief band on high. This got me through the day without acting on my contemplations of how terrifying a death it would be to open the cockpit door and throw myself out. It was an easy flight, but I shouldn't have had so much tea and juice. Bathrooms were becoming beautiful things to me.

One hundred eighty-two minutes after taking off, we landed at a tiny airstrip outside a small town in Louisiana. I hurried inside to find one gray windowless bathroom with an ill-tempered, uncooperative toilet and another with a door that wouldn't latch properly and a rust-stained sink leaking aggressively into a plastic bucket. I adored them both.

We ordered fuel for the airplane from a skinny fellow in coveralls and a dirty cap. Brian asked about a courtesy car and the fellow tossed us keys to an old police car. He followed us outside and in that Southern way of using few words cautioned, "Starts out sluggish, gotta work 'er gas some. Run fine by time you get to town."

We asked about a restaurant.

"Might try Jim's. In town, three… four lights, on the left. The catfish 's good eatin.'"

I opened the back door of the cruiser for Seth and pushed his head down as he got in.

He played along, "You can't prove I done a thing, copper."

"Mind yer manners, boy," I said, "And we might just fix you up with some vittles."

"I'll pass on the catfish," he said.

At fourteen, Seth was still on the short side for his age, but he was athletic. He played on his middle school football team and home on Rancho Del Fuego he could take his BMX bike nearly anywhere I rode my horses. He had light brown hair and though he was my step-son, he looked enough like me to pass as my own. There is a reason for this: his mother and I look surprisingly alike. Brian definitely had a type: petite, blue-eyed blonds with weak chins and passionate, slightly obsessive, personalities.

Seth was an ideal traveling companion. He complained little, assumed responsibility for the twice-daily nuisance of dog-walking, occasionally showed signs of enjoying himself and if he wasn't moving he fell asleep. A couple of times he returned bleary-eyed from dog-walking, having nearly dozed off waiting for Puck to take care of business. We were pleased and proud of such cooperation from a teenager dragged away from his school and best friend of six years: a tall, skinny kid named Andy whose naturally red hair often appeared in various primary colors.

We found Jim's Steakhouse, slid into a booth by a window and ordered two catfish plates and a burger. Waiting for our lunch we turned our attention to a small southern mansion just across the road. Trees draped with Spanish moss shaded half-an-acre of blue-green lawn and partially blocked the view of immense windows and a wide, pillared front porch. Its antebellum beauty seemed more appropriately found on a country lane down a driveway fenced and graced by thoroughbreds. Yet here it was across the street from a steakhouse. I love new places and sights. It's just traveling I dislike.

Back at the airport, we waited out another thunderstorm. Seth and I found the pilots' lounge, a large room with a sofa on one side and a 15" television on the far wall. We watched a black and white John Wayne movie while Puck took advantage of the space to stretch out and Brian talked airplanes with staff and the aviation wannabees that can be found at every small airport.

Brian loved all things aviation and he knew more about airplanes than the men who sell them. He could talk tirelessly about airplanes and was in demand by friends for his knowledge and advice. He learned to fly when he was sixteen, before he learned to drive a car. He soon got his instrument and commercial ratings and later became an instructor. In recent years, he studied formation flying and aerobatics and has flown at air shows including the mother of all air shows at Oshkosh, Wisconsin.

I embraced Brian's passion at first, but eventually when the choice was keep up, sit and watch, or stay home, I found myself increasingly choosing to stay home. I grew to resent the hobby he placed above all else.

Seth munched fresh-popped popcorn from a machine in a corner of the lounge. I gazed on and licked my lips. It would have made me thirsty, but when the weather cleared I'd be saying good-bye to my new disinfectant-scented friends, the bathrooms.

When the storm passed, we flew a pleasant final hop for the day, though the fried catfish made threatening rumbles. By sunset, the sky was clear and we watched the scattered lights of Northern Florida passing below. We landed in Stewart on the East Coast at ten p.m.

There's nothing like seeing the world through the window of a small plane. From five or even ten thousand feet more geography is perceptible than ever could be seen from the cruising altitude of a 747. And, unlike rolling across ribbons of highway in a car or bus, the forest isn't lost for the trees. Hour after hour I've looked down on patchwork quilts of farmland spreading across the Midwest. I've caught glimpses of our plane's shadow slipping playfully through canyons of the badlands of South Dakota, and wondered what it must have been like to cross such arid desolation in a covered wagon. From my window I've seen why they're called the Great Lakes and watched as the Nevada desert suddenly stopped and jagged peaks of the Sierra Nevada tore at the sky, reaching toward our plane. I learned more about the geography of the United States in one cross-country trip than my entire childhood at an elementary school desk. I cherished every opportunity to share the experience with our children. We had five between us and there were usually two or three in the back seat of the plane ... asleep.

Turks and Caicos

We took time in Florida to look at two catamarans for sale. It was there we learned that at marinas power boats are called boats and sailboats are generally referred to as yachts. When you say yacht, I think Onassis and Trump, butlers (or are they stewards) and chefs, champagne and caviar. It sounded pretentious to my middle-class ear to say I was shopping for a yacht.

Seth and I immediately liked the first yacht we toured. Its interior walls gleamed smooth and white, handy cubbyholes lined the seating area of the salon and the bikini closets—thus named by me for their capacity—had smooth, high-gloss, varnished mahogany doors. But, Brian said he saw daylight through the hull in a forward compartment. After a brief debate, Seth and I caved to his argument that hull integrity was more important than cubbies and mahogany. We moved on to a yacht for sale by owner in Fort Lauderdale.

The directions to the next yacht led us through a neighborhood of 1960s architecture and landscaping. The houses featured long straight lines, exaggerated angles and walls of glass. Yards were populated with shrubs sculpted into balls and spires. We were led through the house and out the back door. Our feet squished across the rain-soaked lawn to where the yacht sat tied to a private dock. This guy lived on the Atlantic Intracoastal Waterway.

If the United States wasn't so immense I might be embarrassed to admit ignorance of a major geographic feature. However, it's a forgivable offense in the third largest country on earth so I'm telling you now, I didn't even know there was such a thing as an Atlantic Intracoastal Waterway.

The ICW, if you want to conserve syllables, is 1200 miles of navigable manmade canals, bays, natural river channels and estuaries from Norfolk, Virginia to Key West, Florida, the southern-most point of the continental United States. It passes the likes of Charleston, Savannah, the Kennedy Space Center at Cape Canaveral and West Palm Beach, to name just a few cities along its path. Someday I'm going to cruise the ICW. That will definitely be a hoot.

This yacht told another story altogether, a story titled neglect. While the owner pointed out amenities, we exchanged looks over stained panels of water-damaged wood in the salon. A heavy mildew odor, undiminished by the intermittent wind from an oscillating fan, filled our nostrils and drove us bumping into one another in our hurry to finish the tour. Even allowing for a reduced price, we weren't up to the challenges of such a bargain.

We might have lingered yacht shopping in Florida longer, but were expected in the Turks and Caicos the next day to look at a 48' catamaran. Brian's online research found the web page for the yacht, *Take Two*, some weeks before and in correspondence with her owners he discovered mutual business interests. Excited for the possibilities, we scheduled an overnight stay to check-out the yacht and talk wireless internet.

~~~~

Before taking off from Stewart, Florida, we bought life vests and stowed them within easy reach. If, before we left, anyone had asked if I was nervous about flying out to sea, I would have said yes. But when the time came, it didn't occur to me. There was too much sea to see. The coastline was fringed in white sand, soft blue water and a lacey border of whitecaps drifting between the beach and ever deepening shades of blue ocean.

After the coastline receded, I followed our position on the chart, matching tiny island shapes to the real thing below. When I ran out of islands, I gazed hypnotized at the whitecaps and motion of the surface, or gave my thoughts over to fantasies about desert islands.

Fantasizing isn't as easy as it once was. As a teenager nothing was implausible. In my daydreams I wasn't a skinny, shy girl who stuffed her bra with tissue; in those daydreams I didn't need padding and I didn't need braces. Boys with clear complexions drove Corvettes and competed for my attention; and there was always kissing. Now when I fantasize about life on a desert island and making love in the surf with Indiana Jones, my mind wanders to birth control. Or I picture myself bathing under a waterfall... then I'm thinking how gross my hair would be without shampoo. If I imagine sharing coconut milk with Indiana, it spills onto my bare breasts... suddenly I'm wondering if coconut milk has lactose. Fantasizing, it seems, is one more thing that gets more difficult as we get older.

Conversation in a small plane is a pain. The pilot is listening for air traffic control and transmissions of aircraft that might be in the vicinity. Chatting was regularly interrupted by Brian frantically waving his hand in the air between us, his signal to me to stop talking so he could listen to the radio. He only had to do this two or three times to shut me up for the rest of the flight. This gave me time to think about our decision to move to the Caribbean.

We were hanging a lot on the last threads holding our marriage together. Before we decided to move to St. Thomas, Brian had been researching the possibility of sailing around the world, and I was shopping for a house near my daughter in San Diego. I thought I would fly into major ports to join Brian sailing along some exotic coast until motion sickness or quarreling drove me back to the states. We needed a break from the fighting, but the thought of a second failed marriage was... well, unthinkable; anyway, we still loved each other. And, there was Seth. He'd already been through two divorces.

He was a baby when Brian and his mother split up and six when his mother took the boys away from the step-father Seth had been calling Dad since he learned to talk. He was six and a half when he came to live with us. Now, at the age of fourteen, Seth was facing the very real possibility of his third divorce.

We were motivated to find another solution, but the obvious problem of Brian living on a sailboat and me in a house was we couldn't afford it. He would have to live on fish and seawater and I'd have to get a job, making it difficult to visit him. And, there was Seth. Brian was educated and smart enough to home school him, but Seth deserved a say in the matter too.

When Brian suggested selling Internet access at marinas, Seth and I embraced the new plan.

Four years had passed since delivering our first business into the hands of a buyer and, like childbirth, the memory of the long, painful hours had diminished. I was ready to do it again. I hoped living together on a boat would be easier than living on 92 acres. I wanted to believe we could leave our problems in California where I'd wanted Brian to be more involved in repairs and improvements; where I fought with his oldest son whenever he came home from college, and Brian always sided with him; and I spent hours glancing down the unpaved driveway waiting for Brian to come home, only to have grown angry by the time he eventually showed up.

~~~~

Before leaving Florida, we learned of a curious ruling from the United States Department of Homeland Security: Aircraft leaving the U.S. must stop at an approved country prior to landing at an unapproved country.

This didn't make sense. "You mean before we arrive in the United States Virgin Islands we must come from an approved country," Brian said to the official behind the counter.

"No, when you leave you must go to an approved airport."

"That doesn't make sense. If it's okay for us to land in the Turks and Caicos, why can't we fly directly there?" The official shrugged.

This was too absurd. There must be some confusion, I rephrased the question, "You mean if we want to fly to the Turks and Caicos we have to fly to the Bahamas first?"

"It doesn't have to be the Bahamas. You just have to land at any approved country when you leave the United States."

Brian and I looked at each other, then found another official to ask, and got the same incomprehensible answer.

Technically, I have been to the Bahamas. Mayaguana is the farthest east and least developed Bahama. The port of entry was one of two plain wood 12x12 buildings next to a concrete runway shaved into the south side of the island. We waited an hour leaning against walls anywhere we could find shade. Soon, Seth and I grew bored with leaning and set off exploring. We crossed an empty gravel parking lot and found a shack housing bathrooms; we ventured a few feet into a wooded area behind the restrooms, and that was pretty much it. We were back leaning against the wall before you could say, "I've nothing to declare." A few plastic chairs were inhabited by taciturn locals who showed no interest when we tried to engage them in conversation. Indeed, they showed little sign of life beyond the occasional blink or swatting of a fly. After ninety minutes waiting, a customs official waved Brian inside. He looked at our passports and asked two questions. "What is your aircraft number?"

"November one five kilo Yankee."

"What country did you leave from to come here?"

"The United States. Florida."

"Okay, you may go," he said handing back our passports.

Seth asked to have his passport stamped and was obliged. I wanted mine stamped, too, but was off somewhere swatting flies and missed my chance.

The Turks and Caicos lie half-way between Florida and the Virgin Islands. We landed on Provo (what the locals call Providenciales), and, following a series of signs and instructions through a brief reception as we were processed by smiling, soft-spoken customs officials. When they returned our passports, Seth and I immediately opened them. Finally, I had a stamp from an exotic destination.

The owners of *Take Two*, Allen and Liz, met us in the airport parking lot, with an old Toyota to use while on Provo, and arranged to meet us for dinner.

The forty islands of the Turks and Caicos are part of what's left of the British Empire. Provo, one of eight that are inhabited, is thirty-eight square miles of dismally flat, arid dirt, dappled conservatively with various tropical grasses, flowering plants and cactus, most conspicuously the red-capped Turks Head Cactus.

We found an austere, but charming, hotel with rooms that opened off either side of a wide, Mexican-tiled hallway. Thick, white walls brought to mind a simpler time. A time before building a house required legions of sub-contractors and homeowners supplicating bureaucrats for permission to build a simple tool shed; before electric bills and rolling brown-outs. A time when less was more and the only climate control was shutters opened to the breeze or pulled closed against a storm.

I suppose I'm romanticizing and over-looking the reality of nightly hordes of insects buzzing about oil lamps and palmetto bugs on floors, pillows and dinner plates. It's hard to speculate what life was really like in what we call simpler times.

In our room, in the early twenty-first century, I slid open a glass door and stepped onto a tiny patio. A miniature lizard darted under a cactus. A hundred yards away a regiment of palm trees stood watch over the marina and the blue water of Turtle Cove. A breeze played about the masts of sailboats and branches of the trees on its way to cool my skin and ease my uncertainties about the future.

August is off-season (aka hurricane season) and the hotel restaurant was closed. Liz suggested walking a narrow dirt path to the marina below for dinner at the Shark Bite Bar & Grill. The menu was as entertaining as the food was delicious. Listed with quesadillas and nachos were Chum-Chum Chili, Missing Fingers of chicken, conch or fish, a PADI melt, and Hammerhead Hotdog. I selected, as was my tendency lately, one of the less expensive entrees. The vegetables, mangos and mushrooms of my curry dish were tasty, but after trying a bite from Brian's plate, I wished I had indulged in the Almond Crusted Grouper as he had. The tender piece of fish was resting in a pool of luscious creamy coconut, rum curry sauce.

We talked about business and boats, and walked down the white painted dock for a look at *Take Two*. Since contacting Allen and Liz weeks before, Brian crunched the numbers and concluded he couldn't afford their yacht. But they pressed him to give her a test sail anyway and we were happy to agree. We picked up the tab for dinner and the next day they took us sailing and hosted lunch.

Seth and I did our part getting underway by staying out of the way. We dodged whipping lines and flapping sails until we found safety at the extreme front of the yacht. This was my assigned position most of the day. It worked pretty well considering it's difficult to help while facing forward and keeping an eye on the horizon. I had a wonderful time, but I'll always be envious of people who don't suffer from motion sickness. After a brief squall blew past, soaking everyone, we stopped for lunch and snorkeling. Sand dollars littered the sandy bottom picturesquely as though Neptune himself scattered them just so. Among the sparse distribution of grass tufts and brain coral I spotted a conch shell. Brian plucked it from the bottom for me. Inside the ruffled pink edge a luminous blue and yellow fish, smaller than a hummingbird's tail, darted back and forth. Seth and Brian found another conch and placed it on the swim step to look at later. But Allen spotted a small grey fish gasping for breath inside and returned the fish and its condo to the water.

That evening we drove to the beachside residence where Liz and Allen were house-sitting. Seth paddled a kayak along the marshy shoreline while Liz mixed drinks and Allen barbequed lobster tails and steak on a large deck facing the sunset. Before arriving on the island, we had hoped to be meeting with wealthy, successful entrepreneurs. Clearly Liz and Allen, like most people we knew, were just getting by. But they were just getting by on a tropical island, eating lobster tail and serving rum cocktails on a patio that overlooked the ocean. All things considered, we still felt pretty good about our move to the Caribbean.

Leaving Provo, our flight plan once again required stopping at an approved country prior to our destination, this time St. Thomas in the United States Virgin Islands. Rather than a fuel-consuming back-track to the Bahamas, Brian decided we'd fly to Tortola in the British Virgin Islands where we could apply for a waiver to retrieve the Aztec in ten days. It would mean added inconvenience of dragging duffel bags and the dog on a ferry from Tortola to St. Thomas, but Brian asked at least three officials if it might be possible to get a waiver on short notice and each time the answer was an unambiguous, "No." Brian, however, is not easily discouraged, and while en route to the Virgins he radioed ahead asking for a waiver. They gave it to him then and there over the radio.

I'm saddened and sorry to report that U.S.V.I. Customs was the most unpleasant we encountered. The terse, unsmiling official was neither friendly nor helpful. Though the lobby was not busy nor the hour late the uniformed man was brusque and responded to our exhilaration with impatience. The unwarranted inhospitable nature of our welcome back to American soil completely puzzled us. We headed to the rental car office disappointed in our fellow Americans. Over time we would learn this sort of "customer service" was all too common.

Lesser Geography

The thing about suddenly relocating any great distance from home is you don't know where you are relative to anywhere else. I'd vacationed in the Caribbean before, but didn't learn any geography. The first time was on a cruise ship where time and distance were measured in daiquiris and wardrobe changes. I'd wake in the morning, the ship having floated quietly, almost magically, into the port of St. Whosit during the night. I was far from home, but it didn't matter how far so long as the shops offered either exotic products or lower prices, and the locals spoke with a West Indies accent, but still understood when I asked for lime in my ginger ale.

My second trip to the West Indies, on a family vacation to the British Virgin Islands, introduced our four sons, daughter and niece to the Caribbean. The age range, from ten to twenty, was clustered at the high end and my focus on that trip was not geography, but entertainment director, and then, having found all the hottest night-spots, sleepless parent.

On the family vacation, Puerto Rico had been our last stop before flying into the B.V.I., but I already knew Puerto Rico was somewhere in the Caribbean. All I learned on that trip was the distance between the British Virgin Islands and the U.S. Virgin Islands was so close, Jack LaLane wouldn't bother swimming it on his birthday, not even pulling a barge of sunburned tourists. But it still required a stop at customs. From our chartered boat we could see St. John, the nearest U.S. Island, but we couldn't visit unless we wanted to hassle with customs. Since we already provisioned ourselves with shot glasses, sarongs, and pirate T-shirts, we merely sailed past.

Now that I was living in the islands, I wanted to know whether to react in awed amazement or merely nod understanding when someone related a sailing story that included another island. Too often, I choose the wrong response and the speaker, after a pause to glance at me, would turn slightly more toward Brian to finish the story.

Here's what I learned about Caribbean geography: Miami is hell and gone from the U.S.V.I., nearly a thousand watery miles. In our twin engine airplane, it took as long to fly from Fort Lauderdale to St. Thomas as it would to fly from Seattle to San Diego.

There are twenty-three territories and countries in the Caribbean, with heaven knows how many total islands. The U.K. holds dominion over four territories, France, the Netherlands, and the U.S. retain authority over two each.

The Virgin Islands are smack dab in the middle of the Caribbean enjoying the same balmy latitude 18 weather as Puerto Rico, Hispaniola, and Jamaica. These islands, along with Cuba, are known as the Greater Antilles. Don't ask me what an Antille is and until looking at the West Indies map I thought I knew the difference between Windward and Leeward, but again I was confused.

They like to group their islands down here. The Caribbean page in my atlas might have been filled in during a West Indies equivalent of a N.A.T.O. meeting. I can imagine sand flying and the representative from Grenada pounding the table with his flip-flop while asserting his country's position as a Windward island, while neighboring St. Vincent insisted they are a Lesser Antilles country.

Here's the breakdown of where we were: The U.S. Virgin Islands are part of the Virgin Islands which are Leeward Islands, which are included in the Lesser Antilles also known as the chase your source of revenue away by mugging tourists islands.

The Cayman Islands, alone to the west, and the Bahamas to the north seem to have escaped inclusion in these bewildering categories. Trinidad and Tobago are the southern-most lesser Windward Islands, which puts them hell and really gone from Miami. They hug close enough to the coast of South America to skip a rock, if you can find a really good, flat rock.

One surprise I'm embarrassed to admit, but why stop now, was just how big Cuba is, as Caribbean islands go anyway. There are some very tiny islands in the Caribbean. It might seem a bit presumptuous for eight-mile-long Nevis, even partnering with the slightly larger St. Kitts, to call themselves a country. But there's nothing presumptuous about 700-mile-long Cuba. If you swung Cuba around with one end touching Florida, the other end could reach all the way to Nicaragua which lies halfway between Panama and the southern Mexican border. However, you might prefer to bring it up to Cancún. Of course this is all academic. The chances of Cuba swinging around and making a land bridge to Cancún are only slightly less than either Castro brother is likely to swing open the doors to democracy, or the U.S. government to allow me to legally mail a box of Cohibas to my brother.

Six short weeks after Brian's phone call suggesting we buy a boat and start another business, we were on St. Thomas, our new home and the world famous stop for hundreds of cruise ships every year. The ships come because of the natural deepwater harbor. The passengers flock ashore for tropical beach experiences or souvenirs from the shops in cosmopolitan Charlotte Amalie. Brian came to fulfill his dream of living on a boat. I came hoping for more time with my husband. And we both hoped to rebuild the bank account.

Two hours after landing, we sat beachside eating conch fritters with mango salsa. The fritters were soft balls of corn meal, presumably flavored with conch, but we couldn't tell. The salsa was sweet and hot. Steel drums on the beach played Strangers in the Night, and fruity, orange rum drinks dripped condensation onto our table. Brian turned to me and said, "I promised you wouldn't be bored."

It was a promise he liked to remind me of because he'd kept it well. In twelve years of marriage, he taught me how to swing dance and fly airplanes; we built and sold a business; moved from a condo in Silicon Valley during the dot-com explosion to ninety-two acres in the country; and raised our blended family.

Maybe it wasn't an inspired idea moving a troubled marriage onto a boat, but Brian and I weren't quarrelling. We rarely did away from the house. In our twelve years together, the two vacations Brian and I took—not counting his flying sojourns I tagged along on—were unqualified successes. We each scheduled our choice of activity on alternate days and then enjoyed them together. I wouldn't have thought to rent an airplane to fly around the Hawaiian Islands, but Brian wanted to and we saw Hawaii the way few people do. I had to coax him poolside into the Grand Wailea's mini water-park, but once I did, we played in the water all afternoon. He wanted to fly over the Grand Canyon and I wanted to see it from the ground. Vacationing was something we did well, but unfortunately, not often. Brian preferred going to air shows. He would tell you trips to air shows were also successful, but I wouldn't. I sat ignored and bored by him and his aviation buddies, stayed in the hotel or did the tourist thing alone.

Thus far, our trip had been like a vacation. The sightseeing was incidental, but it added to the excitement of our new undertaking. There was much to discuss and plan. I liked being involved with him again. I wasn't merely a tag-along to a flying clinic, or a nagging wife. At home we argued about housework, money, his time spent at the airport, everything, even whether we argued. I called it arguing, he called it me being angry. My daughter called it the morning show.

On St. Thomas we weren't just away from home, we were homeless.

We spent our first night in the Virgin Islands at the Bolongo Bay Beach Club. It was the only place we found that welcomed pets. We'd gotten good at smuggling Puck into hotels, but preferred not to. Seth could take Puck for long walks if he didn't have to sneak around. I think Seth enjoyed the excuse to get away from the 24x7 parenting. I love my kids and because I love them I want them terrified.

"Be careful at the pool," I'd say, "I saw a news segment about a kid who broke his neck diving."

I shared any story I came across. "Did you see in the paper about the girl who got in a car accident trying to answer her cell phone?" I'd ask my daughter. "She's paralyzed now and her best friend died. I guess they were on their way to hang-out with friends." No story is too horrific, "Have fun at the river, kids. By the way, did you hear about the raft that over-turned last week? A little girl was caught under water. When her dad tried to save her they both drowned while the mother watched helplessly from shore. It said he was a good swimmer too. Terrible. Have fun."

The Bolongo's lobby literature boasted of being just steps from the beach—I don't know any Caribbean resort that is not steps away from the beach. We paid $175 a night for two queen-size beds with just enough room to shinny between them. The bathroom fixtures were dated and the tiny shower stall with its plastic curtain inspired no romantic ideas. It compared to a $65 a night room at the Best Western back home. But, this was the Caribbean and for my part the hibiscus blossom on the stack of white towels in the bathroom made up for much.

From our room at the Bolongo we followed the sound of steel drum music to the beach and Iggy's for conch fritters. It would become a family custom to treat visitors to their first dinner on the island at Iggy's.

Our first full day on-island was a typical September day: warm, mostly overcast and breezy. We stepped from our morning showers into a robe of humidity, the first layer worn most days.

After breakfast we found our way across the island to the marina at Red Hook to introduce ourselves to Cindy, our only contact on St. Thomas. Brian had spoken with her by phone while researching dock space. Cindy was a red-headed God-send with a Southern accent who provided the practical knowledge that couldn't be found in a tote-bag full of guide books. She arranged for Seth to accompany her son to school the next day, showed us where to find the Laundromat, and even knew of a couple with an apartment for rent just uphill from the marina. We became friends with Cindy, her husband, Pete, and son Scott, and never tired of hearing her talk of "fixin" to go places.

We called the apartment landlord and arranged to meet at Molly Malone's, a nearby dockside restaurant. While drinking expensive iced teas from plastic cups that were never refilled, we saw our first iguana. Seth spotted it under a table. I pointed out another and soon we counted several lying in wait for French fries and other food more appealing than what nature spent millions of years evolving for them.

Green iguanas are as thick as tourists on St. Thomas. They look as if they sprang to life from a child's drawing. Their leathery bodies are shades of green and grey with pink mouths. They sport a dorsal row of spiny things like the bent teeth of a comb which starts on its scaly prehistoric head and runs the length of its body. The iguanas we saw were typically two feet long including a tail that dragged behind like toilet paper from a shoe. A large flap of skin, called a dewlap, hangs under the chin of males. I'm told it's flaunted to intimidate enemies and impress females, much the way cash is used by males of the human species.

You'd expect these spiny-backed, bad-ass-looking lizards to be dragging off cats and small dogs, but their favorite food, after French fries, are the bright red and yellow hibiscus blossoms found year round on the islands. Seeing one of them munching on a pretty, pink flower struck me the same as if I'd seen a tattooed biker sipping an icy piña colada.

An iguana's attitude is more aligned with its diet than its looks. They are reserved creatures that would rather scurry up the branches of a mangrove tree than haggle over table scraps. Watching them run, we were reminded of the staccato Flintstones soundtrack as they hiked their bellies off the ground, propelled by legs that appeared to spin in circles. Nevertheless, we heeded the caution that they will bite and kept our distance.

For weeks, Seth and I gaped at these strange reptiles. We spotted them in trees and sunning on rocks. If we happened by Molly Malone's to see kitchen help tossing a washtub of lettuce onto a grassy patch near the dining area we'd linger to count as a dozen or more, in as many shades of green, came running to feast. Once we saw an iguana spit from its nose. I cannot begin to imagine the need for this trait to evolve. There has to be some effect other than to cause homo sapiens to turn to one another in surprise and disgust and chorus "Ewww."

Wilmerdinged

We took the apartment, one of four units in a large house on a hillside. Our landlords, Dike and Inga Wilmerding (formerly of Mr. Roger's neighborhood), gave us the key less than an hour after we met: without application form, credit check or references. They even apologized for not having time to clean the apartment properly. And it did need a lot more cleaning than the half day I spent grimacing and scrubbing in the bathroom and kitchenette. I sprayed a paper-thick layer of disinfectant on surfaces that came in contact with our bare feet and other unprotected body parts. Nevertheless, we were thrilled to have the housing problem solved,

It was a studio apartment, but roomy enough for the three of us and a dog for the few weeks we expected to need it. The large living area was furnished with a queen size bed at one end and a threadbare futon at the other. A nightstand, dresser, coffee table and rocking chair completed the furnishings.

Sunlight streaming in through the two large sliding doors that opened onto a balcony mitigated the general rattiness of the furniture and dingy paneled walls. We kept the doors open day and night to let in the breeze as well as the sun. The daytime temperature at latitude 18 remains in or near the eighties year round, and dips only a few degrees at night. On days when humidity was high, as it often was, the breeze was crucial.

Our studio unit was the smallest in the three-story building. The Wilmerdings occupied the ground floor; a single man with a golden retriever rented the top floor; and our neighbor on the middle floor was a telephone answering machine. The answering machine shared an apartment with a friendly, popular woman named Diane, who happily loaned us appliances, answered our questions and offered her take on the island and islanders. She wasn't around much, so we became very familiar with the ring of her telephone and beep of her answering machine. The arrival of a message heralded hours of beeping until she arrived home. Lying in bed, I found myself counting the seconds between beeps, then wondering who chose thirteen, why not ten seconds, or fifteen, or better still 28,000.

The dog upstairs played a practical joke on us once or twice a day, not often enough for us to catch on quickly. He scratched himself in a way that sounded exactly like someone knocking on our door. He fooled each of us several times before we ignored the knocking, even then we ignored it anxiously, not wanting to miss a West Indian stopping to invite us to some exotic island tradition. Though we stopped answering the knocking dog, we never fully tuned out all the noises on the hillside above Red Hook.

The beeping and knocking were just two elements of the cacophony of life as tenants of the Wilmerding's (someday I'm going to name a cat Wilmerding). The apartment was the acoustic antithesis of our previous home in the middle of ninety-two peaceful acres. Joining the ever-beeping neighbor and practical joking dog, were a barking terrier, horns and engines of ferries and cars, music reverberating up the hillside, and a caustic screeching of a biological nature which we never did identify. I suspected it was iguanas dragging off cats, but it may have been a bird.

The hillside was noisy, but there was no denying it was picturesque. We woke to the sun rising over the hills of St. John Island, its rays hurrying across the Pillsbury Sound to St. Thomas and Red Hook Harbor below. We sat in our pajamas watching the activity, me in T-shirt and boxers, and Brian in T-shirt and the tighty-whities he persisted in wearing in spite of the boxer briefs I brought home for him, and ridicule from the kids. Marlin boats left the harbor and ferries plowed the water to St. John's Cruz Bay and back again. Soon street traffic picked up, the ferry dock crowded with men and women who worked in the resorts on St. John, but couldn't afford the high cost of housing there. Pink-shirted students in their public school uniforms appeared like confetti on the sidewalks as they headed to class at Ivanna Eudora Kean School. Egrets in a small estuary between the bay and the road, hidden from street-level view by mangrove trees, left their nests to feed.

Sometimes, I was aware of a gremlin whispering in the back of my mind. He sounded like Claude Rains as he said there must be some mistake: daughters of hard-working blue-collar fathers don't get to live in paradise; they don't get views like this. Only the very wealthy, or people who have emptied their wallets for a brief heavenly vacation enjoy such things. Then Claude wrung his hands and muttered that somehow I'd get a bill for the sunrises and the hours spent watching egrets in the estuary.

~~~~

When the owners of *Take Two* drove us to the airport to leave the Turks and Caicos, they surprised us by dropping their price. Brian liked its construction and now it was priced to sell. He considered the new price for a couple of days, then, once we settled into the apartment, he made up his mind to buy *Take Two* if she could pass inspection. It was probably as good a decision as a boat can be, she came equipped with everything, including the kitchen sink. Brian particularly liked the water maker. His dreams involved long passages on a circumnavigation of the planet. I agreed that would be nice . . . someday.

I didn't look around much the day we went sailing on *Take Two*, because she was out of our price range. Now, all I remembered was the putty-colored interior. *Take Two* had none of the beautiful mahogany bright work yachts are supposed to have. The walls and ceiling were grey, cupboards were grey, salon cushions were beige. *Take Two* cried out for an extreme make-over.

Before Brian bought any boat he needed a relationship with a marine surveyor. Boats are such risky investments, a competent, trustworthy surveyor is critical. Again, we thought of going to Cindy for advice. We grabbed our sunglasses and car keys. This is where the bill for the apartment's incredible view came due. We lived, and therefore parked, on a hillside. To back out of the driveway, we first had to squeeze out of the corner space we, as the newcomers, had been assigned. Next came the decision to attempt a turn-around on our small concrete platform in the sky, or to back eighty feet up the steep, narrow driveway where the ground dropped sharply on one side and rose just as abruptly on the other. At the top, we had to execute a 180 degree turn, still going backward, still going uphill. Only then would we be facing forward on our narrow road.

Once we got pointed in the right direction, it was smooth sailing to the bottom. Coming back was a little trickier. On stretches where the road was narrowest, the drop-off was on the side of uphill traffic. I took my time driving down, knowing if I met a driver, he'd be the one dangling upside down in his seatbelt if he miscalculated by a inch or two. I dreaded heading uphill, wondering if I was sending cascades of gravel onto houses and swimming pools below.

Our first week on island, I let Brian do the driving. Feminism be damned, the driveway scared me. My grandmothers lived their entire lives without getting behind the wheel of a car. But let's face it, I couldn't get away with that even for a month. And I was having trouble looking myself in the mirror. The truth was: the driveway drove the independence right out of me.

Our third day on island my secret was revealed when I asked Brian to go to the beach with me and Seth.

"No thanks," he said without looking up from his computer.

"I thought we'd go to Magens Bay."

"Go ahead. I'll go next time."

"Well I hoped you'd go with us." He didn't say anything. I turned to Seth and said,

"Maybe we'll go later."

"Go now. You don't need me," Brian said.

"Yeah, maybe, but . . . I just prefer it when you drive. That driveway makes me nervous."

He looked at me. "What? What's wrong with the driveway?"

"Duh, it's steep and narrow."

"So?"

"So, I'd rather not."

"You can do it."

"I know I can. I just don't want to."

"You have to do it sooner or later." Sometimes there was no arguing with him. "In fact you're going to have to tomorrow when you take me to the airport."

"Aw, crap. I forgot about that." I slumped onto the futon with such a look of despair, he took pity and agreed to go along as passenger to lend support and remind me to drive on the left.

The Virgin Islands is the only U.S. possession where driving on the left is practiced. No one seems to know why it's done. The U.S. bought the Virgin Islands from the Dutch in 1917 to keep it from falling into Germans hands during World War I. Left side driving has been blamed on donkeys being too stubborn to switch sides, but I've met West Indians every bit as stubborn as any ass.

Driving on the left is a charming curiosity until you have to do it. Brian did a great job our first week. Only once did we have a near collision because he looked left when he should have looked right. But I was sitting on the right side of the car and Johnny on the spot with a helpful shriek to signal incoming. We learned to look right instead of left before making a right turn, but we were never able to turn across the right lane without wanting needlessly to look back in the direction we just came. In the three weeks renting a Chevy, the only scratch put on it was in that damned driveway.

Seth jumped into his swim-trunks, I squeezed into a swimsuit and Brian grabbed a book. I was delighted to find Brian had backed into our space the night before when our neighbors' cars were gone. I drove straight up the driveway and on to Magens Bay without incident. Once we arrived, I forgot about getting back into the driveway. Brian found a shady place to read and I headed toward the water. Tossing the car keys to Brian, kicking off my flip-flops and dropping my sunglasses into my beach tote, I plunged in.

The water temperature in the islands fluctuates from refreshingly cool to tropically sublime, depending on the time of year. On that hot September day it was blissfully magnificent. Magens Bay is a sheltered horseshoe bay on the island's north side where Atlantic waves don't crash upon the shore, they gently lap the fine white sand. The south coast of the island is the Caribbean side.

When the water reached my hips, I let my feet slip from under me and floated blissfully on my back fanning my hands at my sides, enjoying the feel of the sun on my face and water caressing my temples. I came ashore only to rent snorkel gear for Seth and later to sit with Brian and drink iced tea bought from a pretty waitress strolling the beach in a swimsuit and taking drink orders. Seth donned the snorkel gear and splashed around under water chasing schools of minnows and trumpet fish. Brian read in the shade and listened to steel drum music playing nearby.

While drinking the ice tea, which I paid for with a small handful of diamonds, I remembered visiting a beach like this with my mother a dozen years earlier. It was on a shore excursion from a cruise ship at St. Martin. She wore a caftan to cover the over-weight body menopause had swapped with the trim one she'd had for over fifty years. The body swap happened when she wasn't looking, when she was busy worrying about putting her youngest daughter through college, helping Dad save for retirement, hoping he was happy with his job and the rest of us happy with our lives. I have a photo of her blue caftan billowing in the water around her when she decided the heck with what anyone might think, this water was to be frolicked in, not just gazed at from a beach chair. I knew she'd love Magens Bay and I promised myself I'd bring her here.

Leaving Magens after two hours of floating, splashing and reading was easy only because we could do it again next week. We were trying to establish a work week, or I'd have been back every day. I never wanted to move back to the cold Pacific Coast.

We returned from our afternoon at the beach and found our neighbors at home. I had a decision to make: Did I have the *cajones* to perform the 180-degree turn-around at the top in order to back toward the cliff side and down the driveway into our parking spot, as Brian sometimes does, or to drive straight in today, leaving me to back up the hillside next time I leave? I sat there pulling myself up by the steering wheel to peer over the dash, looking at the driveway, wishing I had the guts to back down, knowing I would sleep better. Brian's patience was beginning to run out when I decided I'd rather back uphill than down. I drove straight into our spot, putting off the inevitable.

Hurricane Glance

I loved life on a tropical island. The warm weather and clean cool breezes made concern for shelter feel like a waste of time. I'd have considered living in the shade of a palm tree with just a hammock, picnic basket and ice chest.

The humidity didn't bother me either, even on days when the air was still and perspiration dampened my shirt. I like warm weather and it no doubt helped that I didn't have to dress formally for work; I could wear tank tops, shorts and sandals every day. Tropical breezes notwithstanding, I pitied the office workers in their dark suits, especially the women. I would not have lasted a month wearing pantyhose to work.

Being new to St. Thomas, it was easy to forget hurricanes were a genuine threat to life and limb. Even Inga Wilmerding's stories of Hurricane Hugo's 200-mile-an-hour winds and Dike's shoulder injury when he was blown across a room by Hurricane Marilyn in 1995, didn't concern us. We enjoyed the stories. Like watching iguanas, they reminded us we were on an adventure far from California. Not even the sight of houses in ruin bothered us.

Only the weather was powerful enough to get our attention. One night a rain shower blew in hard, startling us awake. We jumped from bed, slammed the doors shut, then laid in bed listening to the wind and remembering the Wilmerdings' stories. The rain passed, and the morning breeze was stiffer than usual. I held my newspaper with both hands and smiled as I caught my glasses blowing across the coffee table. But I hadn't forgotten the rain storm. I asked Brian to explain the policy that boats must be taken from the marina in the event of a tropical storm or hurricane.

"It's hard on a boat to be tied to a dock in a storm," he said. "And it's hard on the dock."

"Well . . . yeah . . . but," I faltered, "I'd rather have it sink out from under me at the dock than at sea."

"We won't be at sea. We'll go to a hurricane hole," he explained. "We'll find a deep harbor and tie-up close to shore. If we don't want to stay on the boat, we can check into a hotel."

"Or," I offered, "We could visit my brother in central Washington State 300 miles from the nearest seagull."

"There aren't any seagulls in the Caribbean," Brian said.

"Oh."

~~~~

I didn't back up the driveway the next morning, but it wasn't my courage that failed. Brian planned to meet his marine surveyor at the airport and he was running late, something he does without stress—without stress to him, that is. When he's late, I stand at the door, purse in hand, keys at the ready, making it perfectly clear I'm not the one holding things up. I stand there long enough to absolve myself of blame, then move to a nearby chair to flip through a magazine, or busy myself tidying up. Eventually he appears, looks at me and always, always, asks if I'm ready. Sometimes he tries the, "I was waiting for you." defense. It goes like this:

Me (putting on my shoes): "We should go."

Him (on the computer): "Okay."

Ten minutes later:

Me (folding laundry): "Don't we need to be leaving?"

Him (still typing): "I'm just waiting for you."

Me: "I'm waiting for you, I've been ready for ten minutes."

Him (typing faster): "I have, too."

Then he snaps his laptop shut I grab my purse and we race to be first to the door. Once in the car, I'm tense and snappish, because I'm certain we're going to make a scene walking in late to the movie, wedding, meeting, whatever. We invariably arrive five or ten minutes late, and invariably it makes no difference whatsoever that we did. Still, I've gone to the trouble of being angry, so I fume a while longer.

Because we were in a hurry to get to the airport, Brian jumped into the driver's seat, backed expertly up the hill and we rushed across the island.

St. Thomas is roughly thirteen miles long by four miles wide. It is not one of those flat fossil coral islands like the Bahamas or Anegada. St. Thomas is covered with hills, the highest reaching 1500 feet above beach level. There are 50,000 people who live on its thirty-one square miles. During peak season, the population swells by approximately seventy-centillion tourists all looking the wrong way before crossing in the middle of the block. It's best not to be in a hurry. Nevertheless, we got to the airport and Brian headed off to the Turks and Caicos with a surveyor to give *Take Two* a thorough inspection.

Now it was time for me to drive across the island solo. I was alone fighting my instinct to drive on the right, and my infallible impulse to make wrong turns. I fell in behind a car and followed the flow of traffic. I was feeling confident until I got to the three-way corner by Wendy's, at the east end of downtown. I'd forgotten which way to go. Traffic seemed equally divided. All the road numbers start with three and I couldn't remember whether 30 or 32 or 33 or 35 or 37 or 38 or 39 or, here's a switch, the 302, led to Red Hook at the east end, or to the Tutu Mall, or into the hills where I'd wander until running out of gas outside an illegal dog-fight just in time to witness a murder. Did I mention the St. Thomas per-capita murder rate compares to Washington D.C.?

It would be easier if the roads had names like South Coast Road, Up and Over the Hill Highway, Rutted and Narrow Blvd. I might have gotten worked up to panic if the light hadn't changed and it was time to make a choice. I turned right, on 30.

Right was wrong. I should have taken 38. I turned around, remembering to drive on the left, and followed cars going back toward Charlotte Amalie. I got in the wrong lane and drove past Wendy's, back toward the airport. One more U-turn and up Raphune Hill to the East End where I found our parking lot empty. I drove down and laboriously executed a ninety-seven-point turn to back into our space.

It really wasn't the biggest challenge of my life, but it was in the top three driving challenges, so before descending the concrete steps to our apartment I turned for a satisfied look. I slept well knowing Brian could count on me for a ride home in two days.

When Brian returned to St Thomas, after a three hour flight and ninety minutes in customs, he said *Take Two* looked good and if the surveyor's report pronounced her sound and worth the price, he would buy her.

He got a ride home from the airport with the surveyor, so I met him in the driveway and gestured proudly toward the rented Blazer beside the retaining wall. He set aside his boat-buying excitement to congratulate me.

Cost of Living

The failure rate of marriages, particularly second marriages, is so high, perhaps it's time to look at creative solutions. The divorce rate has climbed steadily and marriage counselors don't seem to be working. My divorced friends have all tried counseling at least once—typically two or three times. Our last marriage counselor, after only five sessions, risked her weekly $120 an hour fee to suggest we consider throwing in the towel. Our quarrels weren't unique: we fought about money, how he spent his time, and occasionally, feeling disrespected.

Brian and I were equally without means when we married. Together we'd had a six-year-old Ford, an eight-year-old Toyota, several rooms of furniture, a small savings account, five kids, and half as much child support coming in for my three as went out for his two. Within a year of getting married his boys were living with us.

Our first years together were a financial tar pit. Debt grew as we tried to build a business while feeding, clothing and straightening the teeth of a houseful of teenagers. Then we sold our business and suddenly we had money. We paid the orthodontist, bought tires, went to the dentist ourselves and took a vacation.

Whoever said money can't buy happiness was probably married. Odds are, any two married people view spending differently. One person's retirement nest egg is another's twin engine airplane. It didn't matter how much Brian and I had, there were always disagreements. We just advanced from arguing if we could afford the cable movie package to if we could afford another airplane. When the stock market turned down, we were left somewhere in between.

Separating our money wouldn't solve all our problems, but I hoped it would help . . . and we needed help. We agreed to each take half of the sale of the ninety-two acres. Brian was going to buy a boat, I planned to buy a house, and together we would fund the start-up.

While Brian was off-island checking out *Take Two*, I looked at the housing market on St. Thomas.

The realtor's office was just around the corner from Red Hook on the road to the Ritz Carlton at the extreme eastern point of the island. The office was a small white house with a bougainvillea canopy over the front porch roof. A receptionist welcomed me in what would have been the living room and directed me to Nick Bailey's office. He and I made the usual chit-chat about why I was on the island and how long he'd lived there.

He suggested *Don't Stop the Carnival* by Herman Wouk, a book about St. Thomas. Though it was first published in 1965, it's still popular, especially in the islands. Frankly much of it is relevant today. My head swelled a little when I told Nick I'm a fan of Wouk's and read *Don't Stop the Carnival* several years ago. I am guilty of having a literary ego. If he was impressed that I'd already read the book, he kept it to himself.

Shopping for real estate is an excellent way to learn about a new town, or in this case, an island. St. Thomas is sectioned into more than fifty areas known as estates. After East End, West End, the North side and Downtown, estates are the next level of finding your way around. Raphune, Mafolie, Peterborg, Contant or Agnes Fancy were typical answers to where someone lived or how far we would have to drive to check out a used car. Few roads have names and fewer still road signs. I learned to keep a map handy. Many of the names were Dutch; my tongue tripped over Frydenhoj, Neltjeberg and Zufriedenheit. Some estates are poorer or seedier neighborhoods to be avoided at night like Anna's Retreat, or

Bovoni where the landfill accepted trash for both St. Thomas and high-rent St. John.

Nick drove me to houses on the North side, where estates Lerkenlund, Misgunst and Elizabeth are especially lush and green. We drove along hillsides swollen dark and green with foliage that thrived in the afternoon shade. A carpet of love vines and anthurium grew low under lacey tamarind trees, taller kapok trees and palms. The plants covered gravel shoulders and nudged parked cars on the narrow roads. The underbrush was thick enough to hide a concrete mixer, and it does. In fact, an abandoned cement mixer, now overgrown and lost in new growth, was once used as a landmark for directions.

Beaches all around the island are lined with black mangroves, seagrape, sea purslane and the white, trumpet-shaped blossoms of datura plants. Any bit of earth that hasn't been scraped bare in recent months or trampled from constant use, is losing ground to lush vegetation, green and ornamented with hibiscus, oleander and alamanda flowers.

But, even the thriving flora of the tropics can't hide human neglect and indifference. Just around the corner from landscaped resorts and pristine National Park beaches are abandoned rusting cars, piles of broken concrete and construction debris, corrugated metal fences and roadside dumpsters overflowing with the islanders' trash. For every home freshly painted a soft shade of coral, yellow or vanilla, there are a several peeling, cracking and blackened by mold.

Nick showed me six houses, each one or more rentable mother-in-law units. Houses with rental units, either detached, on another floor, or simply walled off with separate entry, were common on the island. The nicest units, those with a view or proximity to a beach, were usually rented by the week to vacationers. Others were rented to fishermen for the sport fishing season, to service workers for the tourist season or long term to students or locals.

Everything in my price range was a fixer-upper, or at least needed TLC. Our new start-up business was all the fixer-upper

I wanted just then, and until I got all the sandy beaches kind of TLC I needed, weekends spent refinishing woodwork, replacing windows and painting didn't interest me.

~~~~

Before the surveyor's report came in for *Take Two*, we got a set-back in our plans to live on a yacht. We didn't know whether to feel stupid, angry or frustrated, so we cycled between them. We had done a lot of research before leaving California. I'm a research hound and Brian had been living in cyber-space since the Internet was called the Arpanet. I spent days just investigating the business climate and tax laws, while Brian searched the web for yachts and contacted marinas. Marinas turned out to be the problem. In a call to American Yacht Harbor, Brian was quoted a monthly dock rate of seventy cents per foot for a catamaran: about $35 for 48' *Take Two*. The problem turned out to be that seventy cents was actually the daily rate if paid by the month—big difference. We aren't always complete idiots. We knew this was dirt cheap, but we'd never docked in the Virgin Islands and we didn't look the gift horse in the mouth. Once we learned of our misunderstanding, suddenly it wasn't so affordable planning to stay on a boat while living off savings and starting up another business.

Brian was greatly disappointed. He had lived on a boat in San Diego after college and for some time now had wanted to do it again. I suspect he idealized those days stooped over in a tiny mono-hull, showering in the marina facilities. But it was clear from the way he talked those were his good old days.

Brian listened gloomily to my proposal that I buy a condo and we would live and run the business out of it. He brightened a little when I suggested he look for a smaller boat that he could put on a mooring ball out in the harbor, and we could sail on weekends. I made another appointment with Nick Bailey, and crossed my fingers for an affordable market. I soon learned the price of a condo wasn't going to be the problem.

Nick drove me to Estate Lovenlund on the north side to show me condominiums in the Mahogany Run complex. The north side of St. Thomas offers spectacular down island views of the U.S. and British Virgin Islands. From the hillside you can see St. John, Jost Van Dyke, and the string of five small cays that point toward Tortola.

The condominium's open design was modern and stylish, but not large enough for the three of us. Nick and I moved on to the breezy southeast side of the island in Estate Bolongo. He showed me a small, but bright and well-maintained two bedroom unit with a balcony and a narrow beach view. The living area would have to double as workspace, but that was also true for living on a boat. It was in my price range and conveniently located. I walked from room to room with growing enthusiasm and began to arrange furniture in my mind. Then I remembered to ask Nick about association fees. He consulted his clipboard and said, "Fees on this unit are $900."

I was puzzled. Fees are usually by the month, but, of course, $900 a month was ridiculous for such a small, unexceptional unit. On the other hand, $900 a year was awfully low, and I'd learned the lesson about prices sounding too low to be true. I had to ask. I considered which question would sound less stupid. "That's $900 . . . a month?"

"Yes."

"$900 a month?" I repeated.

"They're pretty high here," he said.

Duh. "Why so high?" I asked, hoping I didn't sound as dumbfounded as I was.

"Insurance mostly."

I glanced at the walls. "Is it about to fall into the sea?" Realtors don't laugh when they're working. He blamed 9/11.

I nodded and wondered what Plan C was going to be.

~~~~

Reality was intruding on our tropical paradise. If we had simply been on vacation, our only problems would have been whether to go snorkeling or sailing. Instead I was fretting over the closing date for the sale of the ranch, which kept slipping; our dwindling line of credit; the cost of living; and it simply wasn't cute stepping over that damn dog anymore.

Puck reacts badly to change. When we moved to the house in the country, he was a nervous wreck, even though he had accompanied us there many times during remodeling. For several weeks after the move, he had nervous fits that set him to trembling all over. If we left a car door open, we'd find him curled up on the floor like a convict bent on escape. I was considering taking him to a doggie shrink, but finally the trembling fits grew less frequent and eventually stopped.

Initially, it was a source of amusement that Puck was positioning himself underfoot in the St. Thomas apartment. Whoever was moving was his target. When I went into the kitchen to cook, he'd be on the rug by the sink. If someone was in the shower, he'd lie against the bathroom door. He amazed us with his instincts. After nearly tripping Brian coming out of the bathroom, Puck moved directly to the floor by the bed where he'd be waiting when Brian sat to put on his watch and belt. We were constantly ordering him out of the way or trying to step over him just as he'd leap to his feet.

Puck was under our feet, and getting ducks in a row was on our minds. We had to buy a car—the rental car was taking a big bite out of our budget. We couldn't cook in the apartment, and we were tired of oriental noodles for dinner. The housing issue was coming to a crisis—we had only two more weeks in the apartment: the Wilmerdings had a new tenant arriving soon for the sport fishing season. The business license application required us to get a tax clearance letter, a zoning compliance review and a police records check. From what I'd been told about the U.S.V.I. government, there would be many delays before we were through the licensing and incorporation processes.

We saw some progress when Brian negotiated slip fees down slightly, and decided to buy *Take Two*. Our living situation still was not solved, it would be weeks before the cash from the ranch was deposited to our account and Brian could pay for the boat and sail her down from the Turks and Caicos. Nevertheless, I was glad to have the decision made and was looking forward to experiencing life on a catamaran.

Painkillers

Brian and I were starting a business once again, and once again, my job was handling the pieces of paper. I was in charge of everything from Post-It phone messages to the Articles of Incorporation.

Brian, along with Dave, our New Hampshire-based partner and long-time friend, handled the technical solutions of establishing satellite Internet access points and wireless connections to our customers. We would contact host sites for our satellite receivers as soon as we got rubber-stamped to conduct business. Other business owners had cautioned us not to accept any customers until all the proper steps were taken and license and permits obtained. We heeded the advice and got to work on the process.

We soon learned going into business in the Virgin Islands was like a home plumbing repair job. In theory, it appeared to be a simple task of inserting information into various bureaucratic pipes. But, the plumbing proved to be deceptively complex and involved several government offices including the Department of Corporations, the Internal Revenue of the V.I., the Department of Business Licensing, and I think one form for the International Brotherhood of Sea Turtles.

Starting a business in the Virgin Islands wasn't as simple as it was in California where Brian and I established and grew our company to a dozen employees before selling it. On St. Thomas there were consultants whose sole business was helping other businesses get started. We saw their clip-art flyers fluttering on the doors of mail centers, secretarial service offices, and delis. They promised to smooth the way through the business license process. Though they only charged a few hundred dollars, I decided to handle things myself since I had plenty of time to stand in lines and fill out forms. At least a dozen times before we got approved, I wished I'd called a service.

~~~~

It rained the Sunday afternoon we drove across the island to a Business Expo at the University of the Virgin Islands. Dark green leaves of wet palm trees swayed against the backdrop of gray sky, potholes filled with water and the visible road narrowed to one lane where water flooded the shoulders.

I felt pleased with myself for seeing the Business Expo notice in the *Daily News*. It would be a perfect chance for networking and to learn about business on the island. We hurried across the parking lot following signs into the gymnasium, where I stopped congratulating myself.

The conference was poorly attended by businesses and visitors alike. Employees of the two local banks and owners of a dozen or so small businesses sat yawning behind folding tables furnished with pamphlets and occasionally a candy dish. A few ambitious businesses covered the table with a tablecloth and set-up cardboard displays. Two or three brought product with them and were selling candles, salsa and jellies.

Aside from the easily overlooked Virgin Islands Dairy, St. Thomas is productively impotent. She is a pretty face of warm weather and sandy beaches, offering no genuine part of her to take home. Nothing noteworthy is grown there or manufactured without benefit of imported materials. A few individuals make perfume or jellies with Caribbean flavor, but a close examination usually reveals they lack locally-grown ingredients to make them authentic St. Thomas.

The highest calling, as Brian put it, seemed to be a position with the government. The odds of securing a government job are favorable. The Virgin Islands Legislature is a weighty thing. Its 374 active employees support a population of approximately 100,000. That's one employee for every 267 men, women and children. By comparison, the Iowa State Legislature supports nearly three million Iowans with about the same number of employees.

We'd heard business owners comment that it was painful to conduct business there. And it was implied corruption is not occasional. The large number of candidates competing for a surprising seventeen senate seats would give credence to the suggestion that the money to be made in the U.S.V.I. is in politics. We couldn't help noticing the government office buildings located in prime real estate on the waterfront in downtown Charlotte Amalie next to stores such as Tommy Hilfiger, Caribbean Emeralds and other high-end shops near the cruise ship dock. Four months after we arrived in the islands, a protest was staged in Charlotte Amalie against large pay raises the senate granted themselves and the governor. The protest turned violent and the raises were eventually vetoed by Governor Turnbull.

The only interesting table at the Expo was hosted by the editor of the *Virgin Island Daily News*, a Pulitzer Prize winning paper. She was an educated and intelligent woman with a genuine interest in running a top quality newspaper. The *Daily News* was published five days a week and a supplement, the *Island Trader*, weekly.

I was eager to learn about St. Thomas, so I left Post-It notes on my purse to remember to buy the paper. There was no such thing as home delivery. It didn't take long to read through the *Daily News*. I read the front page, which for the first eight weeks featured local elections, then I turned inside to local news, skipping international articles about Kellogg recalling mislabeled cereal boxes and Tiger Woods, to read island news, which was generally depressing. The Virgin Islands are not a paradise in every sense. There is a great deal of violent crime. The news was filled with stabbings, robberies, assaults, murders, rapes and more rapes. I carefully read the location reported for these crimes. Names of certain estates appeared most frequently, but few were without incident. In the year we lived on the dock, Duffy's Love Shack across the street was the site of a stabbing and a shooting.

After the expo we drove to St. Thomas's number one local attraction, Coral World Ocean Park. An unexpected memory surprised me as we turned the corner and I recognized the white geodesic dome. I'd forgotten that my mother and I stopped here on our cruise fifteen years earlier. I directed Brian's attention to nearby Coki Beach, where my younger sister slept off a hang-over while Mom and I walked to the marine park. It must have been closed because, I don't remember going in. Brian, Seth and I didn't go in that day either. We learned if we return with proof of residence we'll get a discount off the admission. Until we had an income, we had to budget our cash.

~~~~

Weather comes upon you suddenly in the West Indies. One evening, about six o'clock I put down my book and stepped to the glass door to close it against an aggressive breeze. "Whoa," I said, "can't even see across the bay. Visibility is low." As Brian was suggesting I close both doors, the rain arrived. I closed the one by our bed and by the time I reached the other I was doused by a spray of water as I slammed it shut. In a matter of seconds, rain was sheeting against the glass doors and visibility outside was down to ten feet. We sat, Brian and me on the bed, Seth across the room, marveling and commenting on how quickly the squall moved in.

We were splashed out of our reverie when a determined stream of water abruptly poured from the ceiling onto our printer. With good intentions and little else, I sprinted over and cupped my hands under the flow. Brian grabbed the printer and lifted it out of the waterfall. I pulled the plug and he moved it to the futon. I set a pot in its place on the table and was toweling off the printer when I noticed a small pond developing on the floor. I looked up to see a wide fountain of water sheeting prettily down the paneled wall. Brian set to unplugging other electronics and found our mini-hub and its connecting wires resting in a stream flowing toward the middle of the floor.

Once the valuables were secured and I was mopping away the pond, Seth decided to explore the physical sensations of a tropical storm. He pulled on a thin wind-breaker, tugged the hood into place around his face and stepped onto the balcony. He soon gave up shouting at the wind, but before I could stop him, he reentered through the door by the bed, soaking the sheets half way across. I spent the night spooning with Brian on his side.

Showers came and went while we mopped and bailed until finally we gave up. I moved my books to high ground, leaving a throw rug to hold back the pond. The rain continued through most of the night, which I spent staring at drooping panels in the ceiling.

The throw rug wasn't up to the job of holding back the storm, and we woke to a gulf between the bed and the futon. We resumed mopping with the light of dawn. Then at least the floor was clean.

Brian had been winking at new friends saying that living in this little apartment was a plot to make Seth and me appreciate the spaciousness of a boat. But, even he didn't expect a boat to be dryer as well.

That night we learned of an insurance obstacle that delayed the closing on the ranch. I sulked and Brian called *Take Two*'s owners to pass on the news of the delay. Then Seth accidentally started a stovetop fire and burned my favorite cloth napkins. I sulked more. Soon, however, all was right with the world because Brian downloaded a recipe, made a quick run to the store for coconut crème, pineapple juice, orange juice and nutmeg, and adding this to rum from the welcome basket from Seth's school, made ice cold Painkillers.

The storm swept away the usual evening breeze and left an unpleasant stillness. Walking the dog after dinner was generally an excuse for a few minutes out of the apartment under the stars. Without a breeze, however, the air was stale and musty and the chore tedious. I encouraged Puck to take advantage of the walk. Unfortunately, you can lead a dog to a bush but you can't make him pee. I led Puck to several of his favorite marking spots before he finally made his choice, then I hurried him back inside to escape the squadrons of mosquitoes that sortie when the breeze is low.

The mosquitoes were a nuisance, but we got used to them. We sprouted a bite or two each day and soon every tickle we assumed to be a mosquito. Sitting on the futon, I slapped my face twice that evening to smack mosquitoes. Seth didn't even look up to make fun.

Inner Child

I took my inner child to the beach. She is only about ten-years-old so Brian drove.

There are two ways to leave Red Hook by car: north, going counter-clockwise around the island toward Smith Bay, Coki Point and on to Magens Bay, or south and clockwise toward Bolongo, Frenchman's Bay and eventually Charlotte Amalie. We headed south, but just outside of town we took a sharp left turn onto 322 toward Cabrita Point and the beach at Vessup Bay.

Vessup Beach isn't a privileged beach like Magens or Morningstar Beach by the Marriott. There are no park service or resort employees to wipe the litter from her face. Nor are there restaurants with beachside dining, strolling bikini-clad waitresses or gazebos of musicians playing calypso. There is no leisure body-watching there at Vessup. It doesn't benefit from the popularity Coki enjoys from nearby Coral World or the handful of laid-back businesses leaning against the mangroves. Cruise ship passengers are not dropped off by the truckload. There are no beach chair vendors, or Rastas discretely selling pot.

Vessup's narrow shoreline is broken two or three times by boulders spilling from the thick brush down into the water. The ground between the beach and the parking lot is littered and stinking from trash cans over-flowing with fast-food garbage. Be careful where you sit, Vessup is a popular beach for dog-owners and there are the inevitable piles. But clean spots can be found. The breeze blows just as sweetly as the breeze that stirs umbrellas at the Ritz. The water is the same pure, refreshing blue Atlantic.

I'm not sure if Brian has an inner child or if there's just little difference between the inner child and the outer man. While Brian, the child or the man, read on a small rug in the shade, my inner child splashed in the water with Puck. She found a stick and tested how far from shore Puck would swim to retrieve it before giving the look that said, "I'm not going after that." Then she took Puck for a walk and returned with a sandy handful of tiny seashells.

That evening Brian suggested we accept Cindy's standing invitation to swim in their pool. The air had been still and hot for three days, so we put on swim suits and hiked up the driveway. Pete was out for a night of Marlin fishing, but true to her promise to be ready at a moment's notice, Cindy got into her suit and the three of us spent a magical hour gliding in the moonlit water of their hillside pool over-looking the lights of Red Hook.

~~~~

A write-up in the *Virgin Island Daily News* community events section called for volunteers to join Friends of Coki Beach in a cleanup effort. I cut it out and stuck it on the fridge with a taxi driver's business card magnet. The following Saturday morning, I asked Brian and Seth to go with me. They begged off, so I asked them to do some cleaning in the apartment and went alone. Coki Point is in Estate Frydendahl, just a five minute drive counter-clockwise on the island from our three o'clock position in Red Hook. I pulled into a cratered parking lot behind a smattering of shacks on the beach and ran the nose of the Jeep into the shade of a tall, woody shrub.

Litter grew denser as I approached the cafe and souvenir shacks, and tapered off somewhat near the water. It was nine o'clock, the time specified in the paper, but I saw few people and no cleaning going on. I put down my beach rug and sat for a moment wondering if I was on the right beach. I debated whether to begin on my own or wait for a starting whistle. It's one thing to join a civic-minded group of adults taking back the beach, it's quite another to be perceived as an eccentric middle-aged lady in a shapeless straw hat picking up other people's trash. I didn't want to inspire any locals to bring garbage from home for my sake. A faded sign nailed to a post confirmed this was in fact Coki Beach and a moment later, while still considering what to do, I saw a woman picking up trash and shoving it into already overflowing barrels. She was clearly oblivious to the dangers of looking foolish, so I boldly pulled a trash bag from my duffel and got to work.

The woman was Nancy, a fifty-one-year-old resident of nearby Smith Bay. Like me, Nancy was dressed for the beach. She wore a black two-piece. Her breasts, the shape and nearly the color of eggplants, hung in the top, and her ample midriff shaded the elastic of the bottom piece, which stretched across her behind. She wore her black hair efficiently short, like a newly-sprouted Chia pet.

Sadly, Coki Point didn't have many friends and it wasn't really a clean-up day as much as a clean-up morning. Nancy and I were joined by just one other woman, and though the clean-up day had been Nancy's idea, she had forgotten to bring any trash bags, so she walked along with me picking up straws, plastic bags, Styrofoam clamshells, cigarette wrappers and other refuse. Refuse cast aside by residents who apparently care little for their beaches or for attracting income from tourists who have a choice of more than sixty equally lovely Caribbean islands, all with beaches lapped by the same warm blue water; and refuse left by tourists who travel thousands of miles, look at the sun-kissed sand and see an ashtray.

Eric Johnson from the *Island Trader*, a supplement to the *Daily News*, arrived to photograph the activities. He took two or three shots of us shoulder to shoulder squinting into the sun and made notes about why we were there. Nancy had a lot to say about who she thought were false friends of Coki Point Beach. Friends who party with her and enjoy the riches of her white sand and clear, warm water, but don't answer her call when there's work to be done. She postulated that the small businesses with hand-lettered signs that lined the beach and Coral World at the east end should have shown interest in making the beach a positive reflection of the priorities of the residents.

If the three of us had more stamina or more help, we might have picked up the parking area, too. But after filling a couple of trash bags, we went our own way until next time, leaving a hundred yards of beach far cleaner than we found it and promising we'd be back soon. I left Nancy talking to the reporter and returned to my beach rug. Before heading home, I took a quick swim, then sat a few minutes admiring my work and watching snorkelers bobbing in the water following the abundant fish and coral.

Snorkeling Coki is like an afternoon at the state fair. Instead of cows, goats, suckling pigs and rabbits the size of bed pillows, at Coki you might see goatfish, honeycomb cowfish, blue tangs, parrotfish, hogfish and a variety of damselfish. And, unless your mask fogs over completely, you'll see needlefish and schools of sergeant major and angelfish which are likely to swarm you for handouts which they are used to getting from tour groups of SCUBA divers. There is no agricultural building, but at the east end of the bay, near Coral World, there are as many kinds of coral as there are entries for homemade jam at the fair.

Most snorkeling at Coki takes place at either side of the bay, but it's worth paying attention while swimming from one side to the other. Near the shoreline a careful observer might spot flounder or sand divers hiding in the sand. And I once saw a small white octopus skulking in the crevice of a rock. It wasn't the black, menacing creature I expected, and though I never really believed they grew large enough to threaten submarines, I wasn't expecting something small enough to hide under a slice of bread, either.

Back at the apartment I found Brian and Seth hadn't been completely idle. When I returned, as when I left, they were tapping away at their keyboards, the floor was still dirty and the laundry still piled high behind the chair. But, they were quick to point out, the dog had been bathed. As proof they directed my attention to a soggy, lugubrious Puck dripping on the balcony.

"What shampoo did you use?"

"I dunno, a white bottle," Brian said.

"Did it have French words in fancy script?"

"Yeah, I guess," He said, not seeing where this was going.

Having their judgment and priorities criticized, Brian and Seth logged off their laptops and turned to housework. They tackled the manly chores of sweeping and mopping while I dragged pillow cases of dirty clothes to the Laundromat. By the end of the day, one apartment, one beach, and a dog were cleaner.

~~~~

We devoted the next day to enjoying ourselves at a popular island event: the annual Chili Cook-Off at the Sapphire Beach Hotel. The hotel is only a mile or two from Red Hook, but the sun was high and too hot to walk. We considered walking to the bottom of the hill and catching a taxi from there, but Brian decided he didn't mind searching for parking in a dusty lot, so we drove.

Taxis here are as plentiful as iguanas. Covered kiosks serve as taxi stands, but mostly drivers cruise about offering rides. Besides traditional van and car taxis, the islands have Safari cars: pick-up trucks with bench seats installed in the bed. Steps are cut in the side and canopies protect from the sun and rain. The Safari cars move clockwise around the island charging a dollar per leg. As I understood it, you could generally get from one end of the island to the other for two dollars. A lot of the Safari cars had colorful, creative paint jobs that belied the stoicism demonstrated so often by the locals toward tourists and ex-pats. Jesus and scripture are favorite themes, but many are painted with palm trees, beach sunsets or frolicking dolphins.

With his usual parking karma, Brian found a space right away. We followed other hungry people past a sand volleyball court where a volleyball bounced between swim-suited athletes to a line where tickets were being sold three for a dollar. We figured out, as we mindlessly followed the crowd, that tickets were being traded for tiny sample cups of chili. Brian pulled out his wallet and I ordered three tickets, plenty to make a final choice on where to buy a bowl. Brian bought extra so I got four. What I didn't get was that the only way to get chili was in these tiny cups. Apparently, chili eaters are indecisive souls who must sample everyone's offering. They are also mostly young, beer-drinking, sweaty, and on this hot United States beach, almost illegally undressed.

As Seth called, "See ya," over his shoulder, I grabbed his collar, Brian shoved tickets into his hand and we arranged a rendezvous in an hour at the base of a giant inflatable beer bottle. Brian and I wandered over to a tofu chili booth, but soon got separated. He prefers not to walk while eating chili from a paper pill cup, but I did. Although not very well, it seemed. A bold and indiscreet stranger pointed gleefully to a tomato stain on my halter top and gloated, "You're not supposed to wear the chili."

"You're not supposed to wear it," a woman behind him echoed with a fatuous grin.

"I'm not?" My sarcasm didn't make it through their beer buzz.

"No. You're supposed to eat it." The two of them stared dumbly having offered the wealth of advice at their disposal.

I left them staring as I cringed my way through the crowd of perspiration, beer and chili searching for a fabled hospital booth reported to also be distributing vegetarian chili. Like Shangri la, everyone I asked had heard about the hospital booth, but no one knew where it was. I returned to the tofu booth three times, each time feeling more inept for not locating my mystical goal and, having gotten into the sampler spirit, a bit disappointed.

I adopted a vegetarian diet over the course of several years. I began by eliminating pork because . . . well for the same reason I don't eat dog or dolphins: if they're smart enough to be a pet or find underwater mines, I don't eat them. Before too long, it seemed unfair to discriminate against cows because they were stupid. Then I read an article about the dangers of antibiotics in the beef we consume and heard a news story about cattle waste damage to groundwater. So I gave up hamburgers, which I seldom ate because they're fattening, and prime rib, which I never ate because at the time we couldn't afford expensive restaurants and prime rib is not a food on which to economize. Anyway, there were always the turkey substitutions. I was happily living a poultry and fish-rich life when I heard a news feature about the horrible conditions under which chickens are raised for market. They are crowded tightly into cage stacked upon cage, poop falling ever more noxiously upon the cage below until the poor foul fowl at the bottom grow misshapen feet trying to hold their noses from the smell.

Giving up poultry was the greatest sacrifice yet. Chicken can be eaten seven days a week, but though there are more kinds of fish than poultry, it's all the same, and it takes a more creative chef than I to make fish interesting more than twice a week. Throw in shrimp when you can afford it, and you're still left with three days a week of tofu. I like tofu, but again, I'm not that creative.

I never did find the hospital booth, but it wouldn't hurt me to lose a few pounds anyway, so I gave up and found Brian leaning against a palm tree. Seth met us promptly at the appointed landmark holding up his tickets asking what he was supposed to do with them. We gave him another twenty minutes then, finding ourselves easily overwhelmed by sweaty, drunk tourists and islanders, went home   .

Pseudo Activities

A few days later was Seth's pseudo birthday. When Seth decided to celebrate his birthday on September 26th, rather than on the extraordinarily inconvenient date he was born, December 26th, he had my full support. The hype of global proportions surrounding Christmas for weeks in either direction, can steal the thunder of any event. If you ask me, no responsible adult has unprotected sex between March 20th and April 2nd.

Only after we agreed on the date change did I reveal to Seth a secret birthday guilt his father and I share. Invariably around December 23rd, after weeks of Christmas shopping, decorating, baking, caroling, and wrapping; when the angel hair and the nativity straw are commingled with dust and cookie crumbs; Brian or I would look at the other and exclaim, "Seth's birthday! Did you get him anything?" No, was always the answer. So neither of us being soldier enough to brave the front this close to the advent, we would select one of his Christmas gifts and rewrap it in birthday paper. And by one of us, I mean me.

Brian is neither royalty nor a doctor, but he often assumes the royal "we." "We should update our homeowners insurance" or "We need to wrap the pipes before winter," he would say. Some time would pass and the we would appear as a question, "Did we ever update our insurance policy?" I could only answer for myself, at which point he'd exhale a long-suffering sigh. I helpfully pointed out what he was doing with his pronouns, but it turns out, we were mistaken.

Seth's birthday dinners were generally leftover turkey, or just as often, fast food eaten on the run traveling between relatives. His last birthday was typical. We spent the day flying home from my parents' house in Washington State. After landing we dragged our travel-weary selves into a Mexican restaurant for dinner, then to the local ice cream shop for ice cream cake. My effort to make the day special, besides giving him one less Christmas present, was to call ahead to order a cake decorated with a sports theme and his name written in icing.

We didn't have big plans for the September birthday celebration, but dinner, cake and gifts wouldn't be afterthoughts tossed at him with exhausted smiles. When he got home from school at 4:30, the activities would revolve around our quasi fifteen-year-old.

Seth was the youngest of five kids in our blended family, and Brian and I were exhausted. His older brothers and sister didn't give us a lot of trouble, there was the usual class-ditching, sneaking out of the house and fender benders. But parenting teen-age step-siblings, added to self-employment and a strife-filled marriage had drained us.

Thank heaven, Seth was a solid-gold kid, but even so, like his older siblings the time came when Seth changed from an eager, companionable, open-minded youngster to a moody, grudging, taciturn teen-ager.

The only intelligence shown by any of our kids between the ages of thirteen and seventeen was in the area of logic. Our children became idiot savants excelling in the field of reason and logic.

"Why do I have to leave my bedroom door open when I have a boy over?" our daughter asked.

"It's not appropriate for a boy and girl to be in a bedroom with the door shut."

"What, you think because the door is shut we're having sex in here?"

"No, I—"

"Then why can't I have some privacy?"

"It's a matter of propriety."

"What's that?"

"Appearances," I said.

"So even though you know I'm not doing anything wrong, I can't have my door shut?"

"You can't have your door shut because I said so! Keep arguing with me and I'll have your dad come take it off."

Every trial lawyer should have a fifteen-year-old assistant slouching in the seat beside her.

Seth, however, wasn't typical in every way; his childhood dream of going to the Naval Academy survived the transition to adolescence. His plans to land an appointment motivated him to get good grades and do well in sports. And Seth has a delightful sense of humor. I asked if he wanted any CDs for his birthday.

"No thanks, I get downloads."

"Be careful," I cautioned, "When you're running for President instead of questions about smoking marijuana, they'll be asking if you downloaded illegally."

"It's okay," he said, "I downloaded, but I didn't listen."

Personally, I think he's too clever to be President.

Going out for his birthday we dressed casually. I showered and put on a fresh camisole and shorts, the only style I'd worn since arriving. Brian put on a clean blue shirt and shorts. Seth wore board shorts and a gray Carolina Tar Heels T-shirt. Had we been in California, only Seth would have been in shorts and I'd have insisted he wear a dress shirt.

Birthdays or not, the practicality of life must be dealt with. We preceded Seth's birthday celebration with a quick stop at the Laundromat. A home washer and dryer, like one's health, are taken for granted until one carelessly tosses them away. When we moved our household into storage, I lingered over some items, reluctant to say good-bye to my power tools, my few, but much-loved, paintings and other possessions of convenience or indulgence that wouldn't fit on a boat. I didn't give a second glance to those angel-white appliances that spent their every cycle making my life a cleaner, easier, fluffier existence. I regretted that now. I missed them. I missed their huggable large capacity, their soothing sounds from the gentle swish of the wash cycle to the four extraordinarily loud buzzes announcing the end of a dryer cycle. I was sorry for every time I took a harsh tone and slammed the dryer door declaring, "These aren't dry!" My only consolation was that we didn't sell the Kenmore pair, and one day, years from now perhaps, but one day, I'd move them to a new home, and make it up to them. Never again taking them for granted. We left $7.50 swishing away in three tiny unhuggable machines and walked along the plaza waiting for Seth's stomach, still touchy from a bout of flu the day before, to signal what restaurant tempted it. We'd planned for something special, but his stomach led us to Molly Malone's where he's eaten many times with friends. On Seth's recommendation, we each added a bowl of the conch chowder to our dinner order. It was thick and heavy, without enough flavor to excite or rebuff.

The mosquitoes dined on us while we dined on chowder, so we hurried to the air conditioned Cold Stone Creamery for dessert, stopping to transfer laundry to dryers with equally large appetites for quarters.

Seth told us about the new ice cream place that opened at the American Yacht Harbor complex. Every day Seth walked along the wharf going to catch the ferry to school and coming home. Soon he knew everyone on the docks, and what they were doing. He knew when owners of the mega yachts were in town; and he knew which owners were friendly and which weren't. He knew which sport fishing boats had hard-working live-aboard owners who chartered, and the hired crew who only had to please owners a few days a month. When marlin tournaments were underway, he knew which boats had a good day and who recorded the biggest catch. He eventually gained a reputation as a hard-working kid and made good money washing luxury yachts.

The Cold Stone Creamery was the first of its kind I'd seen. They combined a limited number of ice cream flavors with a vast assortment of toppings, folding them together to make an unlimited combination of ice cream desserts. I chose the German Chocolate Cake from their list. Brian ended up with the same selection due to an error behind the counter and Seth, still nursing a delicate stomach, chose a pink fruit smoothie. Before you feel sorry for Seth, I'll explain that the afternoon before he got sick, he stopped by the newly opened creamery with friends and in place of dinner had an enormous ice cream sundae. It would likely be as much as a week before he'd be able to approach a waffle cone or crumbled candy bars.

Leading to much eye-rolling from Seth, Brian let it be known we were celebrating a birthday. A platoon of employees and customers immediately set to singing Happy Birthday and a magician appeared to perform slight-of-hand tricks.

After Seth opened gifts at the apartment, Brian logged on for a quick check of weather. We were relieved to note the path of Hurricane Lily was going to skirt the Turks and Caicos, avoiding any threat to *Take Two*. The weather looked clear and calm from St. Thomas to there, but we still hadn't closed on the ranch and the window of fair weather would probably pass before Brian was able to fly up to retrieve her.

Brian called the title company to get the update on when we'll be paid for the ranch. We ran out of cash somewhere over Miami, and now were watching our dwindling line of credit with the same faces we had watched the stock market's descent. The latest hold-up was trouble the buyer ran into getting insurance on a property with a recent claim against. That fire that gave Rancho del Fuego its name had come back to bite us in the backside.

We woke before sunrise the next morning to flashes of lightening and the sound of thunder rolling from St. Thomas to the Yucatan. We were getting used to such weather, but Puck wasn't. The thunder still scared the bejeezus out of him. Each new clap set him barking feverishly at the walls then whimpering pitifully to each of us. He'd run from one side of the bed to the other for reassurance and refuge from the approaching doom. When he failed to find shelter, or even identify the enemy, he chose the next logical course of action: to hide. With each storm he pushed deeper into the closet displacing duffel bags and shoe boxes looking for a dark corner safe from the Grim Reaper. This is where we found Puck mornings after a storm.

Rain is welcome by residents of the Virgin Islands. Nearly all of the homes collect rainwater in cisterns. When those are empty and the clouds dry up, water must be bought from the desalination plant and delivered by truck. The morning's thunder brought rain, but no wind, so we, too, were glad. When a strong east wind blew rain against our wall of windows the same wall that let us enjoy breathtaking tropical sunrises became a porous, leaky barrier against the storm.

After breakfast the rain stopped, but clouds lingered, making it a fine day for running errands. I pressed Seth to reconfigure his futon bed back into a sofa, then offering the empty gesture of directing Puck to be a brave dog and watch the apartment we headed out.

Tutu Mall didn't feel like any stateside malls, its anchor is a K-Mart and there are only three or four smaller chain stores familiar to us from the West Coast. The food court was a dimly lit corner with a Kentucky Fried Chicken and Chinese Buffet. The mall always had a semi-deserted feeling about it as if we'd arrived ten minutes before opening. Some of the stores offered depressing collections of merchandise like the shop with walls of sentimental etched glass knick-knacks with testimonials for THE WORLD'S GREATEST GRANDMOTHER. At the bottom of one wall was a single small shelf of scented bath products. I wondered if a box fell from a truck.

It was pitiful, like a child with a lemonade stand. But it's satisfying to buy lemonade from a child who smiles happily and says thank you. You leave feeling charitable, and the child grows up to write books and give seminars on how to make money. I was tempted to buy something to give meaning to the clerk's day, but she wasn't there out of a spirit of entrepreneurship. She probably wasn't even going to smile or say thank you.

Several stores sold strange combinations of products. The front of a fabric shop looked typical enough, but behind the bolts of fabric and shelves of thread and zippers was a small room with two circular clothing racks. No two items were the same style or fabric; the work of the owner? Tag sale items? Who knows? A crowded discount furniture store offered one piece of art the likes of which I haven't seen since the "unclaimed" table in a ceramics class. In a prominent position, just inside the door rested a plaster mermaid the size of a two year old child. Her scales were painted an uninspired flat sky blue; her flesh was flesh colored, her hair yellow and lips pink. For some purpose unguessed by me or Brian this diva of the sea bore a small plastic suction cup on her up-turned elbow. We were tempted to buy it for the next gift exchange event we were tricked into.

I dislike being coerced into buying gifts for strangers. I don't understand why otherwise interesting people will spend tens of hours, hundreds of dollars, and forests of fir boughs throwing a holiday party, will wait until the moment at the height of the evening, when guests are enjoying the fruit of their effort and have settled into amiable, like-minded groups for conversation, to bring the party to a screeching halt by announcing it's time for the gift exchange. They command their captives to step away from the spinach dip, cheese logs, wings and fudge; to leave the bar and punch bowl, stop talking, and come sit four abreast on couches to submissively watch one another unwrap cheap, tasteless—or at the very least, generic gifts. Discarded paper rises like the tide as one hapless recipient after another stammers for something gracious to say about a novelty item, and someone stupidly waives her right to anonymity by explaining that if you press the belly it plays *Grandma Got Run Over by a Reindeer*. And all along everyone wishes they had gotten something as cute as what they brought. The only fun comes at the door when your hostess sees you've forgotten your gift and you scurry down the slippery sidewalk as the slightly drunk hostess turns to find it for you.

Seth headed directly to the Champs Sports store where he selected three jerseys and a pair of shorts to replenish his sports theme wardrobe. He piled them on the counter and I produced my credit card.

"These can be a birthday present," Seth said placing a pair of white Nike's on the pile.

"Another pair! I don't think so. Besides, you already got your birthday present."

"Fine, I'll pay you back."

"When?" I fixed my gaze on him.

"From my birthday money when we get home."

"Okay."

Seth had an athletic shoe fetish. He owned several pairs each indistinguishable from the other: white, laced athletic shoes with the appropriate black swoosh. He didn't even try anymore to convince us that he was outgrowing them.

Next, we drove downtown to a fabric store where I found a beautiful coppery pink and gold fabric I was considering for slip covers for *Take Two*'s salon. So many yacht interiors are upholstered in royal blue and decorated with needlepoint throw pillows sporting cute nautical sayings like: "A Bad Day Sailing is Better than a Good Day at Work;" "Sailors Do It Into the Wind." The one I'd like to see is, "It's Not Seasickness, it's These Insipid Pillows." Boats are surrounded by blue sea and sky, why do so many insist upon blue inside as well. Perhaps there is a Rules and Regulations for Nautical Decorating Guide I wasn't given. Maybe, just below the rules about life vests being orange, it says the interior of a boat will be decorated in blue, if blue fabric is not available, then an innocuous pattern of pastel brush-strokes may be substituted.

Unfortunately, wanting an inspired and beautiful interior and knowing how to pull it off are not one in the same. I lack the Martha Stewart gene, or even a subscription to her magazine. Before buying a dozen yards of upholstery fabric, I needed a lot of encouragement. Furthermore, I had to get past

Brian's response when I pulled the pink and gold roll of fabric from a corner and draped it over my arm. "So, instead of boring and uninspired, you're shooting for Moorish Whorehouse. Okay." I needed to give it more thought so we left the shop and headed toward sub base.

During World War II St. Thomas was developed as a military base. Now the area known as sub base hosts government offices, auto shops, and specialty retailers. After some cruising, Brian found our next stop: Fine Woodworking. There I found a smiling fellow by the name of Jacob. Like nearly everyone we met on St. Thomas, he was from somewhere else. Jacob was born in Guyana where his brother, father, grandfather and great-grandfather were all wood craftsmen.

Seth napped in the car and Brian waited outside while I interrupted Jacob's lunch with his wife to ask about wood for carving. I'd left my power tools behind in California and hoped to satisfy my woodworking interest with small carving projects. Jacob had nothing to sell, but he shared his online resources. Then he showed me around his shop and the cabinet work that made up most of his business. His pretty, dark-haired wife sat quietly eating homemade lunch at a workbench. She watched her husband with admiration as he showed me a binder of furniture he built, and finished the tour pulling a sheet from a beautiful mahogany dining table he was restoring for a customer.

We didn't make it to the art gallery or the fish market, which is really a corner at Coki Point where fishermen offer their morning catch from the back of a pick-up. I stopped once out of curiosity. A big man in faded work clothes left a group of men laughing and drinking beer and met me at the back of his truck. His weathered black face was rough like the surface of a rock. He showed no indication of annoyance at being pulled away just to answer questions.

"Did you catch these?" I asked pointing to a collection of fish lying on the tailgate.

"Yes."

"This morning?"

"Yes, this morning."

"What kind of fish are they?"

He pointed to a red spotted fish and said a word I didn't recognize, then to a grey fish with a yellow stripe and said it was a goatfish.

"What are these?" I asked pointing to several pinkish fish with large staring black eyes.

"Snapper. See the eyes? They are deep water fish."

I asked once more about the red spotted fish and repeated the word he used, hind. At home, I looked it up in my *Corals & Fishes of the Caribbean* book and found red hind and rock hind.

When I told my friends from the States that I stopped at the fish corner, they all looked aghast. Vowing that they'd never eat those fish cautioned me against any foolish ideas, but they couldn't tell me why. I argued there were ways to identify edible fish, to tell if it's fresh, and that it would be bad for business if people died. But they stuck to their beliefs that the fishermen wouldn't hesitate to poison off their customers with diseased fish.

~~~~

Navigating St. Thomas is a game that must be undertaken with a sense of humor. Island maps, your game piece, are available throughout St. Thomas. The game begins when you call for directions to an office, store or restaurant. Your opponent, the clerk or receptionist who takes your call, is awarded points based upon how little information he or she gives. It takes an experienced player to know that the first logical step is to throw away the map. There is no information on the map that will do you any good in this game. The map is clearly marked with road numbers, and signs mark the roads. But the locals have never seen the signs or the map. They use names that are passed from one generation to another, through oral history; names never recorded in print or on street signs.

Your opponent begins by forcing you to admit you don't know any roads by name. One hundred points are issued and they move to the double-score round where they challenge you with local landmarks:

Opponent: "Do you know the Green House?"

You: (unaware of a Green House, a green house, or a greenhouse) "No, I'm sorry."

Opponent: "The left turn by the Department of Flagrant Nepotism?"

You: "Uh, not really."

Opponent: "The ferry terminal?"

You: (hopefully) "Is that near Chase Manhattan?"

Opponent: "You know Wendy's?"

You: (Jackpot!) "Yes! I know Wendy's."

You later learn that Wendy's is always the sign that the game has moved to the final round, DIRECTIONS, for triple points.

Opponent: "Past Wendy's, turn right."

You: "At the light?"

Opponent: "At the corner. Go behind the hospital. Left."

You: "Left behind the hospital? Or left to the hospital?"

Opponent: "The hospital is on the right. It's a pink building."

You: "The hospital is pink, or your building?"

Opponent: "Yes."

You get 1000 points for getting in your car rather than saying screw it. One hundred points are deducted for every wrong turn. One hundred and fifty points are added for understanding why your spouse believes you're a blithering idiot when you're sitting at the corner by Wendy's where there IS a light, and telling him that you're supposed to turn at the corner, not the light.

Finally, you get 200 points for tenacity and not being intimidated by their why are you bothering me with these questions attitude.

~~~~

Another St. Thomas game is called Count the Coincidences!

Soon after we got to St. Thomas, Brian got e-mail from a fellow named Michael, who said Brian's aunt was friends with his wife's aunt. Both aunts had instructed us to get together because we'd all moved to St. Thomas within the past year. What's more, Michael and his wife, Alicia, had lived in Sacramento just twenty miles down the hill from our ninety-two acres.

Well, those were enough coincidences for us, but they were just a start. We arranged to have drinks Sunday evening at our end of the island. We had a delightful time getting to know Mike and Alicia, and discovered they were moving in the next month from a rental house on the North side to a condo that we could see from the balcony of our apartment. We also learned Mike attended the junior college where our daughter took classes for two years. Quite a coincidence, right? But wait! Don't put those fingers and toes away yet. The conversation was just getting interesting.

"You said you lived in Washington. Where ?" Mike asked me.

"Vancouver, across the river from... "

"I know where Vancouver is, I grew up there."

"You're kidding," I said. "That's amazing! What high school did you go to?"

"I graduated from Hudson's Bay in 1987."

"Ha! So did I, in the 70s."

It wasn't until we got back to the apartment that I tried to remember what year my sister graduated. I sent her an e-mail and learned not only did she graduate the same year as Mike, but she remembered him from classes they had together.

I'm not sure exactly how that seven degrees of separation theory works, but I'd say we beat the odds on this one. What's even more amazing is that all evening no one said "Small world."

Jeep Jeep

For several days we'd been shopping for a used car that looked good, ran well, and could carry cargo or people. That meant an SUV. Jeep Cherokees are hugely popular in the islands. We looked at several, enough to acquaint ourselves with the higher prices cars command when shipped in relatively small quantities to an island a thousand miles south of Florida.

After a week of shopping, Brian decided on a 1995 white Jeep Cherokee from a dealer near the airport. He negotiated service to the Jeep and a loaner car while the service was performed. The loaner, a Toyota Echo, had fewer features than I'd seen on a car in years. It took me two minutes of searching for some kind of switch before I figured out the mirrors were adjusted by rolling down the window with a crank handle, grabbing the mirror with my hand and turning it. I did, however, find an interesting radio station. It reminded me of what they say about the weather in Hawaii, if you don't like it, wait a minute and it will change. In half an hour, I heard Garth Brooks, Frank Sinatra, Bob Marley and the Wailers and a steel drum band.

Brian was off island retrieving *Take Two* when the service department called to say the Jeep was ready. I braved rush-hour traffic to the far side of the island to swap the loaner car for our Cherokee. The Jeep was inside a fenced lot, parked under a tree near the service entrance where two men in coveralls stood idly. I swapped keys with the receptionist and climbed in the Jeep. It was dirtier than I remembered and the odometer read 65,000. I thought Brian bought the car with 79,000 miles (Brian also remembered 79,000 and we wondered if we saw it before the odometer was rolled back). The keychain had our name on it and the key started the car, so I shifted into reverse. The Jeep behaved as though it was in neutral. I revved the motor. The car sat without any hint of moving. I put it in park then again in reverse and tried once more. When I climbed out of the car one of the guys in coveralls asked if I needed help. He took the keys and got in with an amused look, probably thinking he had to show me where to find reverse. But a moment later he handed me back the keys to the Echo and said they'd call me when the Jeep was ready. Perhaps the Jeep knew about our drive-way.

~~~~

The day Brian left in the Aztec to get *Take Two* came after an anxious week of waiting and contriving for pieces to fall into place. It was a gray, lightly overcast morning, but ceilings were high, so he expected no trouble. I dropped him at the airport and drove toward town in a gray, lightly overcast mood. The week had resisted planning in spite of Brian's efforts. He needed a sailor to accompany him back with *Take Two*, and a pilot to return the Aztec. Once again I was reminded how convenient it would be for me to get my pilot certification for twin engines. It wasn't until the morning Brian left that he confirmed another sailor for the return voyage and a pilot to fly the Aztec back.

Because of all the uncertainty, and the threat of Brian wanting me to go along for the six hour flight to Providenciales and back, to make sure the hired pilot didn't forget to whom the airplane belonged and wander off to another island offering it to drug dealers, we hadn't discussed whether I might sail back with him on *Take Two*. Once solutions were found and the pilot's references checked (thus letting me off the hook for a vertiginous six-hour ordeal of mistrust), I had time to realize I, too, wanted a blue water sailing adventure. By then it was too late to make arrangements and I left the airport sulking.

There were no cruise ships in Charlotte Amalie's harbor that day and finding a parking place downtown wasn't difficult. I decided to buy myself something. It didn't matter what, because by golly, I had dragged myself thousands of miles from everything I loved, except for what would fit into three duffle bags and two small moving boxes, I deserved something new.

I'm not fond of shopping as a rule and I bristle at the idea that all women love to shop. I have no patience with gray-haired, balding dinosaurs who suggest the women catch the shuttle to the shopping center while the men drag their fists off to their manly hobbies. I enjoy many of the traditionally male-dominated avocations; aviation, astronomy and target-practice to name a few.

Shopping takes a tremendous amount of time or money, and often both. My taste tends to over-reach my self-indulgence and I would rather read a book than wander hours in a weatherless, beige mall searching endlessly for clothes that I can afford and don't accentuate my body flaws, both inherited and evidence of neglect. This day, however, as the Aztec lifted off taking Brian to buy himself a 48' boat, my self-indulgence was feeling unfettered.

Parking near the fabric store, I visited the coral pink upholstery fabric once more. Major decorating decisions such as this are treacherous for the decoratively challenged. A good decision will evoke compliments and self-satisfied smiles for years to come. A bad decision will inspire countless explanations and grimaces every time a visitor's glance lingers. I fingered the fabric for a moment then put off the decision once again.

I strolled along the waterfront in the unhurried manner of someone with an abundance of time and a wish for something interesting to happen. Nothing happened, so I cheerfully chanted, "No thanks," to the cab drivers who didn't notice me dangling my car keys as a sign I'm a local, and got down to business finding something to buy. Nestled among the myriad jewelry stores and shops selling sarongs and bottled sand, I found a gem of a clothing shop, the White House and Black Market. This classy little shop carried a tempting collection of women's clothes that reflect the island's casual approach to dressing-up. With the help of a friendly clerk, I bought a white knit top with a plunging neckline and a pair of embroidered stretch pants that say, "Take me out and show me off, lover boy."

Back at the apartment, I squeezed the car into our corner parking spot. Rain was sprinkling the leaves and pavement unenthusiastically, not serious enough to make this Washington-grown girl dash from car to house. Like so many of my Northwest brothers and sisters I'm more likely to sit in the shade on a sunny beach than I am to bother with an umbrella on a rainy day. That evening Seth had plans with friends and I spent the hours hemming my new pants in front of the television.

The next day I awoke determined to set out on my own adventure, wishing for one to rival Brian's exciting, Columbus-like journey sailing the Western Atlantic. I scattered my collection of guidebooks on the bed. Guide books are a big industry in the Virgin Islands. The pages are crowded with photos of smiling beauties dressed in carnival feathers or designer swimsuits alongside jewelry store and water sport advertisements.

You can learn anything the typical undemanding tourist might care to know: where to find a seafood restaurant and how badly it will damage your vacation budget; the location of beaches and what amenities line their sandy shores; how many bottles of liquor can be taken home duty-free. It's up to you to know how much you can physically carry. Tourists who over-estimate here leave heavy boxes of booze strewn along the corridors of airports like pioneers' pianos abandoned in the foothills of the Rockies.

In the guidebooks all the resorts sound like pearlescent paradises of luxury and beauty staffed by legions of smiling men and women. A piece of advice here: let the price be your guide. If the Azure Beach Grand Island Resort sounds as captivating as the Island Grand Azure Bay Resort but at half the price don't expect both to have neatly-uniformed bell-hops whisking your luggage to sun-bleached rooms where hibiscus flowers adorn mountains of white towels in spacious gleaming bathrooms. At the lesser-priced resort you will probably get the hibiscus, but you'll schlep your own suitcases to dark rooms situated on busy footpaths. If you don't plan to spend a lot of time in your room, does it really matter if the sun-bleached walls are cracked and you find a tiny windowless shower stall cowering behind the door? It's up to you.

If you can't find what you want in one guidebook, give up. Take your towel and go lie on whatever beach you find. There's no use searching through other books, the information is all the same. The thin ones rely on clip-art icons and tables to indicate price, atmosphere, cuisine and location; the thick, more ambitious guides make you read restaurant reviews for the same information. I prefer icons. The reviews are either thinly veiled advertisements or composed by critics who only know of "spectacular views" and "unforgettable dining experiences." Like the resorts, they all sound unforgettable and spectacular even the unkempt, sorrowful little beer-postered spots. However, unforgettable, isn't always good—a meal once gave me food poisoning.

My favorite, The *St. Thomas Guide Book*, published by Great Dane, Inc., is a fun little tome best described as a comic book with advertisements for hotels and restaurants instead of x-ray glasses and hand-buzzers. Charmingly simple drawings accompany droll versions of island history and idiosyncrasies. It was as much fun to read as it surely was to create.

Two prominent options stared back at me from the guide books: Exploring some of the many historic sites of downtown Charlotte Amalie, or finding a place called the Mountain Top. According to a segment that ran seven thousand times a day on the local promote the hell out of St. Thomas television channel, the Mountain Top has a bar

famous for banana daiquiris, a venue for special events, and—
are you sitting down?—shopping. I decided on the historic
walk, preferring to save the Mountain Top discovery and
daiquiri judging for a later visit with Brian. Strolling is best
done without the company of my goal-oriented husband. He
does not wander well, he purposefully walks between point A
and point B. I have an amazingly poor sense of direction
which might be why I wander exceedingly well. I didn't want
to share a desultory walk downtown trotting alongside Brian
trying at every intersection to explain that I didn't have a fixed
itinerary rather I planned to wander about for a few hours in
hopes of stumbling across sites marked by red and white
circles on my map.

I invited Seth to join me, but he declined so after
breakfast I headed to town alone. I drove the long route via
the south side of the island. This road took me past what is
arguably the nicest resort on St. Thomas, the Renaissance
Grand, and through the poorest neighborhoods in Estate
Bovoni near the landfill.

My first stop was at the home of the USVI legislature, an
enchanting green and white building sitting indifferently on the
waterfront. The front of the building gazes over a fountain and
garden toward downtown, to the rear is a parking area, this
leaves a narrow lonely side door opening infrequently to the
beautiful deep-water harbor lapping just yards from its
foundation.

Though it was Saturday the building's docent was on
hand to support campaign activities across the street. He gave
me a thick packet of copied pages: bleary, faded bios for the
current senators, St. Thomas history, and legislative lessons. I
asked to see more of the building and we took a short elevator
ride to an upstairs hallway. The building, originally built in
1828 and reconstructed in 1874, has a handsome interior of
paneled walls and polished beams. The docent's expertise
seemed to lie with biographies and names of governors dating
back to when the island changed hands from US military to
civilian control in 1931.

At home I magnified the blurry six-point Courier in the information packet, and learned this building was the sight of the ceremonies signifying the transfer of ownership from Denmark when the United States bought the islands in 1917 for $25,000,000.

I wanted to see the floor of the senate, but my docent muttered an excuse why we couldn't enter any of the rooms or exit by way of a beautiful exterior stairway that swept in a horseshoe shape to the ground floor entrance with wrought iron railing accompanying the descent. I later learned to be more persistent asking locals to repeat themselves until I understood.

I cautiously crossed Veteran's Drive back toward Fort Christian. Veteran's Drive is a dangerous road along the busy Charlotte Amalie waterfront where cruise ship passengers travel on foot to the shops downtown. Three pedestrians have been killed in recent years. The speed limit, 50 mph, in this high pedestrian area is an example of an apparently indifferent and oblivious St. Thomas government.

Massive Fort Christian stands as a fitting symbol of the epoch of European colonization on St. Thomas. Built by the Danish in the 1670s, this brick red fortress witnessed the coming of plantation owners and the slave ships that made the sugar plantations profitable. Later I would visit Market Square where slaves newly dragged from Africa and other Caribbean islands stood on the auction block. Today descendants of those slaves sell fruits, vegetables and crafts on the same site, but when I arrived shortly after noon the vendors were gone and only a dozen or so West Indians loitered about with apparently nothing to do but stare. What I had hoped would be a moment of reflection over a dismal part of Caribbean and American history became a quick, self-conscious walk past and on to St. Peter and Paul Catholic Church down the street.

Leaving Fort Christian I walked inland from the waterfront toward a sight known as the 99 steps. The guide book said Danish engineers who had never set foot on the island designed a tidy grid layout for the town. The result left the hillsides of Charlotte Amalie beset with steps. I was looking for something grand, not necessarily the Spanish Steps, perhaps like the Lincoln Memorial, but saw only buildings crowded together, separated by narrow crumbling roads and narrower alleys. I found the Grand Galleria which on my map was next to the steps, but I saw no dramatic stairways. The Galleria entrance was blocked by an ornate iron gate which I rattled tentatively. This caused a woman to appear and tell me the restaurant was closed until noon, I also learned I'd find the ninety-nine steps on the corner on my right. I might easily have walked past the tall narrow path of stone steps climbing straight up the hillside. I ascended past bougainvillea and hibiscus growing between the path and the buildings and walled yards lining it. I missed the historic Frederick Lutheran Church which the map indicated was on my right. If it was near the top I may have been too busy breathing to notice.

The view from the top of the steps is said to be lovely. I suppose it was. The lack of oxygen to my brain impaired my short term memory. I glanced up from bending over dragging air into my lungs, then sat on a low, dirty stone wall with my back to the view, but getting a good look at a run-down white building.

Once the oxygen returned to my blood I descended a stairway on the back side. Just for kicks I counted the steps going down. There were more, 180, but unlike the straight, uniform 99 steps, the back side meandered around corners with wide and narrow, deep and shallow steps. They were heavily littered and stank of urine. They ended abruptly on a curb beside a tiny market where I bought a soda and set off for my next historic encounter.

On the way to more history I stopped in a jewelry store along Main Street, which runs parallel to Veteran's Boulevard, one block inland from the water front. I don't know why I go into jewelry stores. I like diamonds and gold as much as the next person, but I am haunted by the gross superficiality of money spent on an ornament when that same money could fly my kids out for a visit.

I visited, again, the coral pink fabric. By now I'm thinking, oh my gosh, make the decision already, but I couldn't. Each time I stopped, I hoped my reaction would be different, decisive. I almost didn't care whether I found myself glad I didn't rush into such a gaudy pink mistake, or sighing at the perfection of the color and know suddenly and forever this match was right for me. Neither such moment occurred, so I went on my way, smiling bravely at the clerk who was probably thinking, oh my gosh, make the decision already.

That evening I heard from Brian. They had work to do on the boat and would be leaving the Turks and Caicos a day later than planned. I was disappointed. I was tired of a temporary home and ready to settle in a place of our own. Though our deadline, to take the boat to Jost Van Dyke for Seth's school camping trip, was a week away. We wanted to sail over and have the comfort of our home, rather than sleeping in a tent.

Yoga Warrior

I heard from Brian the next day as well. *Take Two*'s owner, who was accompanying them to Puerto Rico, had a customs problem to resolve. They would be leaving yet another day later. If Brian and the yacht didn't arrive until Saturday, we could still sail to Jost Van Dyke for the school camp-out barbeque on Sunday. I hoped there'd be no more holdups. Our landlords, the Wilmerdings, had been understanding, but there was little room in the schedule for more delays, their new tenants were moving in in one week.

A new yoga program started on the local television channel one morning. Laying a rug in the only space big enough, between the end table and a chair, I followed along. I've never had much lung capacity, so yoga seemed a perfect exercise alternative. Time would tell. I liked that the positions had names. I could follow along with Up Dog and the Plow; I cheated on Down Dog; and my favorite was the Warrior, which I could hold for several seconds if a breeze didn't come along and tip me over.

I was still pointing at the ground when the instructor's hands were flat, and I didn't know that I'd ever master a position where she sat with one leg straight, one knee bent, and twisted her arm 270 degrees wrapping it upside down and backward around her bent leg clasping her hands together by her butt. I may never understand the need for this particular exercise either.

I did the yoga again the next morning, congratulating myself on remarkable discipline. Not the discipline of two days

in a row so much as the discipline of ignoring another person
in the room, and leaning out of the way when he passed. Yoga,
perhaps most of all exercises, cries out for privacy, or lacking
that, shared humiliation. There should be some sort of Good
Samaritan law making it illegal to witness yoga beginners
without offering a gesture of humiliation such as tripping over
your own feet or an unprovoked coughing spasm.

I got an e-mail from Brian. They didn't get underway until
three days later than scheduled and he estimated they were
four days away. They had problems with cutlass bearings or
something. With Brian gone I relied more than ever on regular
e-mail exchanges with my sisters for companionship. We
chatted about bosses, Friday nights, my older sister's thing for
Jimmy Buffett and other philosophically easy topics. Their
messages always brightened my day, but sometimes my
responses brought me down. Answering a query about my
kids, I got homesick and cried.

I continued with the yoga program each morning, not
realizing until the fourth day they were rerunning the same
program every day. I wondered how long they'd been running
this one half hour segment. I was getting to know the routine,
but it still felt like playing a game of solitaire Twister.

The next day, Brian reported more problems with *Take
Two*'s port engine. This was going to slow them down.
Prevailing winds were right on her nose, so they'd relied on
motoring or motor-sailing. This left them with just the
starboard engine for extended periods. He believed they were
four or five days away. I considered asking if rowing might be
faster, but thought the better of it.

When they reached the Dominican Republic the owner
flew home rather than staying on until Puerto Rico as planned.
Too many explanations for things breaking, perhaps. However,
the marine surveyor stayed on as well as a friend of the owner,
Steve, who came aboard as hired crew to help bring her down.

The next message from Brian reported that one of two
davits holding the dingy broke during the night, so they had to
tow it. That slowed them down another knot.

By now, we'd missed the camping weekend on Jost, and I faced the possibility of moving into a hotel to wait. "Wouldn't that be a grand pain in the ass," I grumbled to myself.

They stopped in San Juan to get fuel and let the surveyor off to catch a flight home. Too many explanations for things breaking, perhaps. As always, they were not allowed to leave the yacht until approved by a customs inspector. Since it was a holiday and no one on duty, they were delayed another day.

You don't live in the islands long before learning to check the holiday schedule prior to heading to the bank or a government office. In addition to U.S. Federal holidays, they add their own. They celebrate Three Kings Day on January sixth; the transfer from Denmark on March twenty-seven; the day before Good Friday is Holy Thursday; and they stay home one day in June in honor of Organic Act Day, which celebrates Congress granting power to the governor. They get twice the bang for their holiday buck in July by taking the third for Emancipation Day; Hurricane Supplication Day is also in July; and Hurricane Thanksgiving Day is the third Monday in October. It must have seemed like too long to wait until November eleventh for a day off, so they celebrate free press on Liberty Day, November first. Finally, they take the busiest shopping day of the year, December twenty-sixth off, ostensibly for Boxing Day. They add nine holidays to the calendar for a total of twenty-four government holidays.

Finally, I woke to an email estimating their arrival that morning. I spent a little more time on my hair and make-up, and was on the dock squinting into the early sun as she slid neatly into our slip at ten minutes after ten.

~~~~

The previous owners didn't turn *Take Two* over to Brian so much as abandon her. They couldn't have left more on board if they'd been driven off at gunpoint. Nearly every compartment was full. Ultimately, we would find almost a dozen household appliances; a veritable hardware store of tools and spare parts for every system on board; an eye-popping assortment of water toys; bed linens to support a large crew through the coldest of climates; and groceries.

I was pleased to find among the kitchen appliances an iron, blender and juicer, all items I had planned to buy. I hadn't planned to buy a television, but Seth would be glad to have the small TV/VCR we found in the center of a large ball of comforters. In between discoveries, I faced the obvious problem of where to put our stuff. Nevertheless, I was still eager to experience living on a yacht and with a certainty of good times to come, I took on the challenge of stowing everything. The clutter was yet to drive me to new depths of frustration.

Brian told me to choose which of the two forward cabins I wanted for my clothes and the few things I'd brought from California. It would also be my space for privacy and to sleep when we didn't want to disturb one another. Each of the catamaran's two hulls had one forward cabin and one aft. I descended the three steps into the starboard hull and turned forward passing through the companion-way. Each hull had a companionway with a narrow upholstered bench on one side and counter space on the other. Two small portholes in the side and a hatch overhead let in light. Each of the forward cabins had a raised sleeping compartment, storage space, and its own bathroom. The only difference between the port and starboard sides was a slightly different storage configuration. I chose starboard for its few extra inches of clothes rod. This arrangement worked out best when Brian discovered he could actually stand up straight in the shower stall on the port side. The ceiling in the starboard master bathroom, where Brian showered on the way down, was slightly lower and his head stuck into the hatch opening. He must have looked like a blue-eyed, graying clam peering from its shell.

Turning aft at the bottom of the steps on each side was a wall of cubbies, a small bathroom and the aft cabin. These cabins were little more than small closets with shelf beds. The floor space compared closely with that of a phone booth. Seth would get one aft cabin, and the other was for guests. In between guest visits, it was piled to the hatch with the kind of clutter that follows people where ever they live.

Like maggots that appear inexplicably on a carcass, clutter appears in space left undisturbed for more than seventy-two hours. Malignant, space-eating clutter in the form of original packaging we hang on to just in case; throw pillows that are still good, but don't match the new blanket; craft supplies pushed aside in a cleaning frenzy and then forgotten; and of course, vacuum attachments that are too much trouble to put back.

I was still sorting through piles of clothes after the sun went down, when I came upon a cockroach expecting to share my starboard cabin. Never in my life have I shrunk from insect battles. Girded with the weapon of choice: tissues for slow bugs, inverted glasses for faster bugs, bigger bugs and bees on windows, cans of RAID for confronting legions of ants, and a vacuum for guerilla warfare with spiders; I've fought my own fights and took pride in not teaching my daughter to be a screamer. I lived my life on the West Coast, the home of innocuous little red ants and killer bees. Never before had I confronted a full-grown, antenna-waving, kitten-sized cockroach staring at me from the bench in my cabin, looking for the world like he was there to ask which side of the bed I preferred. I froze.

The only insects this large I had ever seen were mutated by radiation and chasing Troy Donahue out a cave and down a beach. This was the largest insect I had ever seen and it was in the smallest space I'd ever called a room. I beckoned Brian with such intensity that, to his credit, he came immediately and disposed of the stow-away. While Brian took his captive to a far, far away place, I stood staring weakly at the spot for several minutes. To my credit, I still slept in that cabin.

We were still stepping over Brian's boxes in the salon when he found distraction from putting things away by working on the outboard motor on the dingy. After an hour or two of greasy tinkering and sputtering starts he and Seth took a celebratory lap around the marina. They returned with the news that Pete would be stopping by later with fresh tuna.

When Pete arrived, I had stuffed Brian's things into compartments under cushions, on the sofa in his companionway and anywhere I found space. I put the tuna in the oven and pressed Pete to stay for dinner. Brian opened one of the few bottles of wine we bothered to drag across country and we toasted our new life on *Take Two*.

It Happens

The first things to go wrong that Monday were trivial. I didn't have enough cash at the mail center to pay postage for our daughter's birthday present, my bank card didn't get activated immediately as promised by the perpetually indifferent bank clerk, and I slipped stepping from the boat to the wet dock with an armload of laundry, resulting in a large bruise on my knee. Then the day turned bad.

I called Brian to my cabin where he agreed the odor I'd been complaining of was indeed getting worse. He made inquiries on the dock and learned that hoses carrying waste from the heads often became permeated and need to be replaced. Easy enough. He found the necessary hose and hose clamps at a chandlery and we set to work taking up the carpet from my cabin floor. Moments later, we were grabbing every towel within reach to soak up waste water flowing from the holding tank below onto the floor of my room. The towels became saturated and still the waste was bubbling like a putrid brown fountain into my cabin. I hurried for a bucket and sponge, grateful for a breath of fresh air, while Brian struggled to get the new hose into place. Once the hose clamped tight, we stood, teary-eyed and nostrils constricting, looking morosely at the ankle-deep sewage where he stood. Being the gentleman he is, Brian allowed me the privilege of getting the bilge pump from the cockpit. I returned to find him standing naked and ready for the unspeakably dreadful task of cleaning up. Without a doubt, Brian took the worst of the job. My role was to carry buckets of pee out to the cockpit and discreetly toss it overboard while he stayed below pumping into a bucket and mopping. All told, he must have been over an hour in the foul air without a break. He even kept his sense of humor, at one point muttering, "Well, shit happens." Finally, down to a second or third sponging with disinfectant he let me take over and hurried away to shower. Brian later learned that, though he'd been told otherwise, the galley sink was also draining into the holding tank for my head. Though it should have been less than a quarter full it was completely full and backed up into the hoses.

The day wasn't over, but we had a momentary respite. Having thoroughly scrubbed ourselves and liberally applied fragrant lotions, we felt dinner in a restaurant was not merely earned, but demanded. It was time to try the East End Café in the American Yacht Harbor complex. To call it a café is a bit of a misnomer. The ambiance was simple enough, but the food deserved a more grandiloquent name. From the moment we entered, it was a perfect dining experience. The cafe was neither empty nor crowded, sparing us the noise and poor service that accompany a crowd or the self-conscious feeling of someone always watching you in an empty restaurant. I ordered a glass of red wine and Brian's very specific drink request was received with a friendly desire to accommodate. My red snapper in a berry sauce was superb, its flavor well defined but not over-powering. It is all too rare to experience a dish so masterfully created. Brian's mahi mahi arrived in a gentle, yet flavorful, creamy red pepper sauce. This evening was not for restraint, so we shared—as unrestrained as we get—a creamy canolli for dessert. I praised the food so effusively the chef, Jeff, also an owner of the restaurant, visited our table to thank us personally for the compliments.

We strolled back to the boat mellowed by wine and pleased with our culinary discovery. My cabin was still in disarray when I went below to change for bed. The clothes that were hastily pulled from the closet to expose the hoses were still piled on the bed. On top of the pile of clothes was a cockroach, a big brother to the previous one. This was not a little guy like the two Brian killed in the galley the night before. This bloke was huge… and sitting on my clothes putting wrinkles in them. I called for Brian, but he was off the boat taking out the trash. Seth came quickly, but his attempt to catch the intruder was hampered by his convulsive giggling at my clenching and unclenching fists and stiff-fingered pointing at the roach as it scurried for hiding. Those damned things are freakishly fast. It got away and I broke down. Brian was in the salon when I tumbled in, dropped onto a cushion and cried convulsively. He watched helplessly.

I didn't move from the settee for fifteen hours. I simply fell over on my side and stared at the opposite settee until I fell asleep. First thing in the morning we called an exterminator, but he couldn't come until the next day. I stayed in the salon until the afternoon when I snuck down to my head, showered quickly, then hurried out and slept on the settee again.

Sometimes Brian and I slept in his cabin, sometimes in mine and occasionally we slept alone, but I wasn't going into any confined space where a cockroach, like a fire, could trap you with no avenue of escape.

I don't know why I reacted the way I did that night, probably the size of the roach or the stress of the day, possibly the confined space or that it was on my bed. I killed two cockroaches later, a little one in my bathroom and a slightly larger one in the cockpit. But I was still squeamish about going down into my cabin.

Decorating a Head

The last thing I wanted to do Friday morning was attend a security class at the airport. Friends were coming over that evening for a yacht-warming and *Take Two* was a mess. When the exterminator left late Wednesday afternoon all the cupboards and compartments were open and the contents strewn about. Since then I'd managed to get my cabin returned to an organized state. I'd even added decorative touches. But Brian couldn't be coerced into putting things away.

Decorating a head on a boat is a challenge to send Martha Stewart rowing. No pretty porcelain fixtures or heavy tile there. The toilet was an octopus of hoses and pumping apparatus squeezed into an oval opening that scarcely accommodated my hips. Indeed, the dominant feature of the room, next to its miniature size, is the array of hoses. How does one decorate with a hose theme? If I were clever I might have used them for towel racks or painted them to look like little fishy corridors, but I wanted to hide them. I started with a sheer shower curtain with a lacy pattern. I cut it to size and hung a length of it in the oval opening. Now the toilet looked like a veiled freak at a circus side-show, partially obscured for greater intrigue. I hung another strip under the sink. Again, I could see through it, but now, while sitting on the octopus, I could focus on the lace pattern rather than the plumbing behind, and more importantly, it dried quickly. I added color-coordinated towels and candles. That would have to suffice until I was ready to paint and replace fixtures.

Thursday Brian and I motored the requisite three miles offshore to dump the contents of my holding tank then returned to finish replacing hoses in my compartment. At first blush, the idea of dumping black water (the nautical term) into the ocean awakened the environmentalist within me. I was prepared to wrestle my inner coral-hugger to the ground over an odor-free cabin, but merely pointed out to her that whale guano must surely be as voluminous and no less offensive to unsuspecting marine life swimming carefree in the wrong place at the wrong time.

Friday morning arrived with the salon still in disarray, company due late afternoon and Brian insisting we attend the security class. The class was one of the requirements before we could be issued badges allowing unescorted access to our airplane. Getting a badge was neither quick nor easy. It was already my second and Brian's fourth trip to the security office in pursuit of this elusive ID. We had submitted to fingerprinting and an FBI background check and been directed to return for the security training session.

Ten applicants sat around a rectangular table near a wall of windows over-looking the runway. Brian and I arrived last and took seats opposite one another with his back to the windows and my back toward the center of the room. The class, scheduled for two hours, started forty-five minutes late and ran three hours. It was taught by a tall, uniformed black man who shared his history as a police officer with the VIPD before transferring to the VI Port Authority. He opened the class with a joke that made it clear the morning would not go quickly.

With a serious expression and intimidating tone, he said anyone who did not bring a pen or pencil was to leave immediately. "You would not go to school without something to write with. This is a class. Did you think this would be different?" he said.

I squirmed. I didn't have a pen, but we'd gone to considerable effort to take this class. So seeing a pen in Brian's pocket I figured we'd share it.

A man in a polo shirt on my right asked, "I…I don't have a pen. Do I have to leave?" His voice reflected everyone's incredulity.

"This is a class. If you didn't bring a pen then you don't belong here."

"I don't have anything to write with either," a woman in a business suit muttered.

There was a pause while we all shifted uncomfortably and hoped for another solution. Then my neighbor shook his head and pushed his chair back to rise. Only then did our instructor cackle his amusement and confess to his joke.

He took his authority very seriously, strutting back and forth in the middle of the room, delivering his sermon on airport security. His voice rose to ecclesiastical fist-pounding volume when making an important point. He cautioned us to be watchful and drilled us on the meanings of badge color. In his three hour sermon, he confused us with contradictions, and asked the same questions so many times we hesitated to answer for fear it was another of his jokes.

I enjoyed the position of having my back to him as he swaggered back and forth. I entertained myself making faces and rolling my eyes when Brian looked my way. He stifled snickers as we risked certain banishment from the class. At long last, the sermon ended and everyone paid a twenty-dollar fee. We were photographed and issued our minimum security badges.

Our guests were due in four short hours when we returned with several bags of groceries and no place to set them in the messy salon. I put the food away, begging Brian, "Please, please focus on helping make *Take Two* look good." On the whole, I worked myself up to my usual pre-entertaining histrionics.

It's true, when I invite guests I want the space to be clean and seasonally decorated, and the food home-made and gourmet. I set the bar too high and invariably get stressed. Brian is no less guilty of setting the bar low. Indeed, he leaves it on the floor with everything else; trash, spare parts, the boxes they came in, cleaning agents and paraphernalia he was bullied into using, and crates of personal effects still waiting to be stowed since we moved aboard. We are miles apart in our approach to entertaining, and it should come as no surprise that we quarreled every time.

Inevitably my histrionics are a waste of energy and we have a good time. Friday evening was a success and I can live with the possibility that guests wondered why we didn't bother to clear clutter from the salon when we were expecting company. A dozen friends stopped by and the conversation was animated. The range of sailing experience varied from a few lessons to living aboard for twenty-three years. Everyone had a cockroach story and an It's-a-small-world story. We talked about Tahiti, Panama, fishing off the coast of Alaska and someone even had a cannibal encounter. Our new friends hailed from the four corners of the United States and distant points of the British Commonwealth. The food we offered was simple, but sufficient and Brian made batches of painkillers. I looked forward to doing it again when I'd forgotten the labor pains.

Cockroach II

Just when I thought it was safe to go back into the hull, the cockroaches were alive and skulking on *Take Two*. The day after the exterminator came, we found a couple of small vigorous bugs. I wrote this off to a few resistant beasts. The next day or two were mostly bug-free, and though I still entered my compartment like the first cop through the door of a crime scene, I began to relax a bit on the whole cockroach front. I made my bed with fresh clean sheets, decorated a little, and once again enjoyed organized space of my own. Small quarters are tolerable and can even be pleasant if the space is well-used. Fortunately, I thrive on order. Unfortunately, cockroaches thrive on boats. Another encounter was in my future.

Saturday night yielded an emergency of another kind when I saw all the cushions in one corner of the salon dark with moisture. Brian tracked the problem to a clogged air-conditioning hose. Besides the damage to the cushions, water had collected on the bookshelf in his compartment below the a/c unit and the battery compartment below that. Once again, the salon was in complete disorder with wet books and cushions spread out to dry.

With the salon in chaos, I decided to spend Sunday morning reading on the companionway bench. About ten o'clock, I went to my cabin for my book and glasses. Grabbing my glasses from the bed, I disturbed another large cockroach. The monstrous brown beast raced across my bed, tossing pillows aside as he fled, disappearing into the corner. By now,

Brian recognized the familiar shriek and hurried to my compartment passing me on my way out. He caught the roach with his bare hands; you don't have to be squeamish to prefer not to do that, and tossed it overboard without benefit of a personal floatation device.

Once again, the episode left me somber. I'm willing to sleep in a bed the size of a double-wide coffin with head room. I can even withstand the sandwich-thin mattress. But I insist I only share my bed with mammals: Brian, yes, a cat if I had one, but no insects, especially none tall enough on hind legs to ride the roller coaster at Six Flags.

I recovered more quickly from this encounter and though we never saw cockroaches on Brian's bed I never climbed into either berth without first checking under the sheets and pillows.

I found two more roaches in the kitchen that evening. I shot the first with RAID, wielding the can like an Uzi. But the pesticide clean-up was so much work I used the less satisfying, but effective, inverted cup capture for the next. The exterminator was scheduled to come again the next day, That evening I met the owner of a yacht who said it took three exterminator visits to eradicate his large vessel of roaches. There was hope.

92 Acres to 48 Feet

The American Yacht Harbor wharf jutted out like a wooden five-tooth comb into Red Hook Bay on the east end of St. Thomas. It hosted an impressive collection of sport and pleasure boats. The sport fishing boats were the most plentiful and most imposing. Their uppermost cockpits rose to dizzying heights, tall antennas rose higher still.

Strolling A dock, we talked to three young men, two brothers and a friend, who invested in a charter boat. They lived and worked on their own boat and spent days helping charter guests hook marlin, wahoo and other trophy fish. Like all the men who worked the sport boats, they were tan and muscular. Typically, men on the fishing boats were crew waiting for wealthy owners in silk shirts to fly down from Florida for a few days of fishing, drinking rum and smoking cigars. When the owners flew back to the states the hands washed decks, tuned engines, polished chrome and drank beer.

Most boat owners who lived on their vessels made their living serving the vacationing community one way or another. Catamarans provided charters to snorkeling coves or popular spots like the Soggy Dollar Bar or Foxy's on Jost Van Dyke.

ScubaDoo, a large polished cat offered a gourmet lunch with their day trips. *CoverShot* was a smaller catamaran. Its friendly owner had a more casual approach to chartering. The cabin was kitschy and the food simple, but it provided an outing for the more cost-conscious gourmand.

A few large luxury yachts tied-up on C and D docks. These, too, were occupied full-time by crew, most often a couple, who maintained the boat in between visits from the pampered owners.

At the inside end of each dock "tooth" sat painted rental boat kiosks near their fleets of small powerboats. Tourists could rent small inflatable dinghies with little outboards for puttering around Red Hook and Vessup Bay, or 30', 250-horse-powered speed boats for thundering between islands.

The many islands and cays in the area are mostly green, bumpy and dotted with houses and resorts. I could easily imagine a lost tourist steadied at the helm of a rented boat turning charts upside-down and right-side up again, squinting at every island, trying to navigate by Virgin Gorda's reputation for looking like a reclining woman. For visitors preferring to leave navigating to professionals, hired day trips on large cabin cruisers are also available.

Not everyone living aboard his own yacht was wealthy or in business. E dock was the lower rent neighborhood, located on the innermost tooth of the wharf where the water was shallow and murky. Leaving this dock arm, you passed grimy dumpsters, rather than busy restaurants. E dock vessels were smaller mono-hulls able to negotiate the shallow water when they left the slip, which was not often.

James lived on E dock. He had the same handsome features of Earnest Hemingway, but with a softer boyish quality. He also drank like Papa Hemingway and was a writer. James read his poetry for us if we asked, and when we saw him sitting at one of the dockside bars, which was often, he could easily be coaxed into telling stories of his life. Each story introduced new characters, locations and lifestyles. I often wondered whether he had lived an implausibly full and fascinating life or was trying out material for a new book.

Not all boats tied up at the dock. When slips weren't available, or affordable, yachts hooked up to a mooring in Red Hook Bay. The cost for a mooring ball is cheap once you get it anchored in place, and owners can pay an additional nominal fee to park a dingy at the dock while they're ashore. Cheaper still, free in fact, is anchoring a little farther away in Vessup Bay.

We never seriously considered mooring or anchoring, even though paying for a slip was gutting our budget. The motion of the water with the tide and passing boats would have left me prostrate and unproductive in the cabin twenty-four hours a day. And, unless we could drape a hundred foot extension cable across the bay, there would be no electric hook-up and no air conditioning. Not having a/c is especially intolerable on catamarans which have more heat-conducting windows (which only open a few inches) than a mono-hull.

Anyway, I liked living on the wharf. It was a lively, sociable place. Opportunities for friendship arrived with every yacht. Being first on the spot, as we often were, to catch lines and help a boat into a slip, we frequently knew before introductions if we wanted to get to know owners or crew. Docking can be a tense time for the pilot of a million dollar yacht, and both owners and hired captains often had egos larger than the expansive yachts they piloted. The process revealed personalities better than a high stakes game of Texas hold 'em.

We hadn't lived on D dock long when a sleek 70' power boat approached the slip across from ours. Brian hopped up to help catch lines and soon dock staff appeared. Seth and I hung back gazing at *Mistrel* and breaking at least one of the commandments: We coveted what we saw. With unbridled covetousness we coveted our neighbor's house. We may have even worshipped it a little.

Seth was lured into sin by the sexy, speedy-looking tender—much too glorious to be called a dinghy. It had a helm station just aft of center with a steering wheel and undoubtedly an electric ignition. No tugging the rope on a lawn-mower engine for this sleek fiberglass chariot. Seth stared unashamedly until I took his head in my hands and tilted it up. There on an upper deck sat a glossy blue and white jet ski. Seth found his voice. "A jet ski? They have a cool dingy AND a jet ski? No fair!"

I coveted the boat itself. *Take Two* looked like a homemade sheet cake sitting beside this elegant tiered white wedding cake. *Mistral's* deck gleamed in the sunlight which shot blinding beams off chrome trim. Even the fenders hanging over the side to protect the topsides were white and graceful. Varnished teak chairs and a table sat sturdily in the cockpit. And potted plants! No piles of mildewed life vests, buckets of rags and ropes or tangled nests of snorkel equipment. I couldn't see through the smoked glass to the inside, but I just knew the salon floor was not cluttered with milk crates and boxes spilling over with spare parts.

I repented of my sin to count my blessings before Seth did. He was young. He felt sorry for himself the rest of the evening and now and then for weeks to come.

Brian and I fought about clutter. I can slack on cleanliness, I don't grab a bucket and mop if a damp paper towel will do the trick and I can overlook a blanket of dust as long as nobody writes in it. But, I had a problem with clutter. Brian, on the other hand, had a problem with giving a damn. So, over the years my nagging grew more shrill and frequent, but never more effective. It had been a special hope of mine that living on a boat would be different, but Brian just didn't have it in him to put anything away. But at the end of the day I was responsible for my temper and Brian for his indifference.

While Seth and I lusted, Brian and others called advice to the captain who stood in snow-white shorts, a shirt with epaulets and a cap at the helm on the upper deck. He struggled at the controls of his aft engines and forward thrusters, but couldn't make them do what he wanted. The tide and breeze were on *Mistrel's* bow and nudging her officiously into the slip. He approached and aborted several times having a devil of a time and ignoring all advice. His crew tossed lines to Brian and the others, but they couldn't correct for the captain's mistakes. Finally, after the wind carried off all the advice from the dock and profanities from the helm, *Mistrel* banged into the slip, gouging the platform where the tender sat. The captain proceeded to take his ill temper out on the marina staff with which he already had a reputation for bad manners.

We never did get beyond polite greetings with the occupants of *Mistrel*, but we entertained and were invited aboard several vessels, some elegant and luxurious, some plain and functional, all welcoming. We ate the best nachos I'd ever had on *ScubaDoo*; we got advice for dock living from the crew of *Legacy III*, which occupied the end of D dock during peak season; and we washed down rum cake with smooth aged rum on the magnificent three-story *Sea La Vie*. This was not the cheap rum given away in welcome baskets and good for mixing with pineapple juice, this rum was so smooth Brian didn't realize he and our host nearly emptied the bottle until we got up to leave and the deck seemed to be moving under his feet more than the ocean could account for.

One memorable afternoon, I came home from running errands to find Brian drinking beer with two new friends, David and Jules. Brian found them strolling the dock and started a conversation. He invited them aboard to help reduce the supply of Amstel Light we found in a large cooler in the cockpit. David was a brown-eyed, gregarious Brit with unruly dark hair and a wide, white smile. He had enough class to accept the Amstel in spite of possessing his countrymen's taste for proper beer. Jules was brown-haired, tan, slightly freckled and pretty without a spot of makeup. She was more reserved than David and let him tell the best stories, taking her turn to talk only when the rest of us realized we hadn't given her a chance. David and Jules told entertaining tales of travels on their yacht the *Southern Star* and adventures delivering yachts, one of the ways they made their living.

Like most Americans, we loved listening to their accents, his British and hers Australian. Brian and I jumped from our seats each time business or pleasure brought David and Jules back to St. Thomas and they suddenly appeared on our dock or tossing a line from their dinghy to our stern cleat. David seldom returned without a four-pack of Guinness.

Living at American Yacht Harbor was something of a twist on a lifestyle I've often thought I would enjoy. It was like an apartment in town where one can walk to the post office, pharmacy, market, bookstore, restaurants, and if necessary, find a taxi. Also, like an apartment, our rent entitled us to a parking spot in the nearby marina garage.

Like apartment life, Puck had to be walked twice daily. We took turns leading him to one of the grassy areas nearby. I rustled my plastic bag conspicuously for passers by, as I waited for Puck to decide on all the right spots, lest they think our pet responsible for the piles left behind. Traffic cameras might be more useful redirected to public parks where dog owners don't clean up after their pooches. Rather than fines, they should be issued thin paper bags and sent out on hot days to clean. We reeled in Puck's retractable leash when foot traffic approached and let it out as they passed. Puck was no threat to man nor beast, but for the danger of being knocked off the dock by an excitable border collie who twists his forty pound body into a circle and dances deliriously at the least sign of attention.

The numerous nearby restaurants tempted us, but we dined out infrequently. We were living on savings and well aware the pocket wasn't deep. We would have escaped the confines of *Take Two* for a glass of wine at the East End Café more often, too, but for the same reason. I hoped that once we settled in, emergencies would spread out, and our business would generate enough income for us to become regulars. I wanted the luxury of being recognized by *maitre d's*, ushered to my table and offered "The Usual." The closest I'd come to this was in a Subway sandwich shop when the boy behind the counter once asked, "No peppers, right?" When your job description is putting condiments on bread, you don't have many avenues to excel and clearly this was a young man on his way up. I enjoyed the recognition and ate my tuna without peppers until his well-deserved promotion to, "Is this for here or to go?"

Meanwhile, we sometimes got fish from our friend, Pete. Eating fresh caught mahi mahi off the grill at home was no real hardship.

The marina and nearby shops offered everything a sailor, or live-aboard, could ask. Restaurants with bars draped the dock in music and conversation, but not too loud or too late. The Laundromat was no farther from *Take Two* than our barn was from the house back at Rancho Del Fuego. Tourists browsing the dock were always genial, and opportunity for conversation with owners and crew from neighboring yachts was a regular occurrence.

Dock Life

Some days the best thing about living on the dock was Paulo. Paulo was a dockhand and everything a man with that name should be. He had a handsome, angular face with piercing dark eyes that sparked with a flirtatious twinkle; a quick, dazzling smile; and hair that hung roguishly over his collar. Paulo was too old, in his forties, too handsome and too smart to be a dock hand. But he was a happy man and I liked to hang around him.

Though I'd seen him single-handedly manage the burst of activity of docking large cosseted yachts, Paulo always accepted my offer of help. Even if I merely caught a limp line, his gratitude was effusive. I dropped a line once and, as he scrambled to keep it free from propellers, he swore he would have dropped it too.

I looked forward to his greetings and compliments, though I knew he was promiscuous with them. Paulo cared about people, not money. This explained why most people liked him and also why some of the rich yacht owners, the ones who thought they deserved special treatment, didn't. Money didn't buy his happiness or his favor. He treated everyone the same. Everyone I liked liked Paulo.

One day I found an opening to get to know Paulo better. I heard him speaking French to someone outside the marina office. I found my excuse. The next time I saw him I said, "*J'ai... ecoute... vous parlez le francais. Est ce vous Francais?*"

He smiled and said, "I am Portuguese, but my mother taught me to speak French."

"*Ja'i espere apprendre la Francais*." I hoped I was telling him that I wished to learn French.

"*Bien*. I will help you. I will teach you one word each day."

"Thanks, uh, *merci*. That would be great."

"I will have a word for you tomorrow," he said hurrying off to his next task.

"*Au revoir*," I called after him.

I saw Paulo the next day, he gave me a word, the word for HAND. It sounded like maw. That couldn't be right, I asked him to repeat it as many times as I dared without annoying him. It still sounded like maw. This was not an accelerated learning method. Nevertheless, whenever I ran errands in Red Hook, I kept an eye out for him. When he didn't look busy I'd try some French on him. He was supportive and, fortunately, very understanding.

"*Bonjour*, Paulo," I said one morning.

"Bonjour, madam."

"Comment allez vous?" I asked.

"Ca va, et vous?"

"Uh, *ca va aussi*," I felt confident so I added, "*J'ai vous regarder, hier.*"

He wrinkled his brow and gave me a strange look. I was certain I had simply said I saw him yesterday.

"*Voir*," he said.

"Huh?" I said.

"*J'ai vous voir*. I saw you."

"Isn't that what I said?"

"No. You said you watched me. It's different, watching." He raised his eyebrows.

I blushed. "Oh."

His radio crackled. Lifting it from his belt he smiled and said, "A little mistake." Then he hurried off calling, "*Au revoir*," over his shoulder.

I talked to Paulo often after that, but never again admitted to watching him.

We've all experienced the bewilderment of walking into a room only to wonder why we're there. Magic Tom lived in that state of bewilderment. It may have been from birth, excessive recreational drug use, or an accident. No one seemed to know. But life has played sleight of hand with Magic Tom's memory.

I'd seen Tom roaming the wharf and sidewalks of Red Hook, but hadn't paid much attention to him. There wasn't much to notice. He was thirty-something, average height, slight build, with brown hair and eyes that avoided yours. When he stopped people to show them a card trick, he preferred to do the talking keeping his eyes on the cards.

I met Tom when he wandered onto D dock to watch Brian and the owner of *ScubaDoo* struggling to get two heavy batteries onto the narrow tapered bow of *Take Two*. Tom stood nearby offering encouragement. When the batteries were loaded, I called Brian to dinner and invited Tom. After recovering from the surprise he cheerfully accepted. Seth cautioned me about Tom's mental state and made it clear he thought it risky to feed him. I could see Tom's eccentricity for myself and recognized he might be playing with too many jokers in his deck, but we agreed hospitality shouldn't be denied someone because his sense and memory flickered like lights in a fog.

Tom was garrulous through dinner, sharing bits of trivia and repeatedly praising the deep-fried halibut. The next day he brought a small assortment of wild flowers in a wicker cornucopia, thanking me again. He remembered me and thanked me again every day for the next three days. Then a week passed before we met. When I greeted him by name he looked puzzled and apologized for not remembering me. I reminded him of eating with us on *Take Two*. He thanked me again for dinner and showed me a card trick. We repeated the conversation and card trick a few days later. After that I continued to greet him without confusing him with who I was, or who he was.

Rumors occasionally circulated of celebrities on the dock and at nearby resorts. Once, Brian said hello to Paul Newman on the yacht docked opposite *Take Two*, and Seth excitedly told me he saw Samuel L. Jackson reading on a yacht, but I never saw any.

We hoped for celebrity status for Michael Keown, a clean-cut boy of eighteen who left his job renting boats at the Water's Edge kiosk to audition for American Idol. We knew he could sing because both he and Brian liked to sing karaoke. His biggest hit with the karaoke crowd was Unchained Melody, but we knew him to be a versatile singer and also loved his rendition of Bob Marley's *No Woman No Cry*. Five months after he left the island we saw him on television earning the uncommon praise of Simon and making the cut to compete in Hollywood. We cheered for him. We wanted Michael to see his dream come true as much as we wanted to name-drop and get backstage passes.

~~~~

Life was getting comfortable, holding tanks were doing their job and I hadn't seen a cockroach in days. One night, I hurried down to my compartment to change before going out with friends and standing there by my wire baskets of underwear I realized I'd forgotten a visual sweep of the room before entering. I still jumped at shadows and the occasional lint, but overall I was beginning to think we had sent the beasts to a watery grave…except when Puck caused me to doubt we were alone.

From time to time, always in the evening, Puck would suddenly perk his ears and study the floor intently. Then he would back cautiously from the room, keeping his eyes fixed in the direction of the unseen threat. The first time he behaved like the sign of a gruesome plot change, I jerked my feet from the floor and with hair rising on the back of my neck I mimicked him, insofar as I can perk my ears. This exercise never revealed a cockroach and after several drills I merely glanced down to make certain it was another false alarm. Puck's eleven-year-old eyes were beginning to show cloudiness. It made me sad to think his sight might be failing and he was seeing scary things creeping toward him.

Puck had never been a brave dog. His role in the family was always more of a first alert than of guard dog. When the kids still lived at home a bedroom door banging open and a black streak shooting across the floor to hide under the bed alerted them that Mom was angry about something and the best posture to assume was hunched over school books or out of sight altogether.

Puck was a loyal and affectionate companion in good times and a deserter in bad. Several years back while listening to a recording of Louis Armstrong's *La Vie en Rose*, I decided to learn to play the trumpet. That afternoon Brian came into my office and looked down at an instrument case on the floor. "What's that?"

"It's a trumpet. I rented it from the music store."

"Why?"

It was nice that he showed an interest. "I'm going to learn to play *La Vie en Rose*. Listen." I played the CD. "Isn't that beautiful?" I hummed along.

"Okay."

The kids showed less interest, but they were teenagers. Puck, bless his heart, positioned himself at my feet as I struggled to make a sound come out of the trumpet and succeeding that to make the same sound again. It was a lot harder than it looked. My cheeks hurt, my throat burned and I was getting a headache. But Puck stayed companionably at my feet through the honking and squawking. Then I made a sound that chilled him and awakened an instinctive fear, instantly abolishing all loyalty. Taking a breath between weak, uneven squeaks of air, I softly murmured, "Shit." Puck's ears went flat, he rose slowly to a crouch to creep inconspicuously from the room. I said, "Puck, it's okay. Don't go." But at the sound of his name he shot out of the room and I heard my daughter's bedroom door bang open.

Now before you assume when I get angry I kick dogs, or shut them outside day and night, stop right there. I may be a shouter, but like most screamers we're all bark and no bite. You'd think Puck would understand that.

~~~~

Quiet life or not, one can only go on about cockroaches for so long without boring readers and discouraging visitors. To spice things up and because I like to say yes to new opportunities, I accepted an invitation to participate in a three day venture I was apprehensive about. It came from Pete, when he stopped by *Take Two* to give me a small mahi mahi he'd caught on his last fishing trip. Pete and his crew of two men motored as far as ninety miles south to catch the fish he sold to local restaurants. They usually stayed out for three or four days at a time. This, and that they have a CD for entertainment, is all I knew about what they did. Pete invited Brian to go along, but it didn't interest him, so while filleting the fish for me, he said, "We'll leave Brian, and you go fishing with us."

Maybe I surprised him, but I said, "Okay." Later that evening, dancing at the Renaissance Resort with Pete and Cindy I reiterated my eagerness, probably to convince myself as much as him.

The past fifteen or twenty years, my just-say-yes experiences have been less challenging. The most notable was a twenty-two mile bicycle trek through wine country. This may not sound like an adventure to some, but I hadn't been on a bicycle since before anyone had heard of a ten-speed. I stopped on that bicycle, given to me by my grandfather, by pedaling backward. Some twenty spoke-free years passed with my quadriceps haplessly atrophying. Then I found myself on a bike in the parking lot of a Napa resort. Under the patient and amused gaze of our friends, Curt and Carol, Brian situated me on a borrowed two-wheeler and instructed me in the use of its speed shift. He neglected to remind me of the invention of hand-brakes, so the three of them watched with amusement as I wobbled between cars, pedaling backward and waiting for my brain to remember the 1960s, my brothers' sting-ray bicycles, banana seats and little silver levers next to the hand-grips.

Two other things come to mind when I remember that day: First, after about fifteen miles, when Brian responded to my wish to go back to the hotel with a suggestion that I drink more water, I should have. Second, no one will ever convince me that people who design bicycle seats have ever used one.

The wine was a motivator for that one day excursion. This time the motivator was the excursion itself. My eagerness to crew on a three day commercial fishing trip was like a distant, faint galaxy in the eyepiece of a telescope. If I looked directly at it, it seemed to disappear, but if I glance with averted vision, I could convince myself it was there. Like everything else left scheduled for one of these days, it never happened.

Slipping the Surly Bonds

I made friends more quickly on St. Thomas than anywhere I'd lived. The other people living and working on boats were also far from home, friends and family. When the mood to socialize struck, the walls of a salon closed in, or one partner drove another ashore—this happened on other boats as well as ours—a stroll on the wharf often resulted in an invitation to come aboard for a drink or to admire a new accessory. Failing that, the bars were likely to offer a familiar face or a stranger also in the mood or similarly driven to distraction.

Regrettably, I didn't get to know many native West Indians. They rarely owned or lived on boats and often avoided the water altogether. This was unfathomable to those of us there specifically for the water.

I made frequent trips to the Laundromat and always saw the same older woman staffing the counter and transferring loads between machines. She sold quarters in ten dollar rolls and talked with me if I spoke to her first. But, I found her accent so impenetrable I guessed her side of the conversation on a syllable or two.

"You always seem to be here. Do you ever take a day off?" I asked.

"Saturday ease Friday for chirp with my daugturd. I don't watch clothes of stranglers who leave goats that are furry."

"You, uh, go to church? With your . . . husband?"

"I grow a birch with my dogturd."

"I have a dog. He's outside." I pointed to Puck lying near the door. When I turned around her head was inside a dryer where she stayed until I finished folding.

~~~~

We had many opportunities to entertain on *Take Two*. When on-island friends entertained guests down from the states they'd ask if we'd take them out on the boat. It was a winning situation for all. We welcomed the excuse to take a break from work and they got a private day sail. My lunches were not as photogenic as the professional charters, but I make a mean fish taco and my hurricane cake with fresh coconut was eaten as fast as I could cut it. We asked for nothing in return, but were thanked in many ways: bottles of wine, a cook book, picnic lunches brought by guests, dinner at the Ritz; and we were never allowed to buy our own drinks back at the dock; all this in return for turning passengers into laborers while we sunned ourselves.

Our first overnight away from the dock remains a special *Take Two* memory for me. Friday morning before Seth rushed bleary-eyed out to catch the ferry for school on St. John, we told him not to ride it home because we would pick him up at the St. John wharf. We seldom planned where we would go, it was easier to let the capricious wind decide after we got underway. But Cruz Bay on St. John was a straight shot east across the Pillsbury Sound, so it wasn't far out of the way wherever we went.

Slipping the surly bonds of D Dock was a favorite time of mine. There were chores, but they were the relaxed, easy chores of getting underway. I instructed our guests on how to coil dock lines, pull up fenders and stow them in a hatch on the foredeck. Someone would let out the dingy tow-line and everyone was alert to fend-off any close encounters with other vessels. Our passengers jumped at these chores with the eagerness of volunteers rescuing baby seals. I executed them like a seasoned sailor and still had leisure to smile at envious souls standing on the wharf, seasick from prices on the rental boat flyers clutched in their fists. I gave them a friendly nod to say, yes, we were undertaking the most romantic of all human activities. Later came the hard work, the sweat-and-tail of getting the mainsail raised; straining to deploy the jib or adjust the traveler—careful not to let fingers wander into danger; dislodging violently whipping lines caught on hatches or cleats. But motoring out of the harbor, there was no straining or danger; no problems with motion sickness or the controlled falling that is walking on a rolling deck.

We left D dock twice that afternoon; the first time, with me, Brian, and Paul from California on board. The second time we also had Seth who had forgotten to wait on St. John.

Having company on board generally meant an easy time for me and Seth. We played Tom Sawyer, allowing Paul to join the fun of pulling 730 square feet of the mainsail up the sixty-foot mast and hauling the jib from one side to the other every time Brian called ready-about. Brian liked having company, too, because Paul never responded with, "Again? What's wrong with this direction? I say we keep going this way."

Brian occasionally offered the helm to me and sometimes I accepted. However, he never fully relaxed with someone else there. He's a perfectionist about such things, I'm not. As long as the boat stays upright, I'm unconcerned if the telltales (ribbons attached to the sail to indicate wind flow) are hanging limply, flapping hysterically or streaming the way they should. And I'm not good at shrugging off the tension another person is feeling, so I generally left the steering to him.

The white swivel seat towered above the cockpit for the pilot to see over the salon roof. Like all boats, every space is made useful. The helm seat sat on a two foot post that attached to the box cover of a compartment where we stowed quarts of oil, the hand pump and other messy stuff. Getting into the compartment required removing a pin key and tilting the seat all the way back until it rested horizontally on the stern. I lived in fear of forgetting to replace the pin and what would happen if the seat fell backward at the wrong moment.

Potential danger always triggers my imagination. In a flash, I picture Brian falling backward, cracking his head open, plunging into the water and floating face down while I try to remember the steps of the man-overboard drill and scream for Seth, who is below playing air guitar with headphones on.

Piloting involves less physical strain, but more responsibility. Keeping an airplane on a heading is easier than it is with a sailboat. The method is the same: find a geographic feature in the distance and keep the ship pointed at it or follow a compass heading, but it's harder with a boat. In an airplane you have to counter the effect of wind on the wings, on a sailboat you have the effect of wind on the sail, and water pushing, pulling, raising and lowering the hulls. Like many things in my life, I didn't stick with it long enough to master the skill.

I suggested we take Paul to Trunk Bay to see the underwater park where the National Park Service maintains a snorkel trail. They've placed underwater plaques identifying coral and fish in the bay. Brian agreed and set a heading for the north shore of St. John. We let down the anchor just outside the area marked for swimming.

Seth pulled opened the hatch to the toy box and lifted out the bag of snorkel gear. I sorted through for my favorite mask and flippers while Brian opened another hatch to pull out a toy. Brian wanted to try the Snuba since first finding it on *Take Two*. It ran on a four horsepower Honda lawn-mower engine and came with sixty feet of hose, a flat yellow donut-shaped tube, weight belts, regulators and a small air compressor. Paul inflated the yellow donut and Brian tinkered with the engine. Soon they had the donut floating in the water with the engine putt-putting away in the center, powering the air compressor that sent oxygen through the hoses. Brian and Paul slipped into the water equipped with weight belts, masks and mouthpieces attached to a twenty-foot hose back to the air compressor. I could track their progress away from the boat by the location of the yellow donut that followed them on the surface like a balloon hovering over children at a carnival.

With my snorkel, I frolicked in the voluminous cascade of bubbles that rose to the surface above the Snuba. It felt like snorkeling in a champagne glass. Regrettably, I never did use the Snuba myself. We only brought it out when company sailed with us, and I always deferred to guests, thinking I'd do it another time. When I last left the island, it happened so quickly, there was no chance for such unfinished business.

Most of my snorkeling memories are of sunlight ricocheting off turquoise water where blue tangs, black and yellow sergeant major fish and brilliant damselfish dart ahead of me. Not that day. The temperature, typical for November, was in the low 80s, an overcast sky cast the ocean in a dark shadowless grey and afternoon rain stirred the silty bottom making the water murky. There wasn't much to see as I swam desultorily toward what I guessed to be the park area. While adjusting my mask, I noticed linty white stuff floating on the surface. It may have blown from the trees, or may have been plankton for all I knew. I didn't like it in my hair, so I swam back to *Take Two* to hose off. I was rinsing off on the swim step when I saw a small boat approach the yellow donut. When it motored away, the donut began gliding back toward the yacht. Brian and Paul surfaced at the stern, pinching water from their noses. The park rangers told them no motorized equipment was allowed on park property. So we all rinsed off and headed toward Magens Bay for the night.

With Paul cheerfully crewing for Brian, I took our digital camera to the port bow and sat leaning forward on the lifelines, my legs dangling over the side, my bare feet inches above the water. The noise of the wind about my face and the water breaking on the bows and rushing echoing under the foredeck platform provided a barrier against outside sounds. I took a few photos of water crashing on rocks, but mostly I enjoyed the feeling of isolation from the world, alone with the wind, the water and my imagination.

With only nominal help from me and Seth, we arrived at Magens Bay as the sun set. I moved to the galley while anchoring activities commenced and soon called everyone inside for fish tacos.

There are many ways to make fish tacos. I copied the recipe used by the Tin Fish on the dock at San Diego's Imperial Beach. A soft taco is filled with your fish of choice—I prefer mahi-mahi. Cheese is added to melt on top of the hot grilled fish, then covered with shredded cabbage. The secret of a good fish taco, along with a nice firm piece of fish, is the sauce. The cook behind the counter at the Tin Fish said ranch dressing combined with tomato sauce would bring me close to the flavor of their tacos. I substitute salsa for the tomato sauce and I always get compliments in the form of empty plates brought back for more.

While Seth washed the dishes, Brian and Paul moved to the trampolines at the bow, and I lay in the salon reading a book from the best seller list of last year's *New York Times*. I could hear their voices through the open windows as the day drifted to a tranquil ending. Finishing my book, I joined the men on deck. We watched meteors, possibly left-over Orionids, and a bright quarter moon that looked like the Cheshire cat's smile setting in the west.

It's difficult to describe the serenity of an evening anchored in a sheltered bay. All your senses are at liberty to relax. The clouds and waves pass peacefully, soothing your over-stimulated eyes; a breeze blows gently causing halyards to clang softly against the mast and your hair to play across your cheek; water laps at the hull, whispering so as not to disturb you; the boat rocks your stress into abeyance; and the only fragrance is one of clean perfectly breathable air.

With no dock noises to intrude, we rose a little later than usual the next morning. The sky was clear and the sun beginning to warm the morning when I tiptoed to the bow trampoline to stretch my muscles awake with yoga postures. I washed breakfast dishes then plunged into my swimsuit intent upon snorkeling. Once again, I was disappointed. The guidebooks said Magens Bay was a favorite place to snorkel, but it hadn't specified where. I must have headed in the wrong direction, because I may as well have been looking for fish in a swimming pool. The water was clear and visibility good, but there was nothing to see but a sandy bottom. Nevertheless, I was exercised and felt deserving of a substantial lunch later.

While I was gliding quietly through the water with nothing but the sound of my own breathing for company, Seth was back on the yacht attaching a rope to the rigging, and swinging far out over the lifelines of *Take Two* to drop into the water with a crash. Brian snorkeled, too, but it took him longer to get going. By the time he pulled himself from his morning coffee and found flippers that fit, I'd returned to the boat, showered on the swim-step and was drying in the sun with a hat over my face.

Head Schmed

Living on a boat was pretty much the same as living in our house on Rancho Del Fuego. There was a kitchen, but it was called a galley; bedrooms were cabins; and of course there were bathrooms, but they were called heads. I don't know why a boat kitchen is called a galley. Weren't galley slaves the poor Norse souls who rowed Eric the Bold across the freezing cold of the North Atlantic? Thinking about it, maybe Eric wasn't Bold, maybe he was Eric the relentlessly Sick of Lutefisk.

I ate lutefisk…once. Several years ago, I felt an impulse to explore my heritage and taste life as my great-grandparents knew it before they crossed the ocean to live the American dream as starved, overworked, Midwest farmers. Alas, the Scandinavian culture is dismally barren. All I knew about Swedes and Norwegians was that they used to wear candles on their heads at Christmas. I passed on this tradition certain that my insurance had a clause. And, there were few dishes unique to the region. I made lefse once for my grandfather. Lefse is essentially fried mashed potatoes. I don't think I did it right, because Grandpa never asked again for a plate of dry, crumbling potato chunks. Though I'd heard my grandparents mention lutefisk, my grandfather never asked for it. Mercifully, he was no longer with us when I decided to recreate this tidbit of Norwegian life. He would have been more polite than my family, who fled the kitchen, thumbs and fingers gripping their noses as I pulled the stinking, iron grey fish from the oven. I can only speak for myself, no one else would try it, but dying at sea seems a reasonable risk to find food that doesn't work best with chardonnay and no nasal passages or taste buds.

I suppose, from a certain point of view, galleys of yesteryear—where sweaty men in chains labored day and night crowded in the hull of a ship—compares to the cramped, hot work space of modern day galleys.

Take Two's galley sported all the conveniences of a kitchen crammed into the space necessary for a comfortable recliner, where I'd rather have spent my time. Everything was miniature. The refrigerator was the size of a microwave, the microwave the size of a toaster and the sink just large enough when rinsing a plate to stream water down my pants and across the counter every time. Miniature might be fine if I were feeding miniature people, but six-foot-two Brian and fifteen-year-old Seth expected full-sized meals piled to their chins.

One adjustment I made to galley cooking was to shop more frequently. The Marina Market was just down the street. It was a pleasant stroll along the dock for a hundred yards, saying hello to the bored attendants of the rental boat kiosks, then a few feet of cobblestones to the street. Soon the sidewalk ended and I made my way on a rough shoulder past The Frigate restaurant and the Wok and Roll. The taxi drivers clustered outside the market didn't pay much attention to anyone on their way in.

Getting through the narrow aisles of the produce section inside the door required patience and sometimes determination. Beyond that was a small deli and bakery case filled with tempting salads and desserts. There were only seven or eight grocery aisles, but a large butcher counter filled the back wall along with a door leading to a surprisingly well-stocked wine room.

Sometimes shopping the Marina Market, I'd buy too much forgetting I didn't have a car in the parking lot. Then the short walk home with bulging plastic bags cutting through my fingers and banging against my knees was long enough to exhaust my vocabulary of epithets for cooking on a boat. I learned to use a basket rather than a cart while shopping. When the basket was full, I checked out.

The first time I bought groceries at the Marina Market, I set my basket on the conveyor belt. The clerk was a big girl, at least 5' 8" and 200 pounds. Her hair was greased smooth to ends that stuck out just above her collar. She wore elaborate make-up, her eyelids decorated in lavender and blue, and at least one ring on every finger. She slapped a heavy hand on the conveyor belt by my basket and commanded, "Out of basket." I repositioned my groceries onto the counter while she studied the glitter on her painted nails. Waiting for my change, a cigar box on the counter caught my eye. Hand-lettered on the lid in black felt tip was the word TIPS. "Yeah, right," slipped out of my mouth, but I wouldn't have taken it back if I could.

When we left California, the Safeway grocery chain was in the news because of an aggressively friendly customer service policy. Were the male employees following women home and pushing their way inside to unbag the groceries? Putting beer in women's shopping carts and inviting themselves over? No, they were greeting all customers with a cheerful, "Hi, how are you?" Sometimes, unforgivably, doing so twice to the same shopper. If this behavior drives you to make a formal complaint, your life is too damn easy and you need to get over yourself.

Excessive customer service was not a problem in the islands. On a visit to the bulk food market, I wanted to pick up a case of Guinness. We liked drop-in company, but offering cans of Amstel Light to British friends who came by unannounced said, "Never surprise us again, or you'll regret it." When I found the Guinness, a single case on the floor in front was overlapped by a tall stack behind. I feared pulling the box out lest 144 cans of beer crashed down, sending me to an early, and inauspicious, death. At the check-out stand, my clerk radioed for someone to bring a case forward. She finished ringing up my other purchases when a large man finally appeared from the direction of the beer aisle. We waited as he strolled unhurriedly toward us. The clerk asked if he got the case. Without looking at either of us he said, "She could have gotten it herself," and walked away.

Such is an example of customer service at businesses that don't directly support tourism. Everyone I knew experienced arriving at a store five and even ten minutes before closing and being denied entrance. Seth rapped insistently at the Marina Market door one evening at eight minutes before nine arguing with the clerks inside that it did not take more than eight minutes to buy a gallon of milk. They won, as they always did in these situations.

I didn't mind cooking in a galley or sleeping in a cabin, but peeing in a head somehow didn't sit right. I disliked calling it a head. I found it confusing and a little ridiculous to find myself uttering sentences such as, "I'll be in my head if you need me." "There's a roach in my head." or "My head smells."

I got used to one-handed showering in my head. My shower stall was the head itself. Water drained from an opening in the floor by the sink and the faucet pulled out and rested handily in a holder on the wall. This would have worked peachy-keen if we had any water pressure. In the slip, we used dock water and the pressure wasn't strong enough to wash a spider down the drain, not a stubborn one anyway. If I hung the faucet on its wall hook, water dribbled down from the nozzle. Wetting or rinsing my body involved pressing against the counter to get under the unenthusiastic stream and rotating, as if body painting the front of the counter. As much fun as this might sound, I found it easier to hold the faucet with one hand and rinse myself. Rather like performing your own security check at the airport.

I also got used to sleeping in what was essentially a bunk bed again. Sometimes I slept alone in my compartment to avoid middle of the night wrestling with Brian. Brian was a light sleeper and would lie awake for hours if awakened. I hated waking him, so if I was sleeping by the wall when my full bladder nudged me awake, I'd wait for him to turn over then make my move to climb over him hoping he'd mistake me for a tangled sheet. He never did.

I wasn't, however, used to getting out of bed in the morning. It's not that I had trouble starting my day. I tend to be an early riser. It was the actual getting out of bed that frightened me. The mattress was fifty inches from the cabin floor, the only step was a bench twenty inches high. When I get a pair of pants hemmed I tell the seamstress to make the inseam twenty-nine inches. I didn't like the math. I had to convince my stiff, sleepy leg muscles to catch all one hundred-ahem pounds as I dropped myself from the mattress to the bench. It wasn't a long drop, but I avoid any six a.m. drops. Six-foot-two Brian easily jumped from bed while I scooted on my butt creeping closer and closer to the edge as my toes stretched for the bench. They reached just as my tush slid from the mattress. Next, standing on the bench, I reached across my cabin, approximately twenty-one inches, and grabbed a shelf to steady my twenty inch trepidation to the floor.

I considered building steps, but I saw two problems. First, on the bench, unless I nailed a box to the bench, the chance of it slipping and sending me painting the walls with blood was too great, and if I nailed it there would be nowhere for me to sit. Second, an additional step up to the bench would have created a barrier in the middle of my twenty-one inch wide floor. I could have gotten it out at night and stowed it in the morning, but where. And that gets us to storage on a boat.

Take Two had a tremendous amount of storage so long as you didn't actually need access to your stuff. Large hatches above the swim-steps in the back... pardon me, stern, opened to what Brian told me were called lazarettes. You could stow all Bill and Melinda Gates' money in there and still have room for J.K. Rowling's, but you'd have to climb down a ladder to fetch it and it would have migrated deep into the low recess under the bottom step. Moving forward from the stern was the cockpit, an outside seating area, and the captain's chair. Lids in the cockpit benches opened to more storage for lines, bimini canvas, life vests and tools left by the previous owners. At the bow of each hull another hatch opened to a large storage area accessible via ladder. The port side compartment held our water toys: wake boards, an inflatable kayak, skis, enough snorkel equipment for all the newlyweds in Hawaii and my boogie boards. All, except the boogie boards, were already on the boat when we got it. Undo the latch on the cover to the forward starboard compartment and it would spring open and extra sails would pop out. Also on the foredeck was the hatch to Brian's clubhouse where we stowed fenders while we sailed. We called it the clubhouse because if he wasn't at his desk in the salon we looked in the club house next. There we'd find him squatting in a three foot deep compartment making improvements to *Take Two*'s wiring and plumbing. What started as a Rube Goldberg Habitrail of poorly installed plastic pipe became an efficient system that improved water pressure throughout the boat. That's the run-down of outside storage.

The entrance to the salon was through a sliding door in the cockpit, though you could climb through a hatch directly into your cabin if you were avoiding someone in the salon. To the immediate right inside the salon was Brian's chart table with the galley forward of it. Straight ahead and on your left was the living area. Storage in the galley consisted of a stack of four narrow drawers, a wide pair of cupboards under the chart table and a roomy area under the sink. That's it, except for what I called cubbies. These were small compartments recessed in the counter, with lids not quite flush to the countertop. Brian was too tall to stand up straight in the galley, but could reach into the cubbies in the counter behind the stove, provided I didn't have anything frying too vigorously. I, on the other hand, could stand up in the galley, but was too short to reach inside those cubbies. It forced us to work as a team.

Items we didn't use daily were stored under seats in the salon. Access to these compartments meant getting whoever was sitting there to move, then removing and setting aside the back and bottom cushions, the non-skid mat and a wooden lid. You put all these back and repeated the process around the U-shaped sitting area until you opened the right one.

In addition to team work, functioning on a boat required more patience than I am known for among family, friends and the occasional coupon clipping, check-writing, talker ahead of me in line. Virtually everything you might want to use was underneath or behind something else, probably several something elses. It really did force a measure of patience, even on me.

Night Time

Another difference in our lives after relocating to the West Indies was the abundance of entertainment compatible with our early bedtime. Brian and I were not what you would call party animals. We ate dinner around six, puttered around the boat, bumping into each other and stepping over the dog until eightish, when I started pondering the choice between boxers or pajama pants. By 8:30 or 9 I'd tidied up my compartment, showered and returned to the salon, having made my pajama decision. This done, I might have found Brian dozing at his keyboard or taking a warm-up nap on the settee.

Entertainment to fit such a somnolent schedule isn't usually right around the corner unless you live in Red Hook where it's closer than that. The nearest nightly live entertainment was as close to me as your living room is to your mailbox. The restaurant at the end of D dock employed a musician seven nights a week. With a guitar on his hip, harmonica round his neck and a tambourine wedged on his foot he played The *Unicorn Song*, made popular by the Irish Rovers—the worst thing to happen to Ireland since the potato famine—and other ballads listeners best be inebriated to enjoy. Walk fifty feet and up tiled steps on Friday evening and you would find an unpaid combo jamming blues, jazz and swing numbers on a balcony large enough for an MGM musical. Don't linger too long over dinner, they wrap by nine. Brian and I liked to dance behind the folding chairs or lean on the iron railing while listening to the music and watching boats below. If we were in the mood for strobe lights and a beat heavy enough to tenderize meat it was just across the street at Duffy's Love Shack.

When a nightspot in the Virgin Islands calls itself a shack they aren't being cute, they're being literal. Bomba's Shack on the north shore of Tortola is famous for full-moon parties held in a make-shift structure of flotsam and jetsam literally lashed back together after every major storm. Duffy's wood shack is in the Red Hook Plaza parking lot. After the plaza shops close, two of Duffy's walls disappear and tables and chairs are dragged into the parking lot. You can get appetizers to go with your beer or exotic cocktail, which arrives in a tiki-head mug complete with a tiny orange plastic monkey hanging on the rim. The twenty-something crowd likes Duffy's for the loud music and the nightly appearance of a life-size great white shark head emerging from the wall though machine-generated fog and accompanied by the booming theme from Jaws.

Don't feel like walking? Then fire up the outboard motor and cruise the dingy 100 yards across the harbor to Latitude 18 which hosts the hottest country band and the most lethal sloping dance floor on the island. Thursday and Friday nights were our nights to go dancing. We could count on the music to swing and if the number was fast enough we'd have the dance floor to ourselves. Brian enjoyed seizing the chance to show off his jitterbug steps and enjoy the compliments as we returned to our table.

If we didn't want to go out we could watch a movie. Watching a DVD on a laptop is fine for one person, two can do it if they are friendly, but if three people want to watch they need to shower first.

We were living on the boat when I brought home the *Bourne Identity* DVD. Brian and Seth wanted to watch with me so we slid onto the settee side-by-side-by-side. It was like a two hour hug. The only break came when a rain shower hit. Without a word, Seth jabbed the pause button and we sprang from the settee, rushing to close windows. Brian and I bolted down to the cabins to close hatches while Seth darted from one window to another in the salon and galley. Forty-five seconds later we were shoulder to shoulder again, turning up the sound to hear over rain on the roof.

Bon jour

We woke one Saturday morning with no plans other than to work with repairmen on *Take Two*, but before night fell we'd made new friends and eaten dinner on a French island.

At ten in the morning when Cindy called, Brian and a diesel mechanic were crouching in the port hull hovering over a sputtering engine. On the starboard side, I was watching Jacob install mahogany shelves in my companion-way. Cindy had taken a call in the marina office from a man looking for a ride to St. Marten, and she thought of Brian. My knee-jerk reaction when Brian told me he was thinking of flying this fellow down island was to point out all the reasons he shouldn't. The real reason was my dislike for abrupt changes in plan. As usual, after a few minutes to chew on the idea, my reaction changed to "If you do this, I want to go, too."

Three hours later, I sat tucked in the back seat of our six-place Aztec taking off from Cyril E. King airport for the first time since arriving ten weeks earlier. Up front with Brian was David, a local pilot who had flown the Aztec back from the Turks & Caicos for us. We needed him because Brian was not licensed to fly charter. In the middle seats were the people who wanted the ride: a couple vacationing from Washington D.C. The flight took an easy forty-five minutes, with our passengers holding hands and happily proclaiming the fun of it all at frequent intervals. We pressed our faces to the windows as islands approached then slipped away behind us and the occasional tiny white triangle of a sailboat appeared far below, small and solitary against the dark blue of the ocean.

St. Marten is a unique island a hundred miles east of St. Thomas. Like many of the Caribbean islands it traded hands between European countries many times during the seventeenth century. Then in 1648, when France and The Netherlands agreed to split its 88 km (38 square miles), it became the smallest land mass in the world to be divided between two nations. The French half of the island is part of the archipelago of Guadalupe; the Netherlands side (Sint Maarten) belongs to the five islands of The Netherlands Antilles.

David seemed to know everyone whose voice came on the radio, or whom we passed at the airport on St. Martin. Maybe this was why I saw no sign of French customs and once again I did not get my passport stamped. U.S. customs, however, have never failed to follow strict procedures.

All I can say is I hope I never have to account for the fact that my passport has twice the number of U.S. stamps as all the foreign ones. I swear I was not sneaking into foreign countries with smuggled goods. What would I smuggle out? The rest of the world already has everything we have and it's legal. Amsterdam has legalized pot; several Caribbean islands have legalized 'shrooms; Europe has leading edge pharmacology products years before they're approved in the U.S.; and when they are, Canadians are paying less for them; Cubans—the cigars, not the people—can be bought and carried home by citizens of pretty much every country except the United States. I'm quite sure I wouldn't know what to stuff into the lining of my coat.

While the others strode off in search of a rental car, I popped into a Duty Free shop for something to drink. There, the most amazing thing happened. The clerk didn't speak English. I thought everyone spoke English. Here was my opportunity to use my two semesters of college French. "*Quatre-vingt,*" she said pointing to the .80 digital display on the register. I nodded in French and gave her a dollar. Her tray only had pennies and quarters, so she shrugged and gave me a quarter.

Then I said, "*J'ai cinq.*" and handed her a nickel.

She smiled and said sweetly, "Vous parlez le francais un petite peu."

To which I cleverly replied, "*Oui, merci,*" and left with my *jus d'orange.*

My day was complete and we still hadn't lingered over a beach-side dinner with our new friends, or gazed discreetly over our menus at something else America doesn't have: nude sun-bathers on crowded public beaches.

~~~~

The Sunday before Thanksgiving, I came home from my daily trip to the market with cocoa, baking powder and other items from the baking aisle and announced my intention to bake myself a birthday cake. Brian saw this and asked if I'd like him to bake it. I gaped for a moment, before smiling at the generosity of the impulse. Brian neither cooks nor bakes. When pressed to cook, he will add water to something and boil it, but that is the limit to which he will go. He smiled back with apparent sincerity, so I accepted. The next day, using my favorite chocolate cake recipe, he and Seth baked the cake and Brian frosted it with a homemade chocolate butter cream frosting. Cindy and Scott stopped by, everyone sang *Happy Birthday* and we ate layer cake. The cake was good, but as Samuel Johnson might have said, "It's not whether it was done well, but you are surprised to see it done at all."

While eating cake, we had a conversation about suggestive boat names, and I ended up going to bed angry. Someone mentioned *Shag Me*, a charter boat on C dock, then Brian said he heard a story about a boat named *Blow Me*, "This guy at Molly's," he said, "Heard a radio transmission during a storm off the California coast. A boat radioed for help and the Coast Guard came on and said, 'Vessel calling for help identify yourself.' So the guy says, '*Blow Me.*'" The boys and Cindy burst into giggles.

"Sure," I said skeptically. "A boat named *Blow Me*. I don't think so."

"Really. So the Coast Guard comes back and says, 'Vessel calling for help, repeat.' So the guy says, '*Blow Me*.' And the Coast Guard guy gets mad and says, 'This frequency is for emergency transmissions only.' Finally, the guy says, *Blow Me* is the name of his boat." By now the boys were nearly hysterical.

"I suppose," I said, "It's not that outrageous if you remember it's the name of a sailboat."

Emboldened by Brian's story, Seth said he saw a boat named *Wet Dream*. I glared disapproval at him, but I was outnumbered in my priggish stance and he laughed when Scott said he saw a boat named *Morning Wood*.

I asked what was so evocative about *Morning Wood* and everyone erupted into giggles. No one would explain and I was left to figure it out on my own. I was irritated by their laughter, which drowned out my claims of feeling no shame in possessing a less tainted mind.

I ambushed Brian while we undressed for bed, accusing him and the others of insensitivity, immaturity, and while I was at it, for being a lousy parent, and too tall. As always, he shrugged off the criticism.

People will argue that kids hear that sort of thing in school, so why censor oneself. But if we don't teach them to make a distinction between what is okay in the schoolyard and what is acceptable behavior at home, how will they make more subtle distinctions later when it matters? Perhaps I was being too sensitive when they laughed at me, but I believe if kids are taught a little laughter at someone's expense is harmless, will they figure out on their own when it's not?

~~~~

The Thanksgiving holiday has always been special to me. I was born at 4 a.m. on Thanksgiving morning, so there is the childhood association with blue party dresses, coconut cut-out cakes, and tissue paper packages. However, the best present was the family dinner prepared, wrapped and delivered to the table every year by my mother. She started in the kitchen on Wednesday evening when, after prying frozen giblets from the icy cavity of a twenty-pound turkey, she began sautéing ingredients for the bread stuffing. She scarcely rested until twenty-four hours later, after she whipped the cream for our choice of apple or pumpkin pie.

Decades passed, but little variation crept into our holiday. A daughter-in-law appeared at the table. Sons-in-law came and went, there was that new carrot dish, but nothing much changed, until my young sister became a vegetarian. Even then, because she was simply a late-arriving side dish we just set-aside meatless stuffing for her. Then after years of beef and pork abstinence I, one of the primary contributors to the feast, also gave up poultry and the big change came: Tofurkey. I shouldn't say change, but addition. There is no intolerance at our table, no racism, chauvinism, homophobia, or discrimination of any kind… except soy discrimination. Beside the dripping, golden brown stuffed bird of honor, sat a small tan mound of Tofurkey defended and approached only by the forks of two health-conscious, animal-loving, tree-hugging sisters.

Thirty-six years after she spent her Thanksgiving in the maternity ward, another celebration coincided with Thanksgiving Day. My parents, brothers and sisters traveled hundreds of miles to attend my wedding. We had a small, but elegant, ceremony and for the first time in my life, my family ate dinner on the fourth Thursday of November in a restaurant.

Our Thanksgiving dinner on *Take Two* was different only in size. The turkey was smaller, the side dishes smaller and it was just the three of us. We missed bumping chairs around a crowded family table, but Brian and Seth did something they couldn't do back home, while I prepared our traditional dinner, they strung Christmas lights on *Take Two*'s lifelines.

Caribbean Green

*C*indy invited me to join a small group of women for Sunday brunch. Together we represented a range of middle-aged white women that included the working class, the self-employed and one living on alimony from a marriage to a wealthy New Yorker. On my left, Cindy, a perpetually plump, artificial red-head, tackled a plate of stuffed French toast. On my right, Jane, a skinny, excessively-tanned, blond, chain smoker ordered her third scotch and soda while her scrambled eggs got cold. Next to her, Joan, a pretty, fiftyish landlord sipped her mimosa through lips swollen by cosmetic surgery. Arriving late, was the wealthiest among us, a successful business owner, the oldest and easily the most attractive. She made no secret of being in her late fifties which left no doubt she'd had at least one face lift. It also led to the inkling she's had other work done. I have nothing against breast augmentation, some of my best friends and all that, but D cup, that's just a cry for help. Then there was me, a mimosa-sipping, blond highlighted, self-employed B-cup.

Conversation was stereotypical chick chat. Two of us were married, but all had at least one ex-husband—between us we had eight. Talk was of men, past and present, who was having what work done and shopping.

I asked where, with our only mall anchored by a K-Mart, the others did their shopping. I waited for them to settle down and choose a spokesperson. They appointed Cindy who, on behalf of everyone, insisted I go to San Juan to the Plaza Las America Mall.

Back on *Take Two* I told Brian. He said it would be a short flight in the Aztec to Puerto Rico so we decided to fly over in a few days. I wanted to go Christmas shopping and he wanted to visit the marine supply store.

Everything on St. Thomas was expensive, but particularly marine supplies. The chandlery at Red Hook was convenient and the service friendly and helpful, but like others, it was nicknamed Tiffany's for a reason. Buying two marine toilets on Puerto Rico instead of St. Thomas would save us the cost of fuel for the gas-guzzling Aztec, giving me a free visit to the mall.

We took off and were just out of a rain shower sprinkling the west end of St. Thomas when we approached a small island. It was a pretty little, roundish stepping-stone I guessed to be Vieques, but I saw no signs of the military practice shelling protested on the evening news. Brian consulted his charts and identified it as Culebra. The pilots' guide called Culebra a weekend get-a-way for Puerto Ricans. We agreed it would be nice to land there for lunch one day. Then Brian pointed to a longer land mass to the southwest in the shadow of clouds. That was Vieques. We didn't fly close enough to see whether the practice bombs left scars visible from 4500'. But, I was curious.

~~~~

Next time Crayola wants to rename their colors I'll submit Caribbean Green as the name for their most vivid primary green. The runway at Fajardo, our first stop to get the toilets, was a narrow strip of grey in a Caribbean green field surrounded by green hills on a persistently green island. The breeze at the airport smelled pleasingly of newly mowed grass. I emerged from the Aztec to breathe in the aroma and saw an egret standing elegantly near the runway. Her delicate, pure white body framed by the Caribbean green was magical. I left Brian to secure the airplane as I stared, trying to memorize it. Alas, customs and immigration are not to be kept waiting, so

Brian called me from the masterpiece to accompany him inside.

We stayed in Fajardo just long enough to grab a cab to the marine supply store, buy the toilets, return to the airport and decide it's an enchanting little town. I base this unyielding opinion on a single highway off-ramp. Near West Marine in Fajardo is a park-like off-ramp. A life-size dolphin sculpture greets exiting traffic from the tip of the grassy median. I turned away from the dolphin in time to see a sailing ship sculpture high over-head. At the corner, on our right, bubbled a fountain on a large wall. Water spilled gaily from bowls attached to its face. I didn't see a written message, but I got the message nonetheless that Fajardo means to be a pretty little town and knows how to do it, by-golly. Around the corner, however, there was a message. A banner hanging on an overpass read FELIZ AÑO NUEVO. A pretty and friendly town Fajardo.

Our wheels touching down at the Isla Grande Airport in San Juan was the cue for the sky to open and rain to fall. It fell steadily as we taxied about following directions from ground control, and showed no signs of letting up when we stopped at the transient parking area. In the cockpit, Brian squinted at the dark clouds and the rain pattering impudently at the hull while I fussed about folding charts and tidying pockets. The humidity inside grew dank as wet wool. We traded off for a bit, with Brian refolding the charts and me squinting at the rain. Then we both squinted until puddles of perspiration and humidity developed at our feet and we decided to make a run for it.

My first step on the tarmac soaked my canvas shoes to the laces. I swam through the warm rain, splashed through puddles and burst into a vacant building. Brian dashed in behind me. We opened a number of doors on either side of a long deserted hallway, but found no one. Once more we darted outside, splashed through the puddles and rain and found ourselves in a flight school office. The narrow trailer was crowded with people. They were all talking, and all doing so in a foreign language. If anyone had been counting slowly from one to ten I might have recognized it as Spanish, but this being Puerto Rico, I guessed.

Plaza Las America is much like any other American mall. In between the anchor stores, Macy's, Sears, and JC Penny, dozens of familiar stores crowd one another for space. Restaurant names at the food court were different, but the food was the same. We ate lunch at soggy teriyaki bowl.

After two hours gaping at price tags on board-shorts for Seth, we sat at a window table in a coffee shop refortifying ourselves with lattes. Brian asked the question, "Do Puerto Ricans dress better than Americans?"

"You mean other Americans."

"Yeah," he said.

We studied the foot traffic in the mall and concluded the answer was a definite yes. Fifteen or twenty people would pass before we saw a T-shirt, and then it was generally a nice solid color. In half an hour, we didn't see more than two or three people wearing shorts, and just as few women wearing athletic shoes.

Americans, State-side Americans that is, are terrible dressers. Take away an American's T-shirts and you've emptied his drawers and left him to communicate verbally his profession, hobbies, favorite ball team and prejudices; and to find another method to convince us of his incredible, can-crushing, Harley-riding, flaming skull, bull-dog virility. Take away an American woman's athletic shoes and too often you've left her in flip-flops or clogs.

We glanced down at our shorts and tennis shoes and squirmed. Then complimenting each other on our nice shirts, we returned to our shopping, making stops at clothing stores.

Finally, foot-weary, we sought out the line of taxis waiting at the south entrance to the mall. A cab pulled up as we approached. We climbed into the seat behind the driver: a skinny, deeply-wrinkled, old man with close-cropped white hair and large, age-spotted ears. Old as he obviously was, he might have shared a great deal about San Juan's modern history if he had spoken any English. The taxi dispatcher at the curb repeated Isla Grande three or four times until finally the old man nodded. I don't think the size of his ears made a difference.

Speaking broken Spanish, Brian directed the driver through the maze of poorly lit chain link fences and gates to the general aviation area which we were glad to see was unlocked in spite of the late hour. We thanked the driver and because he was old, I tipped him with the same generosity the Lord showed in giving him ears. Back in the Aztec we found ourselves once more gazing out the windows, not at rain this time, but at a fireworks display. We couldn't guess the reason for the fireworks; the last Puerto Rican holiday I knew of was Discovery of Puerto Rico Day weeks ago, on November nineteenth. Not knowing the reason didn't lessen the fun of the unexpected display.

The day ended, as all good days of flying should, with an uneventful flight home on a clear Caribbean night.

Will You Give me the Woman

They say necessity is the mother of invention and I won't argue, but you should know she is also the sister of adventure, or perhaps experience. It was in the back of my mind for some time that a person shouldn't live on St. Thomas too long without making use of the Safari cars. I knew people who thought nothing of using them to move about the island at least as efficiently as I did in my Jeep, but I had questions. How did I know where the Safari car was going? How did I let the driver know when I wanted off? Anyway, I had a Jeep. Well, most of the time I had a Jeep. Actually, all of the time I had a Jeep, but it didn't necessarily run all of the time.

Watching Jacob build shelves for my companion-way made me home-sick for my wood shop. He took pity on me and helped me do one small project myself. He ordered a half-sheet of mahogany plywood and set me up with the pre-cut solid mahogany trim for three shelves. I would have been better off paying Jacob to do the work, and missing my flush toilet instead. I made so many trips to the hardware store across the street, there was talk of making me repaint the cross-walk. Eventually, I realized Jacob didn't give me any mahogany for the staves. Brian was untangling a nest of wires in his clubhouse, so I jumped in the Jeep and headed to Smith Bay.

Soon I was sitting just shy the crest of a steep hill in a stalled car holding up afternoon rush hour traffic. Although I sat there for a very long minute, maybe two, not one horn honked; no one offered a hand, but to their credit they didn't honk. I got the darn Jeep started, revved it hard, yanked it into gear and crested the hill. It immediately died again and I coasted to a stop in front of a house with a low chain-link fence.

Generally speaking, I like Virgin Islanders, so long as they aren't at work. I reported to my family on the West Coast that the streets and sidewalks were filled with pleasant, courteous people offering a friendly greeting, or drink of milk straight from the coconut when I simply cocked my head curiously; they'd stop thirty mile an hour traffic to let me merge and wait patiently at intersections. But, the moment they arrived at jobs they presumably wanted, they became sour, unsmiling clerks, waitresses, receptionists and public servants. Nevertheless, it was after work so these islanders were in a pleasant frame of mind.

Muttering firmly, I crossed the busy street to a pay phone. Brian could always be counted on to answer his cell phone. He wore it in a holster on his belt along with his PDA, a Leatherman tool and sometimes his glasses case. If Nerds had a Special Forces Unit he'd be captain.

Everyone who drives a car, woman or man, should be able to handle this situation which arises for every poor schmuck sooner or later. Though we had no other car, somewhere deep inside me I hoped, I didn't expect, but I hoped, Brian would say, "Don't worry, sweetheart. Just relax and I'll be there in a minute to take care of everything."

"The stupid Jeep broke down," I said, not bothering to say hello. "What am I supposed to do now, I've got two dollars on me?"

"I'm sorry," he said.

"It's parked in front of someone's house. I'm calling from a liquor store. How am I supposed to get home? I've got two dollars and there are no ATMs."

A moment of silence, "What do you want me to do?"

"Nothing," I said goodbye and hung up the phone, trying to figure out if I could somehow blame this on him.

I looked in the direction of home. I was miles from Red Hook along roads with little or no shoulder. I set off with no particular plan but to stay out of traffic and try to stay out of the late afternoon sun. I hadn't gone more than a hundred yards when a battered grey sedan stopped beside me. The driver announced himself as a taxi. I saw no sign, but taking him at his word I told him I only had two dollars. Brushing papers off the passenger seat, he directed me to get in. I climbed in nudging a Burger King cup out of the way.

It's possible someone with diabolical intent would make such an offer, but I considered it far more likely this guy thought he could pick up an easy ten bucks. When I didn't have money he did the Christian thing (over 90% of Virgin Islanders profess to be Christian) and gave me a lift to the taxi stand a mile down the road.

He answered my questions about the Safari cars, but between Reggae on the radio and his rapid, heavily accented speech, I had no idea what he said.

I waited in the shade at the side of the road for ten minutes passing the time in a one-sided conversation with an iguana swaying in a low bush. Two empty Safari cars sped past without slowing before one finally stopped. The back door of the extended cab swung open and an old man asked, "Are you going weeth us?"

I climbed in and said the island greeting, "Good afternoon," to everyone and "American Yacht Harbor please," to the driver. I glanced around. There were now nine people in the cab, all black except me. A man and a woman with a baby sat in front with the driver. Beside the old man by me were two women. One was pressed against the opposite door cradling a sleeping boy of four or five on her lap. The old man's hair was the color and texture of steel wool and he hadn't shaved in about a week, since Sunday morning probably. He spoke to me with a heavy West Indies accent. "There ees always room for one more. You have room?"

I was snug against the door, but not uncomfortable. "Yes, thanks."

"We make friends riding. Many friends." He looked around the cab at the others for a response, but a listlessness possessed them and they sat as silent and unresponsive as the sleeping child. The cab was hot and all the windows were down.

"We become friends. You can't have too many friends. One special friend. He is a friend to all. Do you know who I am talking about?"

"Who?"

"Jesus. Jesus is everyone's friend."

"That's true," I said.

Someone in the back slapped the side of the truck and the driver stopped to let him hop out.

"Does this car stop at Red Hook?" I asked.

"Yes, yes. It stops. Why do you go to Red Hook?"

"I live there, at the marina." He looked puzzled. "I live on a boat with my husband and our son."

"A boat? You leeve on a boat?"

A bell rang and the driver pulled onto a wide dirt shoulder on our left and more people climbed out of the truck bed. Taxi drivers here do not wait to be hailed. They diligently pursue fares, stopping to ask any weary-looking pedestrian if they want a ride. We drove along the shoulder to where a spaced-out looking man with long black dreadlocks, shabby clothes and dirty bare feet was standing. The driver called to him asking if he wanted a ride.

The shabby fellow gave no indication of hearing him, but looked directly at me and said, "Will you give me the woman?" He moved slowly toward the truck. "Will you give me the woman?" he repeated staring at me. Our driver saw no fare here and turned to look over his shoulder for a gap in traffic. Without taking his eyes off me, the man continued toward my door, "Will you give me the woman?" he said again.

I managed a puzzled smile, pushed the door lock down with my elbow and was eyeing the window knob hoping traffic would clear.

The Safari car lurched back onto the road and the old fellow beside me chuckled, "Imagine heem, wanting you when there are three men here," he gestured to the two men in front and himself, "You haven't given yourself to." The driver and the other fellow in front snickered at this. "Should we have given you to heem?" he asked with a grin and his elbow.

"Only if he was a mechanic," I answered, "My car broke down." All three men exploded into laughter. It didn't seem so funny to me, or apparently, the women in the cab, but the men laughed for another half mile.

I got off in Red Hook and paid the driver. I learned something about how Safari cars operate and that for a dollar it's the best entertainment on the island.

~~~~

We had a number of friends on the island, but many of them were sailors and didn't own cars. It was morning before we were able to borrow a car and drive to where the Jeep sat. Brian got it started and I fell in behind him as he headed to the repair shop.

I was still behind Brian when he made a sharp left turn going uphill. I accelerated for the hill, closing the gap between us. It was not a great time for the Jeep to die, even if it did prove the problem was not my driving or my imagination. I slammed on my brakes and missed hitting him by a foot. Brian got restarted quickly, but in my haste to get my borrowed rear-end out of traffic and up the hill, I missed first gear and killed the engine.

The landscape of St. Thomas does not lend itself to a network of roads that can be intuitively traveled. Brian took the wrong side of a fork in the road about fifty yards ahead. I got restarted and took the right side. Meanwhile, Brian recognized his mistake and turned around. He was behind me, but not close enough to see me make a wrong turn. He proceeded to the repair shop, while I strayed into a run-down neighborhood of poorly maintained apartments, scavenging dogs, and prides of indolent men lounging about like lions on a hot afternoon waiting for a gazelle to wander into sight. I passed just such a group sitting on and around a battered black sedan. I seemed to catch their attention. They sat up and sniffed the air as I drove by. The road narrowed unpromisingly, I turned around in a driveway and once again approached the group. One fellow slouching on the roof of the sedan waved an arm to flag me down. I merely smiled forlornly and kept driving. Two or three frustrating minutes later, I found myself driving by yet again. The same fellow waved me down again. Well now it just felt rude not to say something, so I stopped and put my window half way down.

"Talk to me," he invited jumping from the car and approaching. There are two hair styles for black men on the islands: shaved and dreadlocks. This guy's dreads hung almost to his brown T-shirt.

I shared my problem and he and a shaggy bearded fellow sitting on the ground gestured and offered impossible directions while two others nodded vigorously to indicate informed agreement. Pretending to understand now exactly how to find the repair shop, I thanked them and pulled away.

The crime rate in the Virgin Islands is high and it would be foolish not to remember this. However, like everywhere else, most of the people on St. Thomas, even ragged, poor, possibly stoned, young men, are kind, friendly and enjoy an opportunity to do something nice for a stranger.

I found Brian before running out of gas. And even more amazing, the car got repaired and ready for pick up in time to drive to Charlotte Amalie that evening for the holiday lighted boat parade and dinner with friends, David and Jules, who were on island delivering charter yachts. Overall, things worked out well, I finally tried the Safari cars and I knew the island and the islanders a little better.

On the Hard

For those who believe life on a yacht is all basking in the beauty, mild weather and gentle breezes of a Caribbean winter, picture this: Twenty acres of dirt tramped bare of vegetation and surrounded by chain link fencing. Twenty acres of boats, perhaps seventy or eighty in all, their narrow keels built to glide through the Seven Seas resting painfully on blocks of wood and balanced by over-burdened tri-pods pressing unnaturally against their underbellies. Men and women employing noisy power tools stripping away paint and modesty from boats with names as creative as their designs: *Sea Dreams, Technocat, Sabrina Fair, Quintessence, Yamenja*. Some boats showed damage sure to have stories. Others came and went quickly for routine maintenance.

Brian and I watched as *Take Two* was lifted dripping from the harbor in Nanny Cay, Tortola, and set on blocks behind a two-story building housing yacht outfitters and repair shops. The travel-lift operator climbed down and pointed out a ladder lying in the mud a few feet away. We dragged it over and propped it against the stern. We were now living on the hard.

Living on the hard was like living in a tree house under construction. Whatever water we used drained overboard onto the ground and once or twice onto an irritated laborer. Our limited electrical power came from onboard batteries. We conserved both water and power with Amish-like discipline, cooking one-dish meals and using paper plates, allowing boatyard grit to accumulate on anything that couldn't be shaken clean over the side. Running the air conditioner was out of the question, and though a tropical breeze blew pleasantly from the east, where *Take Two* sat in the boatyard only one small hatch opened in that direction. Inside we sweltered and competed for position near an oscillating fan while Puck lay under the table panting heavily.

The most comfortable space was outside under the boat. A wide, breezy area offered ample head-room free from the heat of the sun. Nevertheless, this was a boatyard and where a soft lawn and old blanket would have offered a snug retreat, gritty mud from expelled dishwater and the night's rainfall commingled with oil, litter, and scrap lumber to give it a post-apocalypse ambiance.

My days were spent drinking gallons of water and sodas then sweating and peeing it all away. The sweating I could do in the discomfort of my own salon, but the marina bathrooms were across the boatyard. On-board toilets were off-limits because on the hard there was no way to empty them. Our ten-rung ladder grew grimy and mud-caked from my frequent trips. It sloped gradually to the ground and I could keep my hands clean by walking up and down with arms outstretched like a gymnast. A gymnast in cargo shorts and tank top. Still, I was no Cathy Rigby and it seemed only a matter of one too many diet Cokes before I'd execute an unintentional dismount.

Two weeks into dry dock living we learned that each time we left Puck on *Take Two* while we went to town for supplies he would howl incessantly. No one enjoys living on the hard and the howling of a dog added to the relentless screaming of power tools and droning of fans could turn the most pleasant person into an angry neighbor. We hoped Puck would be happier on the ground so the next time we went to town Brian found a length of rope and tied Puck in the shade under the boat. Returning with our groceries we listened as we approached. Hearing no howling we exchanged satisfied looks. Then we saw Puck under the boat. He sat forlornly, tangled in his rope, in the mud, soaking wet, under a shower of water spraying from holes he'd chewed in our water supply hose.

Not since making mud pies lost its appeal had I been as dirty as living at Nanny Cay. Traipsing back and forth to the bathroom left me with persistently dirty feet and my calves speckled with bits of mud. We wore flip-flops and stepped out of them on the boat to avoid damage to the deck. After showering I walked slowly across the boatyard stepping like a stork, trying not to fling dirt with each stride. On days when painters worked sanding *Take Two*'s hulls paint dust coated everything blue. My feet were grotesquely brown and blue as the painters went about their work looking like a Blue Man Group production.

There was, however, a dread in the boatyard even greater than filth to the compulsively clean. It is spoken of only in hushed tones and we were not spared that either. *Take Two* was diagnosed with dry-rot. Boat cancer. It wasn't terminal, but required surgery. *Take Two* was basically a wood boat, though the wood was coated with fiberglass. Fortunately, the dry-rot, found in her topsides, had not spread to the hull. The repair shop recommended a particular strong, light-weight plywood. Brian located and ordered what we needed using the Internet. The shipment would arrive in a week and the work would be messy.

Living on a boat was Brian's idea. While he concerned himself with *Take Two* and its equipment, I was decorating with sarongs and spraying for cockroaches, giving no thought to the construction. I'd heard Brian talking about cold-molded this, wood and fiberglass that, but somewhere in the back of my slightly aqua phobic mind, I allowed the notion that great expanses of impenetrable material formed the barrier between me and the danger of rocks, coral reefs and deranged whales— which I'd read about in a book called *Survive the Savage Sea*. All the talk about wood and fiberglass I took to be yachting terms for high-grade steel or whatever they use on the space station. Now there were holes in *Take Two* and I was face-to-face with the ordinary layer of half-inch plywood that lay between me and enough water to drown me several times over.

The floor in my previous home was three-quarter-inch plywood, and the only pressure it bore was a couple of sofas and Seth jumping up and down when the Sacramento Kings won a game. *Take Two* had an entire ocean pressing against her hull. The hull was cedar reinforced with fiberglass, but what if another boat ran into us? If it did, you could bet your Coast Guard approved flotation device it would hit the starboard hull; the one with the cockroach infestation; the one with the perplexing holding tank that would not empty; and the one with the dry rot; my hull. This damage, like all previous problems, affected my compartment exclusively. Brian offered to switch with me, but we couldn't afford any more exterminators, holding tank pump-outs or repairs if the problems followed me.

I might have thought cleaning gutters and repairing sprinklers wasn't so bad and wished I hadn't chucked it all to live on a boat if it weren't for the other side of the chain-link fence. On the other side of the fence surrounding the boatyard on three sides is a road lined with palm trees. Beyond the trees on the east is a beach. Not a big beach, but like all Caribbean beaches the warm waves lapped the shore like a dog prancing at my feet inviting me to play. The shore itself isn't sand, but seashells. Looking down I realized I was walking on millions of tiny shells. I scooped them into my hand and examined their different shapes and sizes. Virgin Island beaches are all beautiful inviting stretches of paradise, but they aren't all alike. I've waded on sandy bottoms, silt, slippery rock, course sand, powder-fine sand and seashells. Some wide beaches reach many yards back to mangroves and palms; and trees tiptoe right down to the water at others. Now and again I find a tide pool, but not always. When I got myself worked-up and stressed about money, business, homesickness or messes on the boat, a walk on the beach cured it all. My stress, like a sand castle, lost form then disappeared altogether the closer I got to the water.

Where the narrow palm-lined road turned inland from the shore sat a small pottery shop alone far from the café,

Laundromat, boutique and other marina shops and businesses. This simple enterprise appealed to me on many levels. I liked the pottery better than what is typically found in shops filled with shelf upon shelf of the same patterns repeated many times over on mugs, pitchers and candy dishes. And, for some time I'd fancied retirement with just such a small retail store with a woodshop in back. In the pottery store, the front and back halves were separated by a low wall. No need to turn over a piece to learn where it was made; it was created right there in the back of the shop by the same person who sold it to you. Instead of worrying about stock performances or 401ks my retirement advice is to learn a craft and buy a little shop slightly off the beaten path. That's my plan.

Friends are made quickly in marinas. Life can be dreary and you never know how long you'll have before someone sails away. Within a few days of arriving we'd gotten to know Gary from Long Island and Rick from Florida. Gary was a boyish, fifty-two-year-old bachelor with a brown ponytail. I eventually got used to his way of helping himself to food he found in the galley. Rick had been flying from Florida to Tortola two weeks a month for several months to work on his hurricane damaged catamaran, *Technocat*. He stopped by often at the end of the day for a drink and chat, generally bringing a couple of beers with him.

~~~~

I pull a muscle whenever I strain to find the bright side of our Christmas on the hard. I was with Seth and we sailed for a few hours, but we were despondent. We knew the elaborate family celebration going on stateside and, absent that, we'd at least preferred to share the day with Brian.

Christmas at my parents' house is a full-sensory celebration beginning on December twenty-second or twenty-third when Dad returns from his first trip to the airport with a daughter or grandchild. He'll make at least one more trip and others arrive by car until the driveway is overflowing. The welcome cheer grows louder for each arrival.

The house is decorated beyond recognition with garland, fir boughs, ceramic Santas representing European nations past and present and porcelain nativities. The regular linens and dishes are replaced with Christmas table-cloths, napkins, doilies, sofa blankets, plates, glasses, mugs and serving dishes. We walk around the house fingering favorite memories from childhood and discovering Mom has spent time on the shopping network again this year. A dozen or more stockings hang from the mantelpiece. At the center of it all is a tall, elegantly trimmed tree with a sprawling Christmas village, twenty-two buildings in all and an O-gauge electric train running through it.

The air is as crowded with kitchen aromas as the floor will be with wrapping paper. Tupperware is stacked and everyone knows which container holds their favorite homemade treat. No one is discouraged from helping themselves and, like the loaves and fishes, they never empty. Mom refills them from a cache in the freezer until she sends the last pieces home with us in foil covered pie tins. The sound track for the week-long event is provided by a stack of CDs playing Christmas classics we first listened to on LPs.

Our attempt to recreate this atmosphere on *Take Two* was feeble at best. We had a pre-lighted twenty-four-inch tree bought from a holiday shop, a dozen miniature ornaments we gave Seth to hang and snowflakes I cut from gold paper and hung from the ceiling. For food we nibbled on Holland cookies, caramel corn and homemade goodies sent by my mom who brightened our holiday from four thousand miles away. She also sent a boxed set of Christmas CDs. Seth opened his presents on Christmas Eve and convinced us he was pleased. We played his new board game, watched a DVD then said good night. The next morning we emptied stockings and I made pancakes.

Like so many of the disappointments and hurt feelings that characterized my marriage, the details include a miscommunication, but the broad picture is one of a difference in values. Brian left after breakfast to join a small group of acquaintances caroling up and down the marina for the enjoyment of the live-aboards and vacationers. Seth didn't want to go and I didn't want to leave him alone, so I stayed behind feeling abandoned. I was homesick and in need of some cheering. I tried not to bring Seth down with me so we accepted an invitation to go sailing. It was a warm day like any other December day in the Virgin Islands. The cloud cover hung a little heavier than usual, but it didn't rain and we passed a pleasant afternoon on the Sir Francis Drake Channel. Nevertheless, Seth and I were in no mood to have fun. We were going to feel sorry for ourselves and that's all there was to it.

When we returned to the boatyard, I walked to the one working pay phone at the far end of the marina. The forty dollars in calling cards I fed into the phone bought me 20 minutes of talk time. I spoke to my two sons and daughter in California for three minutes each then called home and spent the remaining eleven minutes telling a series of family members to stop passing the phone because the call was costing two dollars a minute. This ranked in the top worst Christmases of my life. Brian, however, enjoyed his day of caroling. Life is what you make it.

~~~~

As an orange sun set into the ocean on the last day of the year we celebrated by changing clothes. Instead of putting on a fresh tank top and pair of shorts after my shower I shook the dust from a tropical print skirt and low-cut wrap-around top, and Brian put on an expensive linen shirt. Then we headed to Peg Leg's for New Year's Eve dinner with other souls also stuck in or passing through this corner of the Caribbean. Gary brought a newcomer to the marina, a soft-spoken Brit named Ivan. He was tan and handsome with a broad white smile, sky blue eyes and, at five-foot-eight, seemed built for living on a boat. Ivan recently sold his business and retired to sail the warm water of the Caribbean. He was an entertaining storyteller whose tales of sailing in the frigid wind of the English Channel chilled us to the bone. Ivan was also the best listener at the table and the only one to reach for his wallet when we picked up the check.

Times I wanted to get off *Take Two* I would stop by the *Holly B* which Ivan named for his granddaughter. He always had a cigarette burning, music playing and drinks at the ready.

In mid-January, Ivan invited us to join him and a new crew member, Becky, for a few days sailing. Ivan used websites that connect yacht owners with temporary crew members. Owners can find professional, qualified crew for hire, or inexperienced enthusiasts to share expenses. It's a great way to an exciting and affordable vacation. Some lonely skippers use the websites as a dating sight for sailors. But Ivan welcomed vacationing men and women alike to share expenses, chores, and most importantly, the sailing experience.

For Becky's two week vacation from the London police department Ivan planned to take her navigating the Little Sisters, a string of six or seven small islands south of Tortola.

Brian wanted to stay on *Take Two* to keep an eye on repairs, but I jumped at the chance to get out of the boatyard. The *Holly B* had four cabins, so Gary, who never turned down anything free, came too.

We motored from the shelter of Nanny Cay Marina past the rocky entrance and into a warm breeze under sunny skies in the Sir Francis Drake Channel. Back in England Becky had completed a sailing class to prepare, but was still a novice sailor and new to the Caribbean so Ivan started with an easy sail to White Bay on Peter Island. He puffed on a cigarette at the helm while Becky worked on her tan and asked questions about sailing and Gary fussed with the trim of the sails. I stayed out of the way in a corner of the cockpit on double layer of cushions Ivan brought for me to sit on.

When we put down anchor in White Bay on the south side of Peter Island, Ivan stayed on board, while the rest of us snorkeled toward the shoreline looking for a family of sea turtles reputed to live there. There were few rocks, coral or clumps of grass to darken the white sandy bottom and I remember it as the clearest and brightest bay I ever swam.

When I gave up looking for turtles the four of us motored to shore in the dinghy. At one end of the beach there were several picnic tables and a shack with a small bar, a refrigerator and a large grill. We bought drinks and sat at the tables smoking and talking.

I've never been a smoker, but I will occasionally have a social cigarette with friends. I like holding it between my fingers, putting it to my lips and pulling the smoke in. I don't smoke properly I just hold it a moment in my mouth and entertain myself with different ways of exhaling the smoke. I then spend the rest of the day trying to get the taste out of my mouth.

We had the beach to ourselves until a catamaran, itself the size of some small islands, coasted in and tied up to the dock, depositing dozens of giddy, boozed-up day passengers. Feeling fortunate, and a tiny bit smug, we watched the tourists work on the one souvenir they couldn't go home without: a suntan. They were still enjoying the beach and shallow surf when we returned to the *Holly B* to sail west to anchor at James Bay for the night.

The next day we sailed west to the Indians, a group of four boulders that jut fifty feet above the ocean. The Indians are a popular snorkeling spot near itty bitty Pelican Island. The surf at the Indians was rougher than the calm shorelines I was used to. I'm an insecure swimmer and even snorkeling along a beach if I wander more than a few dozen yards from shore I tether a boogie board to my wrist. If I get tired I rest my elbows on the board while adjusting my mask or catching my breath. I'm neither old nor particularly feeble, but I felt both when I snorkeled with friends who thought nothing of swimming far from shore with just a snorkel and flippers while I dragged my board behind like a security blanket.

Gary and Becky jumped into the water as soon as we hooked one of several available mooring buoys. I didn't have a boogie board with me on the *Holly B*, but I don't embarrass easily so I donned a fat orange life vest over my black swimsuit and slipped in.

I couldn't remember any other time Ivan got in the water, other than to scrape barnacles from the bottom of his yacht, but he put on a life vest and snorkel and joined us. I wondered if he too lacked confidence in the ocean and found it easier to not be the only person wearing a vest. Though there were several swimmers bobbing around us, Ivan and I were the only two wearing adult water wings. But, as I labored against the waves pushing me about, threatening to bounce me off the boulders, and was rapidly running out of energy swimming against the current on the return to the boat, I decided it was worth the risk of looking silly to not feel fear or panic.

The problem of snorkeling with a life vest is that its purpose is, of course, to keep your head out of the water. I had to roll myself firmly forward, with my butt mostly above the water line like an over-inflated inner tube. Only that way could I see the bright orange, purple and yellow coral growing on the sides of the boulders just beneath the surface. I'm not bold enough to dive, although it would have been interesting here where the colors of coral grew steadily paler farther down the boulders.

Our return sail to Nanny Cay was made miserable by Gary's determination to sail hard. He lobbied aggressively for the challenge of sailing in faster wind and Ivan, trying to be a considerate host, acquiesced. We sailed beyond the Little Sisters to where low clouds were dropping rain and the gentle rolling of the Drake Channel turned to white tops in the Flanagan Passage near St. John. Gary trimmed the sails taunt ignoring Ivan's protests that they might tear. They pulled the *Holly B* through the rough water straining against the lines until mild-mannered Ivan was forced to demand Gary adjust them.

Becky and I went below to escape the pelting rain and forage for crackers to calm our queasy stomachs while we waited impatiently to get back to Nanny Cay.

Business on St. Thomas

A few days after Christmas I caught the ferry to St. Thomas to run errands. The deadline for registering the Jeep was only three days away and jumping through the regular governmental hoops was reputed to be enough of a nightmare I had no desire to drive my car through flaming penalty hoops. I was also still running the business license maze.

I always enjoyed riding the ferry, for twenty minutes between St. Thomas and St. John or forty-five minutes from Tortola to U.S. customs at Cruz Bay, I could completely relax. Though inside, even by an open window, the heat wrapped around you like a heavy wool blanket and the droning of the massive engines drowned the sound of the water splashing against the hull, outside, where the breeze lessened the heat of the sun, I could sit comfortably with a shoulder against the rail watching waves responding to the capriciousness of the wind and rolling past the blue painted bow. Sometimes I'd see a frigate bird and I always kept an eye out for sea turtles, dolphins and jumping fish. Ferries beat the hell out of any bus or subway.

Once again Cindy advised me. "You're not going to the DMV are you?"

"I have to," I said. "They need to inspect the Jeep."

"No, no, no. Go across the street to Red Hook Secretarial Services and ask for the guy who does car registrations. I forget his name."

"I can't. It needs to be inspected."

"Trust me," Cindy said. "Just take the paperwork over. There'll be a charge . . . twenty-five dollars I think. But it's worth it. You don't want to stand in those lines."

Cindy hadn't steered me wrong yet, but I couldn't help being a little nervous handing over thirty-three dollars in registration fees, forty dollars for the service and all the evidence the Jeep was mine. The clerk told me she'd give it to Tony who'd have the license back by the thirty-first. On my next trip to St. Thomas I picked up the registration and tags: no waiting in line, vehicle inspection or obsequious smiling at public servants whose whim could cost me another trip. On the island, who you know is everything.

Because I hadn't used a service to help me through the business license process, I spent a lot of time waiting in government offices only to be told to return later to wait some more. Finally after eight weeks, three visits to the business license office, two to the Department of Planning and Natural Resources and one to the Police Department, we had our business license.

We planned to formalize agreements with the host sites for our satellite dishes when we got *Take Two* out of dry dock and back to St. Thomas. We'd install equipment and finally have wireless access not only to sell, but for ourselves. Until then the only public Internet access on the east end was at the Grateful Deli and the marina office. The deli didn't allow personal computers to hook-up and the marina charged ten dollars an hour. When I needed a quick fix I begged use of the phone line for a modem connection at the Water's Edge kiosk on our dock. I'd wait to ask until they weren't busy and they were always willing to accommodate.

It was clear our service would be in demand. The only question was how to make it profitable. The equipment was expensive, but using the phone company to connect to the Internet was out of the question. Their reputation for months-long installation delays and interrupted service was undisputed.

Before catching the ferry back to Tortola I found a patch of shade and called my friend in California. She and her husband had separated two months after I left the States and she was going through the hardest time of her life. I only had a few minutes until I got on the ferry and crossed back into the British Virgin Islands where a phone call home would cost two dollars a minute so we made the most of our call and in the process began speaking in metaphors. That afternoon we compared our marriages to sinking ships, Cohn Brothers' movies, playing catch with my border collie, and mayonnaise.

Nanny Cay

I didn't take enough books. We entered our seventh week on the hard in the backwater neighborhood of Nanny Cay and I was out of good books. When we arrived we thought our stay was going to last three weeks and that Christmas on the hard would be the worst of it. After six weeks, with the end not in sight, not knowing how much longer we had to endure was worse than our Christmas.

Take Two was stripped of her protective paint and a hole gaped in her starboard side Even if we wanted to say, "Ah bugger it, let's go," we couldn't. Getting her back in the water was an event we were beginning to speak of with the same longing and uncertainty as Christians for the Second Coming of Christ.

Long ago I'd finished reading books I eagerly picked up and reluctantly put down. I had moved on to a Nero Wolfe mystery from a second hand store and finally a thin hard-cover mid-twentieth-century novel translated from French that I found on a low shelf in the marina book exchange.

The French novel turned out to be one of those sanctimonious and implausible stories of passionate love sacrificed for the service of God; a worthy life perhaps, but not a satisfying afternoon with a book. Florida Rick occasionally gave me old issues of the *Economist* magazine. When he wasn't in Nanny Cay restoring *TechnoCat* he was a financial advisor. If not for these magazines I'd have been forced to read Brian's science fiction novels, which in large bookstores are found at least half an acre away from the classics or non-fiction I prefer.

We had lived without television before, but then the kids were teenagers and with five kids at home the house was a pinball machine as we bounced off one another, work, school, homework, errands, appointments and hobbies. Art and science projects for five kids kept life interesting. We helped build balsa wood cars and a trebuchet; we provided bubble wrap and raw eggs for physics experiments; helped chart the freezing temperature of salt water; and some weeks spent as much time in the kitchen turning flour into papier mâché and Play-doh, and sugar cubes into Mayan temples as we did cooking. We transported poster-board displays, helped sew home economics projects and I held my daughter's anxious hand as she lay on her back breathing through a straw under a hardening clay mask for extra credit in art class. Then, supplies and entertainment were just a short drive away. It was a different story now. Seth was staying with friends so on Nanny Cay it was just me, Brian and little within walking distance.

One afternoon Brian and I borrowed bicycles and rode Waterfront Drive several miles into Road Town. The terror of trembling down a shoulderless, winding road with blind curves and gravel patches took my mind off Nanny Cay for a few hours. We rested awhile at the Marina Café drinking lemonade and watching yachts come and go. On the way back we stopped for lunch at a spot called Struggling Man's Place. The parking lot, literally a wide spot in the road large enough for three or four cars, was empty. We sat alone on the deck at one of five plastic tables and watched the surf swaying against slippery green rocks a foot below. Minutes passed and no one appeared so we stuck our heads through a doorway into a tiny kitchen. On our right, four-feet of Formica-topped beadboard cabinets led to a small sink. In front of us a narrow white porcelain stove backed up to a wall next to more cabinets. A large black woman with yards of apron tied around her middle and a kerchief on her head stepped from another room and said something that was probably English, but nevertheless unintelligible to our American English ears. We pointed to chicken simmering in a pot on the stove and said, "That looks good." She nodded and brought us plates piled with the stewed chicken, rice and plantains. Everything was brown and soft and delicious. The chicken was expertly infused with a blend of spices. We could not identify them all but between us tasted garlic, ginger, turmeric and pepper. The meat fell from the bone and mixed with the peas and rice that are served with nearly everything in the British islands. We devoured it with the appetite of athletes, leaving on our tongues the taste of delicately sweet, grilled plantains.

~~~~

Every town should have a plaza such as Nanny Cay's. The covered dining area, populated by that ubiquitous ugly white plastic furniture, forms an oasis in the center of the village. The open-air, dining-optional atmosphere overcame the furnishings and drew me. A sidewalk running the length of Nanny Cay from the swimming pool at one end to the boatyard travel-lifts a few hundred meters away bordered the plaza on the front. At the back a tiny bar with three bar stools on a side and a kitchen nearby offered refreshment.

We occasionally ate at the plaza café, we bought lunch there for Seth's real birthday, the day after Christmas, but more often, I simply retreated there from the heat and the noise of *Take Two*. I'd sit, as comfortably as possible on plastic, near the front of the plaza and order iced tea. A refreshing cold drink was part of the escape. However, I always forgot this was the British Virgin Islands and they like their tea inexplicably strong, shockingly bitter to this Yank (in the states this stuff would be controlled by the EPA). I read, said hello to passers-by, and paid two dollars to torture my taste buds.

It was at the plaza where we met most of our friends and where we could find someone to share a cab into town for groceries or to a restaurant on the north side.

One evening I invited Eva, a young Italian woman with long dark hair and brown eyes, to sit with me. She and I met in the restroom. Her English seemed on a level with my two semesters of French so I kept the conversation to subjects covered in those two semesters.

"Where do you live?" I asked.

"I live Florence . . . in Italy."

"My grandmother's name was Florence." What was she going to say, hers wasn't? So I said, "I live on St. Thomas with my husband and our son. Do you have family?" She looked puzzled. I tried some basics, "Mother? Father?"

"Sister. I have sister."

"I have two sisters and two brothers. Do you have brothers?"

"No. No brothers."

"I have four sons and one daughter. Do you have children?" If she didn't have children we'd have to start talking about the furniture or what color our clothes were.

"No children," she said. We both smiled. "I am here one week."

"From Italy," I confirmed.

"Si, from Italy."

"I am here six weeks."

"Six weeks is nice for you."

I was trying to explain how not nice for me it was, using my fingers to indicate climbing a ladder when Brian appeared, and we repeated the part about Italy and sisters for his benefit then sat smiling inanely before she said, "Arrivederci."

Two or three times a week I walked to the swimming pool at the Nanny Cay Resort at the far end of the cay. The pool is built at the ocean's edge where sunbathers can watch boats come and go from the marina. There I'd dropped my sunglasses, tote and hat onto a chaise and step into the cool water. The water temperature perfectly refreshed my wilted frame and invited me to stay. I didn't because grown-ups don't play in water and this grown-up doesn't do laps. So, I'd descend the steps at the shallow end, glide to a ladder across the pool then, holding in my stomach, walk back to my chaise and settle myself, eyes closed to the sun, envying the moms and dads of small children their excuse to play in the water.

All of this, the marina and boatyard, the plaza with its surrounding shops and businesses, and hotel and pool are on a small peninsula. Some afternoons instead of taking the sidewalk to the swimming pool, I walked the back of the peninsula. This took me along the shell-strewn beach and a dirt path that wound near the beach then away past brush and grasses and back again to the sand and shells. My favorite part of the walk was where a narrow channel of seawater flowed, cutting off the extreme end of the peninsula. The depth of the channel rose and fell between three and four feet depending on the tide. On the west side of the peninsula, where the sidewalk ran, an arched concrete bridge crossed the channel. Here on the east side a low, broken, algae-covered, wood slat bridge crossed the water. Eight or ten slats were missing entirely leaving just the two-by-four frame spanning several feet. Even when the tide was low it was a precarious undertaking. When the water was high it covered the bridge to ankle depth and the risk of falling was great. I found this part of the walk exhilarating. My inner child assumed control and though I blush somewhat to admit it I imagined myself deep in the jungle crossing an ancient Mayan footbridge.

~~~~

Just as exhilarating, and often as precarious, were the people we met. People were very important in our dreary entertainment void. We shared cabs with Gary from Boston; drank Painkillers, visited the best island restaurants and begged financial advice of Florida Rick; sailed with Ivan, the most delightful Brit one could hope to close-haul with; and passed time with men and women who had been there so long they actually understood the local rapid-fire, mumbling patois.

Many workdays ended with an assembly of friends sharing a Guinness, or Newkie Brown as Jimmy a retired brewmeister from Manchester preferred, and arm-chairing the world's problems. A favorite aspect of these discussions for me was the sharing of cultural differences. Becky, the policewoman who crewed with Ivan for two weeks confirmed that British police do not typically carry guns and for a citizen to gain permission to own even a hunting rifle is a significant undertaking. We pondered without conclusion whether this leaves the British safer or more vulnerable than Americans whose armed police manage to embroil themselves in questionable shootings every year. On the other hand, Leonardo Hererra, a local laborer, told us in his home country, the still poor Dominican Republic, everyone carries a gun and he considered it no less safe than elsewhere. I can't imagine it's less safe than St. Thomas where the population of approximately 50,000 had eight homicides by February that year and the most common way of obtaining a handgun was to steal it.

I also learned a thing or two about the King's English. While telling us we really ought to call our language American the English will talk about losing their bottle when a Yank would say "losing their nerve." Or showering on deck "in the nut," instead of showering "in the buff," as a woman in the slip next to Ivan's was seen doing. Once Ivan called me a "dippy" as I passed tools to him when he was helping install eye-loops for our trampoline. He claimed this is an English term for an assistant to a skilled laborer. I decided to check with Becky or Jimmy to find out if I was getting a "micky."

Florida Rick knew all the good restaurants on the island and was always looking for someone to share a cab and join him for dinner. A cab ride to Sebastian's on the Beach at Little Apple Bay on the north side cost nearly as much as our seafood dinner. The wait for dinner was long, but we occupied ourselves with rum punch, conversation and watching the sunset behind the hills of St. Thomas.

With Rick we discovered the best barbeque on the island at C&F Bar and Restaurant in Road Town and became well-acquainted with the menu at the Village Cay Dockside Café where we would rendezvous for lunch after sharing a cab to Road Town for provisions. The marina there was the largest one around and made for great people-watching.

On our chartered vacation to the islands five years earlier our stop at Sydney's Peace and Love on Jost Van Dyke taught us that at some restaurants the time you arrive for dinner has no bearing whatsoever on when you will be served. We'd been swimming and hiking at nearby Sandy Cay all afternoon and decided on an early dinner. We anchored in Great Harbor and took the dinghy ashore to Sydney's at 4:30; we were hungry and figured we'd beat the dinner rush. I have a photo of Brian smiling and holding a large lobster he chose from a cage Sydney pulled from the water beside the dock. After selecting our lobsters we ordered drinks and sat on the deck to wait. An hour passed: Brian and I ran out of conversation and the kids ran out of film in the camera. Another hour passed. Brian and I had too much alcohol on empty stomachs and the kids, tired of wandering the dock, sat down to complain. When dinner arrived at 7:00 we were unsmiling, past being hungry and I was angry with the kids for their arguing. We learned later that most restaurants serving the yachting community take dinner orders, usually over the radio, until 4 p.m. for reservations at 7 p.m.

~~~~

It was more common to see men living on boats than women. The docks at Nanny Cay in particular were studded with divorced men made horny and bold by loneliness and sea air. Never before had I been so blatantly propositioned or unexpectedly grabbed. I owned two quarter horses when we lived on Rancho Del Fuego in California and I invited everyone I knew to go riding with me. Besides girlfriends I rode with my ferrier, our realtor, the tree surgeon, men from my Toastmasters club and the office. We rode on beautiful oak-studded hillsides, along secluded ravines and open meadows, and no one ever tried to waylay me in the tack room or explicitly state a desire to slip into my saddle.

Joe was a balding, middle-aged Canadian living alone on a pretty monohull he berthed at the Nanny Cay Marina. We met

Joe when Rick invited us to join the two of them sharing a cab to the north side for dinner. Joe was quiet and seldom joined in the conversation. I saw him now and then on the dock and always took time to chat because I'd formed the impression he was shy and lonely. I'd known Joe for a few weeks when a group of us met on the *Holly B* near his boat for a pre-game drink on Super Bowl Sunday. As we passed his yacht on the way to Peg Leg's to watch the game, I knocked on the hull and invited him to join us. He hurried after and fell into the background at the crowded table. A few days later I saw him working on his deck and stopped to say hello. He invited me aboard to show me repairs he'd made and offer a glass of juice. I accepted the juice feeling it was the nice thing to do. When I got up to leave Joe took me by the shoulders, and completely by surprise, kissing me on the mouth. Before I recovered, he did it again. For a moment I thought I might have to use the knee to the groin and palm to the nose defense my father taught me when I started dating, but I simply pulled away decisively and said, "I'm going now." He didn't chase me and we never said more than hello to each other after that.

Jimmy, on the other hand, wasn't shy, taciturn, or even single. He was a vacationing crewmate on the *Holly B*, his wife stayed home ostensibly preferring a golf cart to a boat. Jimmy was a six-foot tall, one-hundred-seventy-pound British bota bag. He consumed alcohol in astonishing quantities while engaging in his other hobbies of sailing, swimming, and, undoubtedly, fornicating.

We'd known Jimmy a few weeks the evening Brian and I met him and his crewmates on the dock for dinner at Peg Leg's. Brian and the others stopped to look at the rigging on a boat, so Jimmy and I got to the restaurant ahead of them. As we staked out a table Jimmy interrupted our idle chit-chat leaning forward saying, "I want to fuck you."

If there's a proper response to this comment, my mama didn't teach me. What's worse, I'm what the Myer's Briggs personality profile refers to as Feeling, I think about how people feel. This was not a time to worry about how Jimmy would feel. But, rather than the better response of, "You're an offensive drunk and you should screw yourself," I stupidly said, "You do?" And shot a glance toward the door where, to my relief, Brian and the others were heading our way.

Horny males notwithstanding I have never known a more helpful community than the boatyard and dock dwellers at Nanny Cay. One evening we discovered friends from St. Thomas hanging in the travel-lift. They had pulled out just for the night to change oil and perform maintenance on propellers. Unfortunately, the propellers proved problematic and concern grew that they wouldn't finish work by morning. The boatyard rule for this situation is: ready or not the travel-lift operator will lower your yacht back into the water at seven a.m. Over the course of several hours, and well into the night, residents of the yard and marina helped. Along with expert advice and help with the labor. As twilight faded and the moon climbed in the sky they were loaned a drop-light and a grinder; they were given grease and just when it looked like they'd have to go back in the water without completing repairs, Gary ran back to his yacht and returned with an O-ring of precisely the right size. Thanks to help from the community repairs got completed, they were ready to go back in the water on time and even grabbed a couple hours of sleep.

But this was a marina and people came and went. Some weeks all of our friends were either sailing or stateside taking care of the businesses that allowed them to play with boats. It took little more than an hour or two at the plaza to make new acquaintances, which is fortunate because not forgetting the restaurant and bar near the swimming pool, there were only five shops: two souvenir, one dive shop, a grocery and the pottery shed. Such were the distractions of Nanny Cay. Delightful? Absolutely, but for ten weeks? I didn't bring enough books.

I Don't Get it

Brian was gone overnight doing a favor for Gary. He didn't like sailing someone else's boat, but Gary had pressed him to sail his yacht from its slip at Nanny Cay to St. Thomas to meet him when he returned from Boston with several boxes of equipment.

We soon learned that Gary got by in life with more than a little help from his friends. He was quick to ask favors and considered borrowing as good a way to lay hands on money as any other. He seemed to owe money to everyone he came in contact with, including fourteen-year-old Seth. At one point, when Gary was complaining more than usual about money problems, Brian and I checked discreetly with one-another to be sure we were on the same page about not loaning to Gary if he asked. To his credit, and our growing amazement, he never asked. We let him use space in our rented storage locker, but that and a few meals were the extent of our contribution to the care and feeding of our bachelor friend.

In spite of fifty-year-old Gary's propensity for self-pity and indecent habit of hitting on young women—girls actually, I couldn't bring myself to dislike him. Gary was not at all mean-spirited or dishonest, and he was generous with what little he had. He was just extremely adept at making ends meet using someone else's ends.

~~~~

Sometime after lunch on Tuesday, Michael A. from Yacht Restorations stopped by *Take Two* to tell me Brian called on the radio to say the engine failed while returning from St. Thomas and they would be arriving late, perhaps after seven. This was a problem because when they got back to Nanny Cay getting through a crowded harbor into a slip without the aid of an engine was not possible. Michael recommended they call the rescue boat for a tow once they reached the mouth of the harbor. But there was a problem with that, too: the rescue boat people go home at five p.m.

I went about my afternoon not worrying until I began to consider my reaction to Brian not arriving by seven, or possibly at all that night. I walked back over to Yacht Restoration to talk to Michael. He instantly read my face and said, "You're worried about Brian." I asked if I should call someone if Brian didn't come home; or if I should simply presume they were anchored off-shore. And, if I should call someone, I needed to know who. Do the British have a Coast Guard? Is there a listing in the white pages for Beefeater?

We had just about agreed there was no danger when Michael realized the "Gary" that Brian was sailing with. The look that came on his face frightened me.

"What? What's wrong?"

"In my opinion," he chose his words carefully, "He's...reckless. I wouldn't sail with him."

I couldn't argue and anyway it was a little late for that. Nevertheless, Michael assured me, there was no real cause for concern and promised to stay by the phone. Brian had our cell phone and it had been said the Sprint system would work up to a few hundred yards offshore of Nanny Cay.

I walked back to *Take Two* running over the possibilities in my mind. There really was no reason to think they might sink. They'd lost an engine and might drift onto rocks, there were plenty near the harbor, but even if they did the weather wasn't bad. The wind was brisk and there were rain showers, but hardly a perfect storm, more like an adequate downpour. No real concern about making it to shore.

The weather annoyed me all that day, and kept the crew of Yacht Restoration from their work on *Take Two*. I spent the day rushing from hatch to doorway closing them to sudden rain showers only to open them moments later when the rain passed and the stifling heat and humidity inside began to oppress. Even so, since Michael first told me of Brian's call, I wasn't thinking of the inconvenience when I rushed to bang the hatches closed, I was thinking of Brian sailing in it. Also, I didn't want to spend another night alone on *Take Two*. The boat was shrouded in tarps. At night the tarps thrashed in the wind sounding like everything bad an active imagination can construe: horny citizens of the Commonwealth sneaking aboard, cockroaches bent on revenge, underemployed boatyard workers creating more work for themselves. I hardly noticed these sounds when Brian was there.

~~~~

I have to say, I don't get it: sailing that is. I suppose I'm more about destinations than journeys, but sailing? It isn't even a journey so much as costly and stressful pelagic wandering.

Maintaining a sailboat is a constant preoccupation for boat owners. I'd been sailing on *Take Two*, as well as the yachts of friends, perhaps a dozen times since coming to the Caribbean. On four or five of those occasions when we anchored I and other passengers frolicked in a reef or lounged on deck while the captain donned snorkel and mask to spend the afternoon scraping barnacles from the bottom of the boat. Even with all this scraping, boats must be pulled often from the water for new bottom paint, propeller maintenance, hull inspection and general repairs.

These sleek, sexy-looking yachts, carefully crafted from fiberglass or sophisticated combinations of wood and fiberglass, glide gracefully through the water at incredible speeds. Incredible if you're racing against an elderly stroke victim in a row-boat. The Conestoga was a faster mode of transportation. A typical 40' sailboat carries a dizzying array of sails. With enough yardage deployed to wrap the boat and mail it to its destination a yacht will scream along at seven or eight knots. A knot, at 6076 feet, is slightly longer than a mile, so doing ten knots per hour is a little faster than ten miles per hour. I suspect knots were invented because drivers of automobiles laughed out loud when they heard sailors bragging about the speed of their vessels. Until the term was invented sailors had to hide in corners of bars pausing in mid-sentence to look over their shoulder before holding up fingers to indicate boat speed.

Alone with one another, however, sailors boast unabashedly. On a day sail to Norman Island our skipper bobbed up and down alongside his boat scraping barnacles until his knuckles bled and, fearful of sharks, he hurried back aboard. When we got underway he proudly announced, "She's picked up nearly a knot."

Brian spoke up supportively, "Sure, you can feel it."

Another captain on board said, "That much?"

Choosing which sails will optimize speed in any given weather is less science than biased conjecture. Sailors will argue for hours the benefits of a Genoa over an asymmetrical spinnaker, while non-sailors repeatedly say, "Tell me again the difference?"

There are sails for when the wind is too strong, too weak, coming from behind, from the front and from the side. There are even storm sails!

Because experienced and foolhardy sailors alike avoid sailing in foul weather the storm jib is found in the bottom of the sail locker stuffed into a mildew-covered bag. So I'm thinking, when a storm comes up unexpectedly some poor schmuck is digging desperately in the bowels of his boat tossing out soggy bags in a mad scramble for the storm jib. Meanwhile, his wife, shouting over the wind, voices her objections to being at sea at such a time. At this point, he screams at her to shut up and help him hoist the storm jib using line that has stiffened to the pliability of oak. She, clinging to a shroud as the boat welters, demands an explanation as to why he likes sailing so much if it's going to be this cheerless, and can we please go back now. Of course such an exchange is merely speculation on my part.

Sailing in a storm is certainly the worst case scenario, but even on a good day sailing is a stressful undertaking. No sooner does the captain get the sails trimmed for maximum starfish pace and the passengers settle themselves in, or out, of the sun, then the wind shifts and they must quickly tack or come about. This involves jumping out of the way of whipping lines and swinging booms, releasing one line—careful not to lose any fingers—and hauling for all you're worth on another. Soon as you get your beach towel repositioned in, or out, of the sun, there you go doing it again. I don't get it.

There are benefits I'll admit. I have spent idyllic hours leaning back on my palms, raising my chin to the sun and the breeze and contemplating just how clever I was to respond to the suggestion that we move to the Caribbean with, "Okay." It would be better though if it weren't for one other problem I haven't mentioned. If Bill Gates owned a sailboat he wouldn't make the list of the 100 richest men in the greater Redmond, Washington area.

This might be more a Caribbean issue than a boat-ownership issue, I don't know. But I felt as though, aside from friends, nearly every person who set foot on the *Take Two*, and some who had not, did so with the goal of bleeding us of every possible dollar. I was told it was policy for a boatyard to charge ten percent of any work done by boatyard businesses in addition to the several hundred dollars they charge each month to occupy a patch of boatyard dirt. I was told it was policy for our home marina to charge us the full rate for our slip while we are away for extended periods, and policy did not allow us to sublet our slip, but they could, and did, rent it out in our absence.

We were charged extraordinary sums of money for poor, even lawsuit worthy, work. We were promised one price and got another, one completion date and watched it slip past. We were stalled, ignored, and quite possibly cheated by vendors. I felt as though everyone with whom we did business from taxi drivers to marina owners, saw us as rich, gullible suckers to be taken for any sum possible.

Brian is an honest, ethical and fair man. His treatment of others as such has too many times been rewarded with over-priced or poor work. I became quite jaded and began to look on even the occasional fair-minded man with mistrust.

I know there are unethical people everywhere and principled men and women wherever you go, but I'm convinced there was an air of greed there that does not exist on the same level anywhere else I've lived. When we finally cast a Parthian glance at Nanny Cay I was glad to return to St. Thomas, but also had one eye on the not too distant future and our return to the West Coast where I hoped to find a small town and scrupulous people in greater numbers.

Despite financial and other boatyard woes, when I finally heard a call on the VHF radio and knew Brian would soon be back safe and sound, I knew I'd sleep better.

Paradise Pitched

Near the end of my parents' long-anticipated visit, Dad was in the hotel kitchenette making coffee, Mom was in bed and I was sitting on the patio of our beach-side hotel watching the iguanas and thinking of a dream my mother told me about. The night before they arrived she dreamed their visit to St. Thomas was over and Dad was packed and calling her to the cab, but she hadn't been in the water yet. She wanted him to wait until she could wade in the ocean, but there was no time. I was puzzling over the dream because it came true.

Mom hadn't been to the Caribbean since a cruise fifteen years earlier. It was her high school graduation gift to my little sister. My younger sister had the good sense to be born ten years after the next youngest and she therefore got totally cooler gifts. I, quite carelessly, grew up second of five kids. When I graduated high-school, my parents dug out from under a pile of bills to attend the ceremony. Every day the mail box teetered under the weight of invoices for drivers' Ed, orthodontics, car repairs, prom dresses and groceries. I tagged along on the cruise and in the cabin tossed a sideways glance at my sister as I unpacked my Samsonite, my high school graduation gift.

Regardless of age differences, my mother, sister and I enjoyed all the usual, culturally barren cruise experiences. We watched drinking games from our deck chairs; ate breakfast, lunch and dinner with the same group of white Midwesterners; grinned fatuously at one another bouncing in the back of open-air taxis driven by dark men with accents we didn't try too hard to understand. We managed to avoid most of the hazards of cruise travel. No one got sunburned, mugged or lured into talent shows. My sister and I did, however, conga our way to Queen Mary-size hangovers.

Being amateurs in the drinking department, we timed our drunkenness badly; she the night before docking in St. Thomas, and me the night before arriving in St. Martin. Thus we coordinated our hangovers with Mother's unyielding determination to go ashore with her daughters. Bright and early, that is super-nova bright, and can't-you-just-smother-me-with-my-pillow early, Mother shook us awake. No amount of pleading, whining or vomiting would dissuade her insistence that we explore the island together. Mother headed directly to the water, where, even through blood-shot eyes we recognized the most inviting beaches imaginable. Our most vivid memories, along with seeing an actual dead pig at the side of the road, are of frolicking in those emerald waters.

We left promising ourselves a return visit. Mine came ten years later on a catamaran charter with my husband and six nearly-grown kids. On that incomprehensibly foolhardy venture I sometimes thought of my mother, generally in the mornings when the kids were sleeping off their near legal hangovers, and her love of the Caribbean, renewing my promise to return with her.

My mother grew up in the Northwest and raised pale, soggy children in the drizzly Washington State climate where the longest beach in the world stretches along the frigid Pacific for twenty-eight wind-chilled miles. Summer afternoon temperatures on a Northwest beach often linger in the fifties.

As a young mother, she dutifully endured afternoons on the sand watching her blue children flirt with hypothermia in the steel grey water while she sat bundled in a car-coat, a beach blanket wrapped around her legs. SPF in Washington refers to Sweatshirt Protection Factor. Lack of it ruins many a vacation day there as lack of sun-screen does farther south.

Not so living in the Caribbean. The only sweatshirt I owned came out of the closet when we took in a movie at the four-plex. In the parking lot of the theater men, women, and children emerged from cars in T-shirts and shorts carrying coats and sweaters. If you looked closely you'd see wool socks tucked into pockets. Maybe theater managers thought they'd bring in customers from the heat, but setting the air conditioner to the low thirties sometimes backfired. More than once we impetuously considered taking in a movie only to decide against it when we remembered we had no coats or stadium blankets in the car.

Mom and Dad were not coming to take in a movie. Finally, Mom would be back to romp in the warm salty surf, and I would introduce my Dad to the only non-Pacific ocean experience of his life.

The first problem to plague their visit was the persistent and frustrating delays in the work on *Take Two*. After postponing their trip from January to early February, and again to late February, I finally bought tickets for early March hoping for luck to find us in Nanny Cay. Nevertheless, I warned my father that it was possible, just possible, *Take Two* would not yet be back in the water before he returned to work in two weeks. But Mom was staying a month and with confidence I promised a sailing experience for her. It was a promise that became heartbreakingly impossible to keep.

They arrived Wednesday night on schedule. We stopped for dinner at Iggy's where, six months earlier, Brian, Seth and I ate our first meal on St. Thomas. Mom and Dad studied the exotic drinks list. This was not an everyday outing for them. Without a menu, Dad would have to order a long island iced tea, the only mixed drink he knew by name. But, they wanted something exotic, something Caribbean. A Top Banana: yum, *crème de banane*, vodka and orange juice, but one mustn't be too hasty; the Captain's Creole Punch had a great name, but with only three ingredients, it wasn't fancy enough. Maybe a Bushwhacker or a Painkiller, drinks they'd never order back home. Mom eventually ordered a Mango Daiquiri. Dad got the more manly Bushwhacker: equal parts rum, vodka, Kahlua,

Bailey's, amaretto, Frangelico, and *crème de cocoa*. I had my usual rum punch, cheap and effective.

After dinner we drove to a rented condo at Cabrita Point on the east end. The road to the point was a mean-spirited stretch of broken concrete and rutted gravel. A roller coaster ride as I jerked the wheel left and right avoiding pot holes or getting yanked into channels.

The Cabrita Point condominiums are a row of small pink two-story buildings along the pebbled beach of Muller Bay. Each building has four studio units, two up and two down, and a generous patch of grass between buildings. Tossing a pebble into the clear water of the Atlantic while sitting on the small brown patio outside our sliding door required no effort at all.

A partition separated the sleeping and living areas in our unit. Before they went to the bedroom and I opened the sleeper sofa, while Dad channel surfed the limited and fuzzy channels, Mom and I talked about which beaches she wanted to see.

Dad didn't care how we spent our days. If Mom was happy, he was happy. Anyway, he was never completely comfortable if he wasn't working. Even on holidays at home, once presents were opened and turkey eaten, his good shirt was replaced by a flannel shirt, generally with a small tear somewhere, and he'd be under the hood of one of our cars or bagging the holiday trash.

Our first stop the next day was to show Mom the Marina neighborhood. We climbed the concrete stairs to view the harbor from Sopchoppy's Pub on the top floor of the American Yacht Harbor building. Sopchoppy's wouldn't be serving food and drink for hours, but it's an open-air pub. The bar and several bar tables and stools are covered by a large green canvas awning. A beautiful rustic teal, wrought-iron railing runs along the bar and all the way around the building, past the Caribbean Saloon, a souvenir shop and other businesses on this floor and the one below. After fifteen minutes at the marina, while wondering what to do next, we ran into Pete on his way to B dock to take a borrowed power boat to Tortola. He needed to pick up Brian who'd be flying him to San Juan that afternoon. Pete invited us to ride along. He led the way to a collection of rental boats and jumped in the smallest one. Not exactly first class, and it would be a bouncy ride, but he was an experienced captain and we had no other plans so we accepted the invitation.

Dad leaned against the stern, Mom and I sat on a smooth white bench in front of Pete at the center-mounted helm. It was not a fun ride. The water was choppy and there was nothing for us to hold on to. Mom and I bounced uncomfortably with our hair whipping about stinging our faces. We saw a ferry approaching. It thundered across our path. Pete seriously under-estimated the wake trailing this behemoth because he could not have intended to take the plunge we did. At the moment the bow crossed the edge of the wake and I looked with fright at the drop, Pete called out, "Hold on girls!" The boat plunged over the edge and our seat dropped from beneath us. A split second in the air and then we came down hard on the bench and Mom cried out and crumpled over.

She spent five nights in the hospital with a compression fracture in her spine. When she was discharged we moved from the condo to a beach-side hotel room. She refused to let the pain keep her in bed. Each day Dad set up lounge chairs near the water and she walked carefully down to sit and watch others doing what she came to do, enjoy the water. Toddlers ran from waves and giggled at the sand dissolving under their toes, newlyweds—as common in the Caribbean as seashells—stood waist deep clutching one another and bobbing in the surf; old men and women held hands and stepped carefully over the scattered rocks and shifting sand; and pods of snorkelers explored the reef that spread out from the shoreline.

For a week we studied the beach and its inhabitants: the pink, the white and the brown. Nearly all the women under sixty wore two-piece swimsuits regardless of figure, from skinny flat stomachs to large round ones looking like risen dough ready to be punched down and shaped into loaves. No pre-menopausal midriffs were spared the ultra-violet rays of the sun or the gaze, sometimes admiring, sometimes tortured, of fellow tourists. I wear one-piece swimsuits. My weight is appropriate for my height, but I bear the signs of motherhood, which I am clearly more self-conscious of than most.

We noticed that women with European accents showed no sign of tan lines, and wondered if they thought us puritanical. Deeply tanned middle-age women, with thighs that brought to mind crisp, cooked Thanksgiving turkeys, always seemed to be accompanied by pale, paunchy men.

We observed the loose-fitting swim trunks men wore got shorter as they got older. Teenage boys and twenty-somethings wore long, baggie board-shorts that would have been considered modest in Victorian times; the fathers of those teenagers wore swimsuits that reached just to their knees, and the granddads' swim trunks stopped half way to their knobby, white knees.

One couple stood-out from the rest. They strolled the beach for a few hours one afternoon. We noticed her because of her lovely figure. Nature had been good to her without showing off. Her swimsuit was sexy, but not slutty. We noticed her partner because his swimsuit was slutty. Can men be slutty? His Speedo was smaller than the bottom of her sexy two-piece. He wasn't fat, but love-handles around his middle argued against the likelihood he was an athlete about to go for a swim.

Mom's greatest concern was for Dad to enjoy himself. While she was in the hospital, she insisted he go sight-seeing. He reluctantly left her side twice a day. We visited Coral World, walked past historic sites; sat on the beach with my friends; and snorkeled at Coki Beach. One day Brian caught the ferry from Tortola and took Dad for an aerial tour of the islands. I know Mom was never off his mind. I wonder if he remembers any of the sights.

St. Thomas is the place to be if you want to shop for jewelry, fish for marlin, or enjoy a beach vacation, but we had serious reservations about the care Mom would receive at the Roy Lester Schneider hospital. We need not have been concerned. The medical staff was competent and caring. Mother was treated respectfully and made as comfortable as possible by a friendly, professional nursing staff. Her only complaint was the food service staff's habit of placing her food tray out of reach and scurrying from the room before she could ask them to move it nearer. In her condition, hunger was more desirable than the agonizing pain associated with the movement necessary to retrieve it.

We changed Mom's ticket so she could accompany Dad home. As in her dream, she never waded into the friendly blue ocean. When she left I promised she'd come again in a few months when her back was healed. With a little luck maybe *Take Two* would be back in the water then.

Willie T.

When I left Nanny Cay for my parents' visit, I hoped never to return to the boatyard. Alas, having seen Mom and Dad to their plane, with nowhere else to go, I turned reluctantly toward Tortola to resume life on the hard on *Take Two* where work was in its twelfth week.

People who have half a million dollars to spend on a boat don't live on it full time, and if they don't live nearby they leave it in the care of a part-time skipper who is encouraged to take her out and blow dust off the engines from time to time. This was how I got back to Tortola by way of a stop at the *Willie T.*

Pete was the on-call skipper for a pretty little cabin cruiser whose owners lived Stateside. Pete and Cindy, along with friends, Brent and Lee, were taking the boat to a popular BVI nightspot for the evening. They offered to drop me in Nanny Cay on their way home, around midnight.

Sailboats and powerboats each have advantages. When *Take Two*'s sails were trimmed and there was time to relax, the ride was smooth and restful. Leaning on the side of the cabin or sitting on deck, we scanned the water for dolphins or turtles, lost ourselves in thought or talked. Sometimes we talked about the places we would like to visit, but were too far away. Weekend sailing destinations fell within a very small circle on our Virgin Islands chart, but the circle widened considerably for powerboat users.

We would have been leaning on the side of *Take Two*'s cabin for several hours sailing to the Willie. T., but that afternoon we spent forty minutes bouncing to our destination. If I have to choose, I prefer peacefully skimming the water to thundering across miles of waves in a powerboat shouting, "This is nice," over the roar of engines as you clutch your hat with one hand and maintain a white-knuckle grip on the boat with the other.

The William Thornton is a 100' schooner anchored in The Bight of Norman Island. It's a popular nightspot in the British Virgin Islands about fifteen miles east of St. Thomas. Visitors to the *Willie T.* anchor in the harbor and take a dinghy to the floating dock attached to its hull. If you don't arrive early the dock is crowded, sometimes two-deep, with dinghies. A long line is tossed to the dock and you must fling yourself from one bobbing dinghy to another to reach the dock.

We arrived early and took seats at a picnic table in the belly of the ship. I scanned the menu, saw the price tag of a mahi mahi sandwich and suppressed an inclination to buy my host's meal. The bar was still empty after dinner when I secured a barstool and asked for a ginger ale. I needed to pace my alcohol intake; it was going to be a long evening for someone whose original party clothes included bell-bottom hip-huggers.

The bar eventually filled and the alcohol flowed. I switched to nursing a sea breeze while watching the action from my perch where I had a ringside view of the circus. In the center ring, the bar, troupes of men and women tossed back shot-skis with bravado. A shot-ski is a five-foot long ski with four shot glasses lodged in holes and drunk by four people in unison. It's an effective way to keep the drinking equal. Occasionally, there was confusion as to whether to drink on three, or say three and then drink, but this generally happened later in the evening when the alcohol was best dumped on the floor anyway.

This act sequenced with temporary tattoos being applied at one side of the bar. Men wanted tattoos on their arms and women wanted them on their cleavage; the one exposed area where it was least likely to be noticed. At the other end of the bar a bored-looking bartender set up body shots, hand-cuffing women to a column for boyfriends (pure conjecture on my part) to lick salt from the woman's thigh, drink alcohol from her navel and suck a lime wedge she held in her teeth.

Meanwhile in another ring, a *Willie T.* tradition carried on. Women jumped from the stern like rats leaving a burning ship. For this *Willie T.* rewarded them with a free T-shirt. Strictly applied, to earn a T-shirt jumpers must be naked, but from my coveted position on a barstool I couldn't see whether they were discarding their clothes as well as their dignity. The bartenders took each jumper's word for nudity. To stop pouring and witness would have been costlier than handing over cheap T-shirts; and from the bored expression on the bartenders' faces, it held no allure for them.

This circus had no popcorn vendors, but that isn't to say I wasn't approached by men with something to sell. Being possibly the only woman at the bar old enough to know better than to offer myself as a shot glass, in public anyway, I attracted every man old enough to know he didn't have a chance with the ones who did. It helped pass the time during intermissions and I'd like to respond here with probity I was too polite to show at the time. To that first fellow on the barstool, the small guy in the large tank top with arm holes open to his belt, it wasn't just because I was with friends that I didn't come see the bathtub perfectly suited for bubble baths, on your yacht. To the guy vacationing from Chicago who bragged on himself for forty minutes, thanks for the ginger ale, but you're going to have to wear a nicer shirt if I'm supposed to believe you have eight million dollars to buy an island. And you'll get a lot further with women if you show more interest in her and less in yourself. The one piece of advice I would give to any man who is trying to impress a woman, for whatever reason, is to listen more...a lot more. If you are impressive, she'll figure it out, if you're not and you boast, she'll figure that out sooner. There may be exceptions, but if a woman falls for a man blowing his own horn, he'd better be able to back it up. She'll be expecting a four-star dinner and after dinner drinks in a house she'll fall asleep wishing was hers. Bringing her back to an 800 square foot apartment strikes a pretty sour note and unless she's very naïve or in denial, she won't buy your excuse whatever it is. Finally, John, not very tall, nicely dressed and interested without being pushy; you seemed like a nice guy and I really did hope you would stop by *Take Two* to say hello sometime.

We didn't leave the *Willie T.* until after one o'clock. The skipper decided he was in no condition to operate a half a million dollar boat that didn't belong to him, so the decision was made to sleep it off. There were five of us, one bed, and no extra blankets on the boat. Pete and Cindy climbed into the bed, under a blanket no doubt, Lee passed out in the salon, and Brent dozed outside near the swim-step for easy access to vomiting overboard. I spent half the sleepless night shivering in the frigid air conditioned cabin on a vinyl bench curled in the fetal position under a beach towel, and the second half on a short L-shaped bench outside where the air was warmer, but I'd fall off if I fell asleep.

I have never been on anyone's speed dial for party friends, and a cold, sleepless night notwithstanding, I'm glad I get dragged along from time to time.

Nanny !#%^ Cay

I was back in the boatyard. The explanation of being understaffed was wearing thin as we approach the end of our third month. Most days were frustratingly quiet with workmen appearing for brief periods, if at all. When the work would be completed, it will have amounted to perhaps half the time we languished there. Meanwhile, Nanny Cay Marina—motto: Welcome to Tortola. Put your wallets and jewelry into the bag and wait over there—was charging over $900 a month for a patch of dirt, minimal water, electricity and the use of cold public showers.

The feeling of helplessness Brian and I suffered under took a toll. We wanted desperately to leave that wretched place and the untenable cost of the work and merely taking up space. Also, we needed to get back to St. Thomas where our business lay dormant. And we wanted our son back.

Our friends, Pete and Cindy, sent to us by the benevolent gods who watch over abandoned dogs, lunatics and boat owners, had been housing Seth since Christmas break ended. He slept on their sofa and caught the ferry to school on St. John. It would have cost $200 a week, and involved customs delays for him to ride the ferry from Tortola to school on St. John every day. Seth came to Nanny Cay some Saturdays, but weekends were when he could hang-out with friends. When we called to ask which ferry he would arrive on, he generally offered a series of reasons why he couldn't come. We suggested solutions to the proffered problems until he pulled an insolvable one from his hat or we took pity and he further enjoyed their hospitality.

On top of that, Seth's basketball team also practiced on weekends and the team needed him. They needed all the players. Seth, like virtually all children who moved to the Virgin Islands attended a private school. The public schools were poorly managed institutions that, because of failure to give even the most rudimentary education, had lost their accreditation. We followed news about the re-accreditation efforts in the paper, but saw little progress.

We had two private schools from which to choose, Antilles on St. Thomas and Coral Bay on St. John. Antilles' enrolled 500 students in grades kindergarten through high school. Coral Bay was a young school with only sixty students in grades seven through eleven. Tuition for either school carried a hefty price tag, considerably more than the tuition for my daughter at San Diego State University. We choose Coral Bay on St. John because Cindy's son attended it and, more importantly, Brian felt he could be more involved.

There were drawbacks to attending such a small school; chief in Seth's eyes was the athletic program. He participated in a drive to form the school basketball team that consisted of five boys and one girl. Their average height was 5'8". When the team returned from a severe beating by the Antilles basketball team he complained of two 6' 6" ringers brought over from South Africa. We missed the game because we were on Tortola. I can't imagine the starting ball-toss. The Coral Bay team was without a victory all season, but undefeated in morale and winners of our admiration.

There was no reason to subject Seth to our boatyard stress which manifested in sleeplessness for Brian, and an eye twitch for me, which was funnier in the Pink Panther movies. Brian managed a few hours sleep each night, but seldom enough. During the day he was drowsy and his thinking muddled. Or maybe my thinking was muddled. It was hard to tell with all the chemicals wafting on the air. There we sat twitching and staring into space as the hole in our boat rendered our desperation impotent.

Puck was living on the hard, too, and his presence added another level of hell to the experience. Every morning and evening we walked him along the road between the beach and the boatyard. It was a pleasant time for all. But before we knew what was happening we were infested with ticks. We found ticks on the dog, on the salon cushions, on our clothes and, to my horror, on my pillow. I shrieked hostility to every tick I found and lived in a constant state of alarm and anxiety, insisting hourly that Brian examine my scalp. Initially, we fought back with a tick collar, but the creatures chuckled at this, and chest-bumped each new tick that hopped aboard. We needed to take more drastic measures.

Brian found a bottle of the most lethal tick shampoo made then looked for a place to perform the exorcism. Dogs were not allowed in the marina showers and we had no large tubs. Clearly we had to break the rules. We waited until late at night when businesses were closed and other live-aboards had showered and returned to their vermin-free yachts. I grabbed a bucket and a pair of rubber gloves from under the sink, Brian tucked towels under his arm and called an unsuspecting Puck. Flipping a coin we chose the men's shower. The moment we opened the shampoo bottle our eyes began tearing. We poured a measure of it into the bucket and I massaged it into Puck's thick coat, wishing desperately to be able to hold my nose. The smell was over-powering in the enclosed space. Our eyes stung and we took our breath in gulps. Brian flinched and protested every time the toxic solution splashed his bare legs as he tried to coax a despairing and futilely repentant Puck off his back. Puck smelled of tick shampoo for days, but we won the battle and rid ourselves of ticks.

The tick bath was reminiscent of an episode on the ranch. One evening Brian and I were watching television when we noticed the smell of skunk. Unthinking, Brian opened the front door and skunk odor burst into the house like a vaporous SWAT team. Puck sat on the doormat looking up at him pitiably.

I called the vet to inquire if tomato juice was really the solution for this situation, and was told to bathe Puck in a mixture of peroxide, baking soda and dish soap. I collected the ingredients and called Brian and Seth to help.

"I don't know what to do," Brian claimed.

"Yeah, and I got a degree in dog bathing. Come on, you're helping."

We shoved the dog into the shower stall in the shop bathroom, pouring buckets of the mixture over him. He darted out of the shower and shook before we could dry him with towels, so we used them on ourselves. Puck slept in the laundry room that night instead of at the foot of Seth's bed.

Nanny Cay reminded us of California in other ways as well. Rolling blackouts, like the ones in California in 2001 and 2002 that caused much fuss and hand-wringing from the pampered population were common on Tortola where power outages were an accepted part of most days. Whether they lasted a few minutes or several hours, hardly a word was said as everyone went about their routine without benefit of fans, radios, office equipment or power tools.

~~~~

Twelve weeks we'd been fugging (it's a word) around on *Take Two*, waiting to get back in the water. We were nearing the end of our stay and I took inventory of my time. My activities had been diverse in both recreational value and productivity.

I tried new recipes from a cookbook given to us by friends as a thank you for a sunset sail. On the hard I couldn't use the oven and was limited to one burner at a time on the stove top, so I stuck with easy recipes. One of the easiest was chocolate rum mousse. This perfect island dessert called for only six ingredients: rum, semi-sweet chocolate, cream, eggs, sugar and vanilla. But this was Nanny #$%^ Cay and even six ingredients was a challenge. The first time I set my mind and taste-buds on chocolate rum mousse my package of chocolate chips was too small. I was three ounces short. I'm not one of those cooks who can ad-lib in the kitchen. Cooking came so naturally to my mother she assumed I, too, would be able to flip the refrigerator upside down and turn what fell out into a mouthwatering meal. Down the ladder and off to the Marina Market. Apparently, however, baking was not high on the itinerary of the charter customers who made up most of its traffic. I stood sulking over the cost of a cab ride into town when my eyes fell on a display of food found in every store from Austria to Zimbabwe: candy bars. What is a Three Musketeers bar anyway but stiff mousse. I brought it back to the boat, cut it into little pieces, and stuffed the wrapper in the trash. I have no ego as a cook, so I wasn't afraid to share the improvised dessert with visitors. Regardless, no one living on the hard is going to examine any small pleasure too closely.

Many afternoons I fled the stifling heat of *Take Two* for a dip in the marina pool and to lie in the sun. As a result, for the first time since I was a child of twelve, I had a discernable tan—even without holding my arm next to the arm of an eighty-year-old shut-in. I am of Norwegian and Swedish descent; a tan Scandinavian is a rare thing.

In my teens and twenties I tried to tan. I spent long hot hours lying on plastic chairs in a pool of sweat, looking at my watch every twenty seconds to see if an hour had passed. My sister and I basted ourselves with every kind of tanning aide including baby oil with iodine. We must have read about the baby oil solution in the magazine where we also learned to spray diluted lemon juice on our mousey brown hair to lighten it in the sun. The result was sticky brown hair, slippery white bodies, and pupils the size of decimal points. Sometimes we'd get burned, but even after a sunburn the pigment-challenged bodies in my family stubbornly return to their natural shade of ice-flow white.

I've since learned about the dangers of sun exposure and usually hide under a hat and sunscreen, but I didn't plan to stay in the Caribbean long, so I rationalized taking advantage that one time would be all right. The tan looked good on me. Nevertheless, I would no more make an annual practice of getting a tan than I would take up smoking asbestos cigarettes.

Not all my time was devoted to self-indulgent, superficial goals. The mood to accomplish something lasting seized me occasionally. When this happened I dug through a crate of wood scraps we found on *Take Two* until inspiration spoke. Once it did and I walked into Yacht Restoration with an armload of scrap mahogany. I stammered something about the wood speaking to me, and the handsome Miles squeaked, "Cut me, cut me."

Miles was the cabinet expert at Yacht Restoration. He was over six foot tall, tan with wavy brown hair. When I passed the shop and found him sanding or planing a board I'd pull up a stool and we'd talk about wood, boats or life in the islands. Miles encouraged my woodworking interest and invited me to see his cabinetry work on Rock Me, a spectacular 94' sloop with acres of mahogany and teak throughout. Besides the finest woodwork I've seen on a boat, the galley was roomy and well-equipped. Each of five spacious cabins had state of the art flat-screen televisions with its own satellite receiver.

Miles helped cut my scrap to lengths which I assembled into a little counter-top crate we used for easy access to our booze. Easy access to alcohol is as necessary to life on the hard as a good fan and shower shoes.

When the wood didn't speak to me I would find a piece that needed sanding. *Take Two* sported a minimum of bright-work, but sadly, what she did possess was anything but bright. It was dry, weathered and badly split in places. I couldn't help where it was split, but a vigorous sanding improved other pieces considerably.

One morning while sanding on the foredeck, I overheard three boatyard workers engaged in a friendly disagreement over scripture. I was sitting astride a piece of teak that ran between the bow trampolines. They were below me mixing paint in the shade of a building. All three were black men, the youngest, Ron was in his twenties. He had short hair and a muscular build. The oldest I guessed to be in his fifties. The third was a little older than Ron, and not as muscular. They disagreed as to whether someone had to work to get into Heaven. The older man held a Bible open to a passage. He read the verse saying faith without works is dead. Ron, sitting on a paint can near the port bow, didn't have a bible, but he believed the way to salvation was through faith in Jesus. I spoke in support of Ron's position quoting a verse from "Ephesians," "By grace are ye saved through faith." They glanced up at me, but didn't acknowledge my comment. I turned my attention back to sanding. A few minutes later, two of them left and Ron began singing a hymn I knew from my Baptist upbringing. His voice was deep and rich. He faltered over the second verse, and once again, I chimed in. He smiled up at me, and together we sang "Where He Leads Me I Will Follow." The next day I passed Ron in the boatyard and said, "You have a beautiful voice. I enjoy listening to you sing."

Ron grinned broadly and lifting his chin toward the sky he sang as he walked away, "I love to sing. Thank you for the compliment."

No sane person lives in dry dock if they can avoid it. Only those who live exclusively on their boats and can't afford a hotel would be willing to live at the top of a ladder and tolerate the menace of public toilets, dirt, noise and all the rest. People usually came and went quickly. A family with four small children lived next to us in the boatyard for what was surely a very long week. Rick flew down from Miami once a month to live and work on his boat, staying only a week or two at a time. Our three-month stay on the hard seemed interminable and we pitied ourselves, except when we thought about Tom and Leslie.

Tom worked at Yacht Restoration during the day and on their own yacht evenings and weekends. Their cutter, *Kobbe*, was on blocks behind the shop. A ladder leaned steeply against its side reaching to the deck high above the ground like a viewing platform. Leslie, Tom's long-suffering wife, lived on the hard with him. We saw their boat transformed by a new coat of Kelly green paint and watched the positioning of a tall, solid wood mast, until finally, after they'd been living on the hard for a year, we witnessed Tom and Leslie's return to the water.

Nanny Cay was unquestionably an experience I won't forget. And, I can't imagine ever again taking simple luxuries for granted. Merely staying in touch and conducting routine business was a challenge. The phone company charged two dollars a minute to call the States and one dollar a minute to call St. Thomas fourteen miles away. They captured our cell phone signal to add a surcharge of $3.50 for each minute. We depended on Seth to bring the mail each weekend, but he didn't always remember, and he didn't always come. We had only intermittent Internet access. And while I'm complaining, I missed having my own bathroom, doing my own laundry, and showering barefoot; I missed my oven, and I definitely missed access to my car and all the freedom and convenience built into it. Put simply, if I ever got out I was not going to miss Nanny Cay.

Ten Seconds to Papa Up and Gun

When we arrived at the boatyard before Christmas, it didn't occur to us to mention our obligation as committee boat for the Rolex Regatta. But, by March first we were lobbing daily reminders to the staff of Yacht Restoration who lobbed back promises that we'd be back in the water in time. We passed these assurances on to the nervous race committee, which was considering looking for another boat. The regatta was scheduled to begin Friday, March twenty-ninth at the St. Thomas Yacht Club. The race committee wanted us anchored offshore of the club in Cowpet Bay on Tuesday. As the days of March progressed, the pace of work on *Take Two* picked up. We tried not to dwell on the problems we'd face if any new conditions were diagnosed.

Yacht Restoration kept their promise with no time to spare. Painters were kneeling on the deck applying a final coat when the travel-lift lowered our home back into the water Tuesday before the race. She floated, still in the straps of the travel-lift, while the staff scurried throughout checking compartments for leaks. They pronounced her water-tight and we waited anxiously for the painters to finish so we could hoist sail for St. Thomas.

When we arrived in Nanny Cay thirteen weeks earlier, *Take Two* was Brian's yacht. When we left it was ours. It had been necessary to use some of my money to pay for repairs. A lot, in fact. This put a strain on our marriage that had been temporarily removed when we divided the profit from the ranch. For a few months we didn't have to agree on what was affordable or necessary. There were no arguments when Brian wanted to buy parts or contract for service I thought could be postponed, or even just grab fast food when there were groceries in the fridge. We were now living off my share and when it was gone we would have nothing left from the sale of the ranch but a boat, which Brian admitted was a luxury, not an investment, and equipment in a start-up company that had yet to prove its viability.

Many arguments were ahead, but just then we were happy to be on the water and headed back to Red Hook. We trimmed the sails and settled down with smiles as we watched Tortola's West End slip behind us. Then Lovengo Cay, the eastern most of a string of small cays between the U.S. and British islands, appeared ahead. Thirty minutes out it occurred to us that this was the first time we'd ever sailed alone. The first thought to cross my mind was to sunbathe nude. This wasn't Brian's first thought . . . so sunbathing came second. A ferry passed a hundred yards to starboard as we enjoyed our private sail. I felt self-conscience for a moment, then decided if anyone preferred watching us to watching the surrounding islands and sea then so be it. They weren't close enough for video, so what the hell.

Returning from Nanny Cay, friends hailed *Take Two* from dockside boats and hurried to catch lines and welcome us back to Red Hook. We made it into the water just in time for the regatta and *Take Two* was worthy of her role as committee boat. Her topsides shimmered with a new mirror-like coat of marine blue paint, and her name was re-appliquéd in a more graceful serif lettering than the previous stencil-style block font. She also sported a new blue canvas lazy-jack to hide and protect the main sail when lowered.

Take Two was beautiful, but she was a mess. We had one day to wash the boatyard grime from her deck and sort through the trash, spare parts and tools that cluttered the cockpit and littered the upholstered settee in the salon. The race committee representative sighed relief that *Take Two* was back and asked us to have her in Cowpet Bay seven a.m. on Thursday.

Wednesday morning we were introduced to Dan in town from Chicago to volunteer on a marker boat. He needed a place to stay close to the regatta action and we were happy to offer our guest cabin. Dan tossed his bag onto the bunk and immediately set to work helping get *Take Two* cleaned up.

Before the race, I had no idea what a race committee did, but I woke the morning of the first day ready for a good time. I ignored the echo of voices from recent months asking, "How did you get roped into that?" The concept, as I understood it, seemed simple enough: Clean up the boat then stay handy and out of the way at the same time. A breeze blew through the salon and a quick look at the sky showed only a few puffy white spectator clouds. My friend Alicia arrived early to learn with us what it meant to host a race committee. We learned they are an amazing coterie that pulls off the feat of coordinating dozens of boats under sail to gather simultaneously at a starting line, then records often crowded finishes with indisputable accuracy.

We motored to Cowpet Bay and shortly after hooking a mooring ball we heard a dingy approach. It brought large shopping bags of sandwiches, cans of soda and enough bottled water to float a fleet. Two more visits by the dinghy and the race committee was on board. *Take Two* was as crowded as we had ever seen her.

With an eye on the sky and a finger to the wind, the Principal Race Officer (PRO) immediately set to work with Brian examining charts and discussing where to position *Take Two* for the day's races. With a quick motion, the flag bearer unrolled a long blue bundle onto the deck and selected flags for the day; the gunner, a big man with a rough black beard, set up a toy-size red cannon near the starboard stern; and the IT guy plugged his laptop into power at the chart table. People were laying flag poles on the deck, attaching a white board to the boom, and placing directors chairs for the judges. I tried to look busy, but there is only so much activity involved in putting sodas in a cooler. After fetching tape for the white board, a stapler for a judge and more standing around, I decided to get out of everyone's way and enjoy the event. I sat with my legs hanging over the side of *Take Two*, enthralled by the colorful commotion.

Nearly a hundred sailboats circled *Take Two* like Native Americans in their grandest head-dresses and war paint. The race committee hastily took down boat numbers while I took pictures. A few times I jerked my toes to safety as a clutch of boats crowded past close enough to pass me an empty. In truth, I saw no alcohol drinking during the race day. Night was a different matter, everyone drank like they were putting out a fire, but they still managed to be back for Day Two.

Our daughter, Rose, and her roommate, Jamie, were also on board for Day Two. They arrived Friday night for spring break ready to share the experience her teenage brother simply rolled his eyes at.

Seth behaved like a typical bored teenager all weekend. Even when the deck of *Take Two* erupted in cheers over the flying finish of a beach cat soaring past the yellow finish marker, its crew stretching far over the edge as one hull flew above the water, Seth yawned and slouched onto the settee.

Probably the best part of co-parenting is having someone to help you over the nagging late-night fear that your son will forever be a surly, torpid, sport-drink-guzzling off-spring, spilling Cheetos on the couch, chuckling along with Beavis and Butthead, even as his beard grows in and his hairline recedes. Brian and I assured one another that someday soon, Seth would look back from law school regretting his indifferent attitude toward this rare opportunity.

The organization that goes into each race is complex and critically timed. Course information must be displayed on a white board; a sequence of flags are raised and lowered and a horn or gun signals milestones in the sequence. Everything is strictly timed to the second. While dozens of boats bob and sway on the water, tacking and jockeying for position, countdown is playing out on the deck of the committee boat.

The timer counts the seconds and issues orders to the flag raiser, gun shooter, and (with love to Dr. Seuss) horn honker. Starting several minutes before a race, the timer, with the mental discipline of a monk, tunes out all the activity on the deck and water around her and the sequence begins . . . "One minute to papa up and horn . . . thirty seconds to papa up and horn . . . ten seconds to papa up and horn . . . nine . . . eight . . ." Colorful flags go up on cue, remain for an exact number of minutes and are soon replaced with a flag conveying the next piece of information. Flags and horns tell the sailors which class is racing and how many minutes to the starting gun.

Coordination was just as critical for finishes. After a brief break, the committee moved chairs to the starboard hull to prepare, as well as anyone could, for what was to come. The PRO selected a line of site between himself and the finish-line marker buoy; one volunteer grabbed a clipboard, another a stop-watch, and another the horn which he would blow when the first of a racing class crossed the finish line. I was recruited to help keep track of which classes had already crossed.

It's elementary to distinguish a yacht sailing with a spinnaker (a huge roundish, often colorful, sail that billows ahead of the bow) from one sailing a main and jib, but another thing altogether to know a racing yacht from a cruising yacht. Fortunately for me, each class flew a different colored flag. Nine classes raced. They ranged from lightweight little Beach Cats to the over 50' class, and included Spinnaker Racing, Spinnaker Racing/Cruising, Non-spinnaker Racing, and something known as J 24.

I would hate to have to choose my favorite class of yacht. The Beach Cats are the sport cars of sailboats, small, fast and highly maneuverable with two quick-moving crew members. The beach cat starts were the most fun.

Beach cats are sporty, but the monohulls are sexy. It's a beautiful thing when the ocean reflects in the polished hull of a sailboat heeling close to the water; jib and main fat with the wind, moving with confidence and the elegance of a swan. The spinnaker classes painted the prettiest horizon. My camera clicked repeatedly as we watched a broken rainbow of colors scattered on the water racing toward us. The rainbow grew larger and more vivid until they flew past *Take Two* in a prismatic explosion of color and cheering voices.

Team work is involved on every boat, but none more than the over 50' class where a dozen men (and occasionally a woman) on each of the two big boats entered responded to the feel of the vessel and orders from the captain.

Many finishes were exciting. Everyone got involved when a crowd of tightly clustered yachts approached. The PRO called out one yacht identification number after another, the timer called out the time and the information was scribbled onto forms. Anyone without a job backed up or doubled-checked the work of someone else. Once the rush passed, everyone took a breath and notes were compared to ensure accuracy.

Each of the three race days proceeded differently. Day two brought stiffer breezes and rain, and the PRO called for a single race over a long course. Milder weather returned Sunday and the PRO squeezed in three races before reluctantly admitting it was time to call it a day.

Even though I normally don't get it when it comes to sailing, then I did. I recognized how fine a thing traveling across open water propelled by nothing but the wind; to make a sport of a skill that is so much more than sport. A skill that can carry a man around the world the way men have been traveling for thousands of years. To know the wind and just how to catch it, to know your vessel, what she's capable of and how to bring out the best in her while exercising the best in yourself. That is competition at its finest.

Saturday night, after the second day of races, I stepped into a cocktail dress for the first time since arriving in the Caribbean. Brian and I left Seth and the girls enjoying themselves under the Regatta Village Tent at the yacht club. Seth hit the buffet line while Rose and Jamie got in line at the Cruzan Rum booth for their first buckets of voodoo juice—a blend of four tropical flavored rums, cranberry juice, orange juice, and pineapple juice topped with a floater of dark rum and served in a plastic bucket.

Brian and I had been invited to an exclusive dinner party hosted by the local Rolex distributors. The dinner was a magical evening at a private estate on Hassel Island, a 135 acre island in Charlotte Amalie Harbor. We felt hosted by royalty when two handsome brothers greeted us at the Danish Wharf and invited us to make ourselves at home on their expansive and elegant patio. The entire evening passed as all dinner parties should: with tireless conversation, excellent and exotic food, and perfectly suited music lingering in the background. There were no self-conscious moments standing outside a circle, no chatting up the bartenders to pass the time or pretending fascination with potted plants. All evening we were engaged with interesting men and women, and thus convinced we too must be interesting.

One more thing, and though I must sound like a hick saying this, the bathroom was amazing. It was so spacious I had to look for the toilet. I found it around the corner from the basin stand on a long wall past a shower stall large enough for a horseshoe pitch. It felt strange sitting there in a sparsely furnished room the size of my living room back home. I thought someone might walk in on me. On the boat, indeed in several of the bathrooms I've called mine, this was not a problem. To prevent unwanted company, I merely stuck out my foot to keep the door from opening.

The final race day ended with an award ceremony filled with much cheering and pride all around. They didn't award a pair of Rolexes to us for providing the committee boat—we didn't think they would, but you never know. Nevertheless, we hoped to get roped into it again next year.

Latitude Lassitude

We were told it was a wet spring for the Virgin Islands. Temperatures didn't waiver much from the year-'round highs in the eighties, but our daughter's spring break visit was notable for sogginess. Aside from sleeping off hangovers, there wasn't a lot for college girls to do on rainy days. Once they'd spent an hour or two in Coral World, they'd hit the highlights of indoor daytime activities.

After a soggy Monday spent watching *Weekend at Bernie's* on DVD, we jumped at a break in the clouds and headed to nearby Coki Beach. We splashed in unusually rough surf for a short time until the clouds returned and soon we were back on *Take Two* watching *Weekend at Bernie's II*.

We spent the next afternoon in downtown Charlotte Amalie, but we weren't interested in jewelry, so after darting through the rain from one T-shirt shop to another, we dripped into the Hard Rock Café for lunch. We drank in honor of my sister's birthday, then it was back to the boat to play a board game and grouse about the rain.

Our slip on American Yacht Harbor was stumbling distance from seven or eight bars, so the girls' nighttime activities proceeded unimpeded by the weather. Duffy's Love Shack in the Red Hook Plaza parking lot was the only bar affected by the relentless rain. At Duffy's only the kitchen, bar, and space for dancing were under cover. Tables were dragged out into the parking lot each afternoon when they opened for business. Gathered around a table one night with two or three friends and eight or nine strangers, someone commented that

Duffy's reminded her of high school drinking sitting on cars in a Dairy Queen parking lot. We all agreed.

I'm told that when Duffy's collects tables and shuts down the shark and fog machine around two a.m., everyone heads over to the East End Café which converts from the finest restaurant on the east end into the hottest late-night spot. Another option is the Warehouse, just down the street. It's popular for its pool tables and two-dollar pour your own drinks. The pour your own drink concept has been outlawed in California, but when it comes to drinking, the Virgin Islands are a galaxy far, far away. Customers are allowed to carry open cups or bottles of beer with them when leaving and it's believable that the average sixteen-year-old would not be carded or challenged in any way upon sidling up to a barstool and ordering a cold one.

While late night partying at the East End Café, the girls met friends of the owner of *FanSea Pants*, a beautiful cabin cruiser also slipped on D dock. They were invited to be guests for a cruise the next day, weather permitting. The girls rose mid-morning to sunny skies, and immediately set to the task of making deck jewelry of themselves.

While they showered, shampooed, shaved and brushed the lashes of flirtatiously feminine eyes, I sat in the companionway lecturing them on safety at sea and the dangers of boating with strangers. I elicited promises not to drink before getting into the water, and to trust their instincts if anything appeared unsafe. I told them every boating accident story I could remember and made up details of some I forgot. I offered potentially fatal scenarios of drinking and swimming. When they still didn't look terrified, or even aware of my presence, I said, "You girls look very pretty. You would be very valuable to a white slave trader."

"What?" Rose challenged.

"I heard a segment on NPR about the white slave trade."

"Can I take this yellow towel?"

"Sure."

She said, "Thanks," and left me believing she was thanking me for the advice as well as the towel. It's possible.

Anyone who can turn a key can drive a boat. If you can write a check for a powerful boat you can speed through the water as carelessly as stupidity or testosterone persuades. It requires no license, no training or permission of any kind. There are boating safety courses, but in spite of the potential for injury—even death—they've only recently been mandated in the Virgin Islands, and then only for minors.

Twice in the year we lived on D dock Brian helped rescue a sinking boat. The first time was the result of a common oversight, a dock line fell into the water and tangled in a propeller. When it happened, the boat was being piloted not by the owner, or the part-time skipper, but the skipper's wife, Cindy. When I learned the boat had run into rocks and was taking on water before Cindy saved it from sinking by beaching it, I had mixed feelings. My first reaction was how dreadful it would be to inform the owners who lived Stateside that their boat had been seriously damaged while the skipper's wife was taking her girlfriends out for a day on the water. My second thought was, why hadn't Cindy invited me along?

Just two weeks later, Brian and I were lying in bed late in the evening when we heard insistent knocking on our hull. Our neighbor on the dock, Phil, an entrepreneur with a small fishing boat, was desperate. His boat had struck coral and was taking on water. He and Brian hurried back in Phil's dinghy to where the boat was slowly sinking just off shore. They climbed aboard and beached it in time to save it.

The girls sat on the deck of *Take Two* waiting for the guy who invited them along on *FanSea Pants* to show up. He never did, but just prior to casting off, Tony, another new bar buddy, saw Rose and Jamie tanning on *Take Two* and called to them to come along. The girls grabbed their totes and I got one quick photo before they sped away for a day of sunning, swimming and daiquiris.

They returned safe, happy, tan and bubbling anecdotes of their day aboard a beautiful boat. Rose kept in touch and saw

Tony and Bill, the owner of *FanSea Pants*, again when she returned to the island after graduating. Such is the way of St. Thomas. Friends are made quickly over memories that last forever.

Rose and Jamie's last day on island dawned soggy again. Final days of vacations are not to be spent watching movies, so we found our raincoats and climbed into the Jeep looking for entertainment. We stopped for a photo-op at Drake's Seat, a view point on Route 40 on the north side. The guidebooks say the red bench is where Sir Francis Drake, the English-sanctioned pirate who plundered Spanish ships in the 1500s, sat to admire his armada and watch for the enemy. On a clear day the down island view from Drake's seat is magnificent and serene, but even with clouds and low visibility it was worth the stop.

Windshield wipers slapping away, we followed small signs pointing up narrow roads to The Mountaintop. We knew of the spot from a local television program that promoted St. Thomas attractions. Surprisingly, a white woman was the spokesperson for this program. She had walnut-colored hair and wore tropical prints. Speaking in a syrupy, soporific stage voice she made sweeping show-room gestures as she pointed to views and attractions. The Mountaintop is located on 1500-foot-high Crown Mountain, the highest point in the Virgin Islands. The roads were slippery, steep, narrow and rutted. Our traction faltered once or twice on hairpin corners. I was glad Brian was driving.

Rain had washed clean the thick green foliage lining the road. It was like driving through a soft, jade tunnel lit occasionally by light wafting through the canopy of palm trees. Royal palm leaves the size of elephant ears and platter-size leaves of the heartleaf anthuriums swayed overhead. Love vines climbed the trunks of palm and tamarind trees and mingled with the elite leaves that had a view of the sky and looked down on the thick undergrowth.

We arrived at the Mountain Top to find only a few cars in the parking lot. We didn't see an obvious entrance, so the five of us darted in different directions. We all found a way inside where we pushed off wet hoods and shook open raincoats. Clearly, the tourist channel over-stated the fun to be had. It was simply an over-rated shopping venue with a bar and twenty-five cent telescopes anchored on the deck. We fingered a few T-shirts and postcards, then settled into the bar and ordered their specialty, banana daiquiris.

We tried to liven things by engaging the bartender in conversation. He would have none of it. He refused to smile at our jokes, answered our questions with a minimum of syllables and effort, and otherwise mutely prepared and served our daiquiris.

Having emptied our glasses, thus exhausting the entertainment options, we once again browsed the predictable merchandise on the way out. We left with yet more shot glasses.

The next morning the girls packed their clothes and souvenirs into duffel bags and we drove them to the airport under sunny skies.

Carnival

April is carnival month on St. Thomas and festivities abound. Sewing machines and glue guns across the island work overtime on costumes, decorations and floats for the parade of events that winds through the month from beginning to end.

I followed events through the local paper. The month began with pageantry. The couple that won the Carnival Prince and Princess competition was a seven-year-old boy and eight-year-old girl. They also won the award for Most Cooperative and the Talent Award for his ability to play bongos while she "…maneuvered a low limbo stick." I wasn't there so I can't comment on the judges' choice of bongos and limbo over a fire-twirling psychic, a Sponge Bob Squarepants act, calypso dancers, or one couple both of whom played instruments and sang.

There was also an article on the selection of the Carnival Queen. Six seventeen- and eighteen-year-old contestants demonstrated their talent and competed in swimwear, evening wear and cultural wear. I regretted not attending this event when I read in the *Daily News* that in the cultural wear competition the winner, "…carried on her back an enormous replica of an historic cookhouse." The only photo accompanying the article was of the winner playing the saxophone. The *Virgin Island Daily News* is an excellent paper, but if you ask me, the photo editor missed an opportunity.

The Queen won a $3500 scholarship and the honor of representing the American Virgin Islands in the Miss World

Competition. I wondered if she was going to take the cookhouse.

I experienced the Cultural Food Fair first-hand. It was held in Emancipation Garden instead of the traditional site at the Market Square Pavilion because less than two weeks earlier a Mack truck destroyed the Pavilion turning the site of the former slave market into a pile of rubble now surrounded by chain link fencing. I hoped they would rebuild it to accommodate the farmers' market vendors as it had for nearly a hundred years.

The air at Emancipation Garden was filled with the aroma of callaloo. Dozens of vendors offered their version of the soup made famous in Herman Wouk's book *Don't Stop the Carnival* and the Jimmy Buffett musical of the same name. It is named for a leafy green plant called callaloo, but most of the vendors used spinach as their main ingredient. I peered into pots and read hand-lettered signs. The broth was greenish brown, greener in some, browner in others, none looked very tempting. Some recipes included chicken, most were vegetarian. I laid down two dollars at a booth that included a piece of bread and took my Styrofoam cup out of the way of foot traffic to people-watch while blowing on it. The women selling the callaloo, and other supposed island food, wore colorful skirts and scarves tied around their heads. They may have been in costume, but I'd seen the style on the street as well. After eating the callaloo, which tasted the way you'd expect vegetable broth, greens, onions and a minimum of spices to taste, there wasn't much to do. I looked for something to spend money on, but found nothing tempting.

The island rocked with music all month. There were beer-sponsored calypso events, a steel band jamboree and school bands playing at all the parades. Bands also played for the pre-teen tramp and senior tramp (these are events not titles), and of course, *j'ouvert.*

J'ouvert is promoted as a multi-cultural pre-dawn event that attracts people from all walks of life to dance in the street behind live bands. That's not entirely true. I was told that nothing happened before seven or eight at the earliest. This came from a friend who, the year before, after a night of partying, rose at five a.m.. to find the streets empty of all but a scattering of red-eyed people.

At seven-thirty, I met friends parked near the cemetery at the west end of town and we joined the throng of people heading east on Veteran's Blvd.

I read somewhere that white people in the Virgin Islands make up about 15% of the population. That may be true of people living on St. Thomas, but it wasn't true of the population of *j'ouvert*. We fell in with a sea of mostly young, all black, men and women surging down the street. It was easy to keep track of one another, we had the only natural blonds and redhead in the crowd.

The final misrepresentation of *j'ouvert* was the music. Some trucks carried musicians playing live music, but mostly canned music blasted from giant speakers attached to stereos. This was a disappointment to us, but the crowd didn't seem to mind, it was festive and well-behaved. The good manners may have been, in part, a reaction to the heavy police presence.

I swayed along, letting my shoulders dance to the music, while some partiers rocked with their entire bodies, bending snapping fingers to the ground then raising arms high overhead waving to the sky. We accepted free bottled water and juice handed down from a truck, and tramped along for an hour enjoying the energy of the crowd and being a part of something unique in our experience.

The climax of the month's activities was the adult parade, with more than fifty bands, majorette and dance troupes, mocko jumbies—best described as clowns on stilts—and all manner of elected royalty riding in convertibles and on floats. Several troupes had more than a hundred members. It was a grand parade even by the standards of a much larger population. Brian found a parking space one block from Main Street and we hurried to find a patch of sidewalk shaded from the blistering sun. We stood near the beginning of the procession that moved in fits and starts while participants perspired in the heat. A squad of baton twirlers in blue and gold lamé uniforms and, heaven help them, pantyhose, waited with bored expressions for the convertibles ahead to move. We saw those same bored expressions on faces throughout the parade. Twirlers, dancers and musicians ambled down Main Street as though under court order. I took dozens of photos and captured very few smiles. The mocko jumbies appeared to be having the best time. They lurched overhead waving gaily and shaking hands with the crowd, reaching down from high stilts draped in yards of vivid patchwork fabric and fluttering ribbons. The expert mocko jumbies danced and bounced in time to music, but even the novices moved with confidence.

Royalty smiled and waved gloved hands from rides swathed in miles of long metallic fringe. There were princes and princesses, a Festival Queen, Miss French Heritage and a dozen others whose titles I have forgotten. Some had parasols the others were surely melting beneath their silk and satin.

Some costumes were fully as elaborate and nearly as large as the floats. One ambitious young man with wide red cuffs on sleeveless muscular arms and a headdress painted in great red flames, shouldered a magnificent goldfish costume with gossamer fins spanning six feet across, and an orange body waving fluidly behind. Other costumes appeared to be merely fanciful creations of gauzy fabric festooned with feathers, sequins, rhinestones and glitter.

Music cascaded from double-decker buses rambling the parade route carrying steel drum bands. Decorated band members wore billowing sleeves of sheer rainbow-colored ruffles or shirts fringed in red and gold. Bus canopies matched band member uniforms and displayed slogans on banners draped over the sides encouraging hard work and achievement.

Carnival is a great time to visit St. Thomas. There are events all through April and into May. And, many resorts and charter boat operators discount prices during this shoulder season that follows the winter peak.

St. Thomas is a great place to visit, but I'm not sure it's the right place to live with children. Kids don't appreciate the opportunities of living on a tropical island. We hoped Seth would take an interest in learning to sail, but like most teenage boys he lusted after jet-skis and powerboats. It wasn't until years later, when his older brother and sister moved to St. Thomas all three got their SCUBA certification and dove the wreck of the R. M. S. Rhone, a popular dive site in the British Virgin Islands.

The expatriate population was predominately young and yet to enjoy the rewards of parenting, or they were middle-aged and rediscovering an empty nest. The younger generation was generally content living in small, sparsely-furnished apartments used only to change clothes or sleep. All their spare time and money being spent on partying, which on St. Thomas can be done even on a budget. Rum drinks were cheap and an effective means to inebriation, if that's your goal.

The Cruzan Rum Distillery on St. Croix is what's left of a thriving sugar-based economy, rum is made primarily from sugar cane. Before slavery was abolished, sugar cane plantations flourished in the Virgin Islands. At one time there were twenty-five on St. John alone. Ruins of Danish colonial sugar mills still dot the islands. In April I visited the ruins of the Catherineberg Sugar Mill off of route 10 on St. John. The narrow, deeply rutted road led past the mill into the National Park. All that was left of the Catherineberg mill was a thirty-foot-high, round stone building tapering slightly from the ground up, with a stone ramp that climbed to an opening ten feet above the ground. From inside through thick arched openings, I took photos of foliage and curving trunks of forest trees that grew close to the building. Outside I peered into small dark dens through low entrances around the base. I was alone and would have lingered longer running my hands over the stones and imagining the life and times of an eighteenth century sugar mill, but mosquitoes drove me back to my car and on my way.

The high cost of groceries balanced out any savings on rum . . . for most of us. Homeowners insurance was also high, extraordinarily high, but car insurance was low. We were delighted when the insurance bill for our Jeep came in at a third what we would have paid in California. I suppose it's harder to total a car when there are no freeways. Nevertheless, it amazed me that the combination of partying and winding narrow roads didn't result in more accidents. And, housing prices were lower than in California, but not so much as to be irresistible.

May Gray

With the regatta and Rose's visit behind us, there was plenty of work to do. It was good to be back in business. I wrote web content, collaborated with our web designer and tested his work. We drafted contracts, met with lawyers and owners of host sites. Brian installed and tested equipment and our partner wrote and debugged software. Soon we would be signing up customers for our wireless internet access service.

We had the life we wanted: satisfying work and time to enjoy weekends in our tropical island home. After spending three dreary months in dry dock, we wanted to sail. Sailboats are far too expensive to own and inconvenient to live on if you aren't going to sail them. There were still countless coves and bays we hadn't visited. I'd heard the snorkeling was good at Waterlemon Bay and Cinnamon Bay on St. John's north side and at Flanagan Island just off the east coast; I wanted to see if the White Cliffs on the south side of St. John really were white.

We hadn't even begun to explore all the sailing destinations around St. Thomas. Buck Island Cove was a popular location for snorkeling and diving because of two shallow wrecks. This was the place to see a ship wreck for someone who didn't want to dive.

Snorkeling I love, but I have never wanted to SCUBA dive. I blame this on the television show *Sea Hunt*. I was too young and impressionable to handle Lloyd Bridges as Mike Nelson being ruthlessly attacked underwater week after week. It didn't matter to me whether he was brave, careless or just unlucky. Each week, deep beneath the surface of the ocean, someone or something managed to cut his air hose or otherwise sabotage his air supply. It was terrifying. His companion, either a beautiful treasure hunter or scientist, was always hysterical and had to be slapped silly so they could buddy breathe, leaving yet another set of Mike's tanks sinking to the ocean floor.

I was too young to appreciate the environmental message Bridges tried to convey. All I took away from *Sea Hunt*, other than the closing speech about three-fifths of the Earth's surface being covered by water, was that the ocean was an alarmingly dangerous place where, unless you were with Mike Nelson, you'd quickly be done in by unscrupulous villains, sharks, or something with the nightmarish name of "the bends."

Twenty-five years after the last *Sea Hunt* episode was aired, I set aside my fears to go on a dive . . . sort of. It was on the Caribbean cruise with my mother and sister. I signed up for a snorkeling trip and got talked into upgrading to a SCUBA dive. My sister was sleeping off a margarita hang-over and my mother was shopping, so I stood companionless in a circle of instructors and honeymooners. Feeling quite alone, I listened to the ninety-second course and examined the hoses dangling from my gear. Apparently, all you really need to know about diving is the function of three hoses. One you put in your mouth to breathe, one tells you how much air you have left and one will pump air into your buoyancy belt thingy. There are more instructions printed on my washing machine lid, and my reds still bleed. If I bled in the ocean there'd be nothing left to throw into the rag box after sharks finished me off.

Soon the young instructors were leading our group of handholding lovers, and me, on our first diving experience. The instructors produced kibble from plastic baggies and fish appeared like pigeons in a park. I was still trying to decide if being swarmed by schools of begging fish was cool or creepy when pressure built up in my ears. I fell behind when I stopped to try various techniques to clear them. I couldn't hold my nose, but I filled my cheeks with air and tried to blow it out my ears. Nothing. I swam a few yards trying to keep up with the group, then stopped to tilt my head and whack on it. Now my ears hurt and my mask was crooked. I was getting desperate, my ears throbbed and it was clear no one had been assigned to look after the pathetic girl without a boyfriend. I tried the only other method I knew for unplugging ears, I opened my mouth into the widest yawn I could force. The hose end that goes in my mouth came out and floated somewhere out of my sight. Now my ears hurt and I was going to drown. I scooped at the water behind me trying to locate my air supply. I caught the buoyancy belt pump thingy. I snagged the air level indicator, it seemed there would be plenty of air left for the next diver. I waved for help toward twenty retreating flippers and remembered descriptions of torturous deaths of divers who surfaced too rapidly. Time was running out for me to make my decision between drowning and a slow death by bends, when an instructor appeared and surfaced with me. Apparently, eight feet isn't enough to cause the bends.

All I needed was help finding my regulator, but I was deemed incompetent and Wally was hailed from the beach to take me ashore. It would have been a good time to tell me that this happens to a lot of people and that you can't be too careful about the bends. I was turned over to Wally who swam beside me without comment and left me at the beach with no instructions for rendezvousing with my group or reassurance that I wasn't dumber than a flounder.

While walking along the beach trying very hard to be proud of myself for making the effort I stepped on a rusty nail. The honeymooners finished playing find the sea cucumber and we all caught the shuttle back. I limped aboard to the ship's doctor for a bandage and tetanus shot. Yup, Mike Nelson was tougher than me.

Take Two was out of dry dock, but we still couldn't go sailing. Shortly after the regatta Brian discovered a small area of dry rot on the deck. I was in no hurry to incur more repair bills and said so, but Brian immediately called Jacob of Fine Woodworking. Jacob showed up within hours to give us an estimate, and started the job two days later. He cut away the damaged area and glued a new piece of wood in its place. After the glue dried he would return to apply the first of several coats of protective finish. The glue dried, but Jacob didn't return. We were stuck on the dock because Brian didn't want to risk further damage by taking *Take Two* on the ocean. His caution seemed excessive, I wanted to sail.

The following week Jacob was still busy with larger jobs and once again the weekend came and went and we couldn't sail. I was frustrated beyond words, or possibly to a profusion of words, I felt the repair should have been postponed until we had income and I wanted to get off the dock for some fun. We talked about flying the Aztec to glamorous St. Barts, Dominica or even having lunch on nearby Cuelbra, but the wind is free, fuel for the airplane is not and the Aztec was a fuel hog.

I particularly wanted to fly to Dominica, an incomparable island I'd read about the year before. I wanted to snorkel at Champagne Beach, where geothermal vents expel tiny bubbles into the sea, and walk in the rainforest to the twin falls of Trafalgar Falls. I knew it would be a shame to live in the Caribbean and own an airplane without seeing some of the islands and by the next weekend I was ready to spend the money on gas, but I'd missed my chance, Brian had arranged to meet the air conditioner repairman on Saturday. I never did get to Dominica, we always seemed to be waiting for one contractor or another to perform repairs, which we invariably argued the necessity of.

Keeping *Take Two* in proper working condition and improving the efficiency of her systems was more interesting to Brian than office work. As a result an increasingly large part of my role in the company became getting Brian focused. Though unquestionably brilliant at building networks, he avoided the business side of things. Motivating him to do the boring stuff he hated tested my abilities of persuasion like never before. Generally, I saw little success and caused yet more arguments.

June Gloom

Our June calendar was filling up. We were supporting the trial members of our Internet service; scheduled to launch on the eighth; I had family arriving on the tenth; more arriving on the twelfth; and on the thirteenth, when Seth's school dismissed for the summer, we were sailing to the British Virgin Islands.

A troubled marriage is not the best host for a family vacation, but after ten months in the Caribbean and only the disastrous visit by my parents and a rainy spring break for my daughter we looked forward to showing someone a vacation to remember. I did my best to lock away my resentments and anger.

I was ready for our two weeks with family when Mom and her friend Audrey arrived early in the afternoon. *Take Two* was gleaming, the galley was stocked with rum, fresh mangos, prawns and ingredients for fish tacos, chocolate rum mousse and other favorites. I'd cleaned and decorated my cabin for them, laying out my thickest, yellow beach towels and an assortment of sarongs for wearing or sleeping under.

The nighttime temperatures generally lingered in the 70's and I preferred to sleep with the air conditioner off, the hatches open and a loosely draped sarong for covers.

My sister Christine and Aaron, her husband of less than a year, planned to stay on *Take Two* for a few days then move to the greater privacy of a hotel so I cleared clutter from the guest cabin and its tiny closet, placing a few books and fragrant candles on the narrow shelf by the bed. I added color with a couple of throw pillows and more sarongs.

I drove our first guests directly from the airport to the yacht for *Take Two*'s signature drink, Painkillers. It seemed appropriate for Mom. The next day I had work to do so I dropped them at Magens Bay, introducing them to a favorite pastime: sitting at the edge of the surf in a low beach chair. This is one of the best ways to enjoy a tropical beach: with a drink in your hand and warm waves sloshing over outstretched legs.

I hate clamoring clumsily onto an uncooperative air mattress, then constantly checking to make sure I'm not drifting to out to sea, only to wear myself out paddling back toward shore in a zig-zag pattern, correcting direction every ten or twelve strokes when I realize I've turned parallel to shore. Also, my mother doesn't swim and has never been completely comfortable in water more than four-feet deep. She will use an air mattress if my dad, an excellent swimmer, is nearby. But even then, panic is not more than a whitecap away. On a Hawaiian vacation a few years earlier she and Dad took air mattresses into the water at Waikiki Beach. Mom, in her black, skirted swimsuit, and Dad, in his turquoise trunks—the only suit I ever remember seeing him wear—and farmer's tan, paddled past the low waves breaking on the sand. They floated lazily in the warm water until a bigger wave appeared suddenly, lifting them like pancakes and flipping them over. Mom, terrified of losing her only means of staying afloat wrapped arms and legs around her now upside-down air mattress and held her breath as she clung on for her life. Meanwhile, Dad stood at her side laughing until he nearly lost footing in the three-foot-deep water.

Two days after Mom landed, the newlyweds arrived and the next day we threw off dock lines, heading out for their first-ever weekend of sailing. Christine, Aaron and Seth stretched out on the foredeck trampolines, the coveted real estate when *Take Two* is underway. The sailing experience is most dramatic there. The water rushes beneath, echoing between the dual hulls, and the wind rushes past not yet caught by sails. When a bow dips passengers are dampened, but never the mood.

Our first stop was at White Bay on Jost Van Dyke at the Soggy Dollar Bar where Painkillers were invented. We snorkeled in the reef that cuts across the bay then dried ourselves in the sun on the beach. One and two at a time we returned to the boat to shower and change for dinner. We arrived at the Sandcastle Restaurant already worn-out from sailing and swimming. By the time our food arrived much later we'd grown uncharacteristically churlish. We snapped at one another, throwing a wet towel over the evening, even before the sizable bill arrived. I went to bed annoyed with myself .

~~~~

It's a funny, and good, thing that no matter how angry I might be with Brian or he with me when someone else upsets one of us, the other steps up to be supportive. I may rail against Brian until I'm out of breath, but if someone else voices a criticism I change sides. It sounds perverse, but that's the way it should be. It's a loyalty thing.

We'd just weighed anchor and left White Bay; Seth and my brother-in-law were on the swim step letting out the dinghy's tow line. Standard practice if a yacht doesn't have a lift for carrying the dinghy out of the water while underway, is to let out fifteen or twenty feet of rope so the dinghy can follow in the calmer water beyond the wake of the yacht. Your tender takes less of a beating that way. Brian called instructions back to Seth and Aaron and, in the time it takes the wind to change, words were exchanged, tempers flared and Seth followed his uncle Aaron storming into the Salon. Leaving Brian and me to handle our 48' catamaran.

As I said, quarrels between members of my family are extremely rare. The few we have don't last long and bad feelings are quickly left behind. But, for the moment, I knew the five people in the salon were all some combination of angry, tense and uncomfortable. The main and jib were up and secured. Brian could have used the autopilot and handled the winches himself, but I wanted him to know he had an ally on board so I assumed the position of crew, dashing from starboard winch to port releasing one and tightening the other with each tack. To take my mind off the emotional situation I let myself feel a little pride at how well the two of us were handling the yacht. But, as my mother often says and her mother before her said, when things go wrong, "Cheer up, things could be worse. So I cheered up and sure enough, things got worse." And, indeed minutes later I felt worse.

I'd just fallen into the routine of first mate when Brian glanced back and noticed the outboard on the dinghy had not been locked in the up position. It was banging up and down as the boat bounced along behind. He said, "We should fall-off and take care of that." He was proposing coming to a full stop on the water when I wanted nothing more than to get back to the dock at Red Hook as soon as possible. Everyone needed time apart and that meant getting off the boat.

I said, "Now?" The dismay in my voice was obvious and he didn't stop. Brian nearly always insists on being efficient and doing things the right way regardless of inconvenience to me or anyone. He surprised me this time when he continued without fixing the problem. Minutes later we were both angry with ourselves when Brian glanced back again and saw the outboard was gone. It had fallen off somewhere in the Sir Francis Drake Channel. A few weeks later when we drove across the island for a new one we learned it would take $900 from our rapidly dwindling savings to replace.

Back at Red Hook our passengers were in their shoes and clutching purses before Paulo even caught a line. They hurried from *Take Two* like women and children from the *Titanic*. The newlyweds moved up their hotel reservation and left with suitcases packed and in hand.

The quarrel fouled the air for the rest of the day then floated off with the night wind leaving plenty of time yet to enjoy St. Thomas and one another. My sister and her husband checked off a list of must-do activities for his first visit to the Caribbean: They rented snorkel gear to explore the reef near their hotel, went SCUBA diving at Coral World and, with the family gathered below to watch, my brother-in-law para-sailed high above Sapphire Beach.

We all celebrated Brian's birthday at Karaoke night at Iggy's. Karaoke is the most fun you can have on the island for the cost of a rum punch. Brian had become a true enthusiast; he and his buddy Roger knew where to find Karaoke any night of the week. Brian knew he had a good singing voice and he required no coaxing onto the stage. I stayed firmly in the audience when I tagged along nights he and Roger went out to sing. Their version of *Bye Bye Love* was as good as Karaoke gets.

It was a typical Iggy's crowd that night. We recognized a few locals, but most seemed to be vacationers. We found a table in the middle of the room and ordered drinks to take a bit of the hard out of the wood benches we sat on. I asked Brian to sing Elton John's *Your Song* for me and then after much coaxing from my mother I joined him for a duet of *I Got You Babe*. I was half-way through the song—singing to Brian while he sang to the audience—before I realized the lyrics were color-coded for the duet. I'd been singing both parts. My brother-in-law, a Texan and former rodeo bull-rider, treated the audience to *Mammas Don't Let Your Babies Grow Up to be Cowboys*, and two white girls entertained us with a hysterical version of *Baby Got Back*. One girl sang while the other, backside to the crowd, gyrated until both were completely out of breath. We laughed so hard it was dangerous to take a drink.. Next, a father coaxed his four children onto the stage for the theme from Gilligan's Island.

The last full day before everyone was scheduled to leave for home I asked Brian to fly us to St. Croix. It was my first time on St. Croix, the other of the three largest U. S. Virgin Islands. At eighty-four square miles in size, St. Croix is more than fifty square miles larger than St. Thomas, but its highest peak reaches only two thirds as high at St. Thomas's Crown Mountain.

The Cruzan Distillery and one of the world's largest oil refineries are on St. Croix. There are casinos, too, but the economy took a tremendous hit when crime against cruise ship passengers and crew increased until nearly all major cruise lines discontinued service to the island. I doubt if the crime on St. Croix is any greater than on St. Thomas, but St. Thomas has the lure of superior shopping at Charlotte Amalie.

We caught a taxi to explore Christiansted and soon discovered there was little to explore. We moved quickly through T-shirt and souvenir shops at Kings Alley and along the boardwalk to lunch at Fort Christian Brew Pub. Regrettably, we didn't have time to visit the real St. Croix treasure: a rainforest on the Northwest corner of the island.

Back at the airport we waited on the tarmac for Brian to settle the bill for airplane fuel. Before we left *Take Two* I had taken a Dramamine. I had let myself run out of the non-drowsy tablets. Now I was so drowsy I was gazing at the ground through half-closed eyes seriously considering lying down on the warm concrete for a nap when Brian finally emerged from the building and told us to climb in. There's an understanding in the flying community that anyone with a pilot's license sits in front. It just makes sense, but that afternoon, I relinquished my right to a front seat and fell asleep before our wheels left the tarmac.

Independence Day

The Fourth of July fell on a Friday and, going to St. John to join friends, we nearly missed the car ferry. We were on foot and going over just for the evening, but Pat and Nicole paid the $42 round-trip fee for their car which was packed to the dome light with camping equipment for the weekend. More than half of St. John's twelve thousand acres, and thousands more underwater, belong to the National Park Service. Pat and Nicole had reservations to camp on the north side at the Cinnamon Bay campground and they'd invited us to join them and campmates to their campfire dinner.

The ferry crew finished directing the last car onto the ramp when we ran up out of breath. We pointed toward the viewing platform and said we were meeting friends. They waved us on without question.

Pat and Nicole's reserved cottage was not a quaint Hansel & Gretel cottage or even a rustic summer cabin, but a cold gray fifteen- by fifteen-foot room with concrete walls on two sides and screened walls front and back. What the rooms lacked in privacy they made up for in austerity. The unit had four twin beds, a fan and a single small cupboard above a tiny counter. The back door opened onto a concrete patio with a large wood picnic table and charcoal grill, the front to a gravel path leading from the parking area. As camping goes, it would beat sleeping on the ground and dinner of cold cuts, but not by much. Anyway, Brian and I were only there for the evening.

Once we found the assigned cottage we wanted to head straight for the beach, but there was unloading to be done. The screen door banged percussively as six of us carried boxes of groceries, bags of paper products, ice chests, sleeping bags, tote bags, duffle bags and more into the relatively vermin-free sanctuary of the cottage. The screened walls bulged with camping paraphernalia when we left the cottage for the beach. The narrow sandy path wound timidly through the trees, I fell behind—Brian often forgot I was around when talking with others—and lost the path altogether once or twice until finally lurching through the underbrush in the direction of voices and onto the beach nearly tumbling over a family sitting on a log. The sun was low and the entire beach, which extends only a few hundred feet before it gets interrupted on either side by rough boulders spilling from the brush into the water, was in the shadow of trees.

I couldn't swim with the others because I hadn't brought a change of clothes so I sat swatting mosquitoes and sand fleas and wondering how long before dinner.

Hours later everyone climbed back into Pat and Nicole's Jeep to drive to Cruz Bay for the fireworks display. For such a small island it was a surprisingly long drive back winding along North Shore Road.

A crowd lined the narrow beach facing west toward St. Thomas. Once again I got separated from the others so when the fireworks began I found a patch of sand to sit alone and watch the brief display.

I won't deny my tendency to remember too well all the times my feelings were hurt, but when you're starving it's hard to get past the gnawing hunger to remember the time you had a cookie. I didn't get married to have breakfast on the patio by myself; or to be ready to praise, compliment, share or seduce only to have fallen asleep or given in to hurt and anger while waiting; to go along and still be left behind; or watch fireworks alone.

Sadly, such a thing wasn't unusual enough to evoke more than a cheerless, "Where were you?" when we met in the line for the ferry.

Tropical Depression

After the Saturday night when Roger, our neighbor on *Cover Shot*, stuck his head in the door and asked if we were following the progress of Tropical Depression Six he and Brian huddled over satellite images and prediction charts on the computer for nearly an hour. I went to bed and dreamed of being in a hurricane.

I woke before Brian and navigated my way through the NOAA website to the prediction graphic. Nothing had changed much overnight. We were still within the path of rough weather if the depression didn't run out of steam on its way across the Atlantic or veer off its present course.

A tropical depression would make for a rough day, but nothing we couldn't ride out on the dock. However, if TD6 reached winds over thirty-nine mph it would become a tropical storm. They would name it and we would have to leave the dock and seek shelter in a protected cove. There was some consolation in knowing that TD6 would be upon us before it had time to become a full-blown hurricane.

A tropical storm graduates to hurricane when its sustained surface wind surpasses seventy-four m.p.h. And that's just a baby-size category one hurricane. Hurricanes come in all shapes, sizes and temperaments. Andrew was a small, but furious category five with sustained winds that reached 145 mph when it hit Florida in 1992. But, Andrew was a slow-poke compared to category three Gloria, which in 1985 raced across the eastern U.S. at thirty miles per hour. Katrina was a category three and traveling fifteen miles per hour when it made landfall in the Gulf in 2005.

A short walk taking kitchen trash to the dumpster afforded several opportunities to talk about the weather. There wasn't much concern about TD6, but Roger decided to play it safe and left the dock to get a good spot for his Seawind 1000 in a lagoon southeast of Red Hook. Brian and I stowed the bimini, secured potential flotsam and filled the water tanks, just in case. We'd been told that after Marilyn, a category two hurricane, hit in 1995 some places in St. Thomas were without power and water for weeks.

Another look after lunch at the prediction table showed increased chance of the USVI falling in the path of the depression, and sooner than expected. The marina office manager stopped by *Take Two* to thank us for following the weather, and remind us of marina policy that no boats are allowed to remain on the dock if the Virgins are in the warning area for a named storm.

Meanwhile closer to home, tropical depression Connie struck as I pondered the problems we would face if an honest-to-goodness storm headed our way. We didn't need a distraction from the work of promoting our Internet service business which was off to a slower than expected start, and since losing our outboard in the Drake Channel we were still dinghy-less.

In the event of a hurricane, our plan was to take *Take Two* to a hurricane hole and put down all the anchors, an exercise which requires a dinghy. Then we would make the choice to either stay with the boat or go to a hotel . . . which, unless we wanted to make a raft of our luggage, also required a dinghy. Finally, we'd still have to get the airplane someplace safe. We would probably split up, with Brian flying the Aztec out of harm's way and me staying on the island to deal with any boat-related issues. All the scenarios I imagined caused anxiety. Riding out a hurricane, even on a catamaran in a deep harbor, offered no appeal; neither did abandoning our home or counting on the construction of a hotel built on an island where every acquaintance offered a shortcut around building codes and standards.

We had been shopping rather half-heartedly for outboards, but the price-tag on even a small four- or eight-horsepower motor was enough to cause procrastination. The same money could buy a ticket home for Christmas, or pay for fuel and hotel expenses for a weekend in Dominica. We were trying to adopt a life is too short attitude and not beat ourselves up over losing the outboard, but sometimes we couldn't resist a little self-flagellation.

By mid-afternoon activity was picking up on the wharf. The sounds of dock carts clunking along the dock taking bottles of water and other provisions to yachts; boats leaving their moorings; and the rumble of engines idling spoke of something coming. The crackle of the VHF radio broke the silence inside the cabin with transmissions from boats calling the fuel dock and radioing ahead for slips in safer marinas. Brian raised *Cover Shot* on the radio and arranged to join them in the morning to raft our catamarans together. This would be unnecessary if TD6 remained a depression, but if it approached with the attitude of a storm at least we had a plan.

By evening TD6 didn't show signs of growing intensity, not before passing the Virgins anyway, and it had veered slightly south, putting us at the very edge of its path. I stopped my hourly checking of the weather websites, which were updated every six hours. We went to bed hoping the morning would bring blue sky, encouraging news from NOAA, and a return to worrying about lesser things—like whether our younger friends think we're old because we always have an excuse to go home by ten p.m.

By morning the forecast hadn't changed; it looked like we could stay on the dock. But, if TD6 turned into a storm just before arriving we'd be forced to leave the dock at the worst possible time. We checked its wind speed, still thirty-five m.p.h, moving twenty-three m.p.h. I left for a dentist appointment with the understanding I might find Brian, Seth and *Take Two* gone when I returned. CNN was on the television hanging from the ceiling over the dentist chair. Squinting between the drill and the suction tube, I saw a report that the Tropical Depression in the Caribbean was growing. I almost forgot about the drilling.

Two hours later, back on *Take Two*, sucking milkshake through a narrow straw with lips unevenly numb, I checked the weather charts. The Virgin Islands showed up just outside the prediction path. We decided to stay put, but drove to the far side of the island to tie-down the Aztec. We got back to the boat just ahead of the rain, and quietly celebrated the five p.m. report of Tropical Depression Six dissipating.

I expected to go through this drill several more times by the end of hurricane season in November . . . , but I didn't. Events led me to leave the islands before hurricane season was through.

Looking for Rose Petals

The biggest drawback of living on St. Thomas was being without family. I missed my kids, my parents, my brothers and sisters: all living on the West Coast of the United States.

The kids were attending college and working, until my middle son's plans changed. Josh had been contentedly ambling his way toward whatever degree the unlikely combination of karate, critical thinking and real estate principles might lead. He didn't yet know how he wanted to apply his rare gift of enjoying people. While gaining the esteem of supervisors at the San Diego Community Center Box Office, a merger cut his hours to twenty a week. In a phone call he told me the money he saved taking dates to free performances wasn't enough and he was looking for a new job. I offered a suggestion. Three weeks later he was installed in our guest cabin and working at Molly Malone's, a marina restaurant a hundred feet from his hatch on *Take Two*, and attending classes at the University.

Signing Josh up for classes at the University of the Virgin Islands was bewilderingly easy. We hurried across the island on the last day of fall semester registration to sign him up for an evening class in hotel and restaurant management. We walked up to a table in the gymnasium at three-thirty Friday afternoon. The following Monday Josh began a full load of classes as a marketing major.

Leaving the gymnasium, Brian and I looked to one another for reassurance. Was it true that our junior college 'C' student really was a marketing major at an honest to goodness university. It seems the UVI was desperate to get warm bodies into seats. Higher education is not a higher priority for many on the island. The seemingly officious St. Thomas Rotary offered a scholarship the previous year. It was awarded to the sole applicant.

Seth was happy to have a brother on board and on his team. If Seth asked for a ride to the mall and Brian and I suggested he take a Safari car, his brother stepped up to give him a lift. If he wanted to go joy riding in the dinghy but we disapproved of wasting fuel, Josh suggested they take Puck to Vessup Beach for exercise and they'd be gone for hours.

Though step-brothers, Josh and Seth were cut from the same denim. Eight years older, Josh had blazed a black and blue trail of rope swings, roller blades and bike ramps that Seth eagerly followed.

Both were hard-workers. Seth was earning a reputation among the local yacht owners as dependable and diligent. He could earn as much money in one day washing a luxury yacht as Josh made in a weekend serving beer and conch chowder to tourists. Josh supplemented his income putting the Snuba to work making money scraping moss and barnacles from boat bottoms.

~~~~

Josh wasn't even tan yet when my marriage reached its lowest point. Brian and I had moved four thousand miles from Rancho Del Fuego, but our problems found root in tropical soil and grew as vigorously as mangroves on the beach. I became increasingly critical and angry.

The combination of a dwindling bank account and Brian's intractable procrastination on business responsibilities was driving me to new levels of bitchiness. Just to make matters interesting, the stress seemed to have jumpstarted me into an early menopause. Eventually, the only reason I needed to be angry or crying was to be awake.

On one of what had already become regular midnight chats with Joshua after his shift ended, I told him that Brian and I needed a break from one another and I would be leaving the island. There was no reason Josh shouldn't stay, Brian wouldn't care one way or the other, and Josh could be there for Seth.

Brian and I said good-bye at the San Juan airport thinking this might be the last time. It was.

I joined my daughter in San Diego. After a brief, somewhat alarming period of falling apart, I rented an apartment and got a job. All my new acquaintances required the usual get acquainted conversations. I dreaded these exchanges. I was both ashamed and incredulous that I was soon to be divorced . . . again.

Somehow my life got swapped with that of another. Somewhere, a woman is growing old with a man she loves and respects, a man willing to compromise and for whom she is happy to make concessions. They have raised their children together and hand-in-hand turn pages of the calendar. They watched one another's bodies' age and are intimate without self-consciousness. He was there when the children were born, he'll be at her side when they marry.

Finding a more grown-up way of introducing a fifty-year-old man than as my boyfriend, will never be a problem for this woman who is living my life. Nor, does she wonder if it isn't foolish to think someone new can fit into a life so far along. She doesn't grow disgusted with online profiles of single, middle-aged men who are looking for the love of their lives, but can't be bothered to spell-check or take a photo they don't have to cut their last girlfriend out of. Her children won't ever refer to someone as Mom's husband or feel like guests in their mother's house.

Twice, divorce erased someone from my life. I was looking for a happy ending and to wake from a bad dream to find rose petals in my pocket and the life I imagined all those years ago in high school... maybe minus the part about me being a world-famous Triple Crown jockey.

You can not change the direction of the wind, but you can adjust your sails.

Epilogue

It took life yanking away my air mattress to teach me I could float on my own. It didn't happen overnight, and I went under a couple of times. I had help, but the important adjustments came alone in the dark when I turned off my light, lay my head on my pillow and, unbidden, the cheerless question, "So, this is it?" saddened me. It rarely comes to me now and, like something from a Hollywood script, I'm seeing Ivan, from Nanny Cay.

After a few half-hearted match.com efforts, I realized, with no regrets, that I was simply too happy to spend the time, effort and emotional energy to search for a lover. But, I hadn't forgotten the pleasant, attractive Ivan. I found him on facebook. He'd sold the *Holly B* and was posting his latest adventures as crew on a yacht delivery. I messaged him and four days later dragged my suitcase onto a plane to El Salvador to spend a week with him and the skipper he was sailing with. We connected on a new level and though his home is in London, and it's as long-distance as a relationship can be, a generous, considerate man is worth going the distance for.

In the months after leaving St. Thomas, I continued to provide support to our business venture, but it had been floundering before I left, and Brian soon crafted an arrangement with a local company to take it over.

Brian stayed on St. Thomas for two years, then sailed *Take Two* to Fort Lauderdale, leaving it with a yacht broker for sale. He's back in the Sacramento area. Seth moved into a dorm room in Washington D.C. where he had been accepted as a page at the U.S. House of Representatives and is now at the Naval Academy.

Josh helped sail *Take Two* to Florida then hopped a plane back to St. Thomas where he'd fallen in love with a girl he met at the university. I've been back to the islands a few times, even ran into Gary once, but I live and work in Sacramento. Now, after answering the question, "What would it be like to live on a Caribbean island?" I'm just an occasional visitor with a special connection to the Islands.

The Author

Connie Fleenor lives in Sacramento, CA

www.ingramcontent.com/pod-product-compliance
Lightning Source LLC
Chambersburg PA
CBHW031952040426
42448CB00006B/329